P9-DCL-886

You grew up in a good family;
hardworking dad and a mom who
was there when you needed her.

They taught you and your little
b rother to share and sho wed you
how to pray every night before bed.

In Sunday school, you learned about
Jesus and sang all the songs with
                     the rest of the kids.

There was Noah and his ark, Moses
and the Ten Commandments, and little
baby Jesus asleep on the hay.

You learned about the blessing
that was America and were grateful
to live in a country led by good
Christian leaders.

With a hand over your heart or above your brow, you pledged allegiance to

God and Country,

for the Lord was at work in this holy nation.

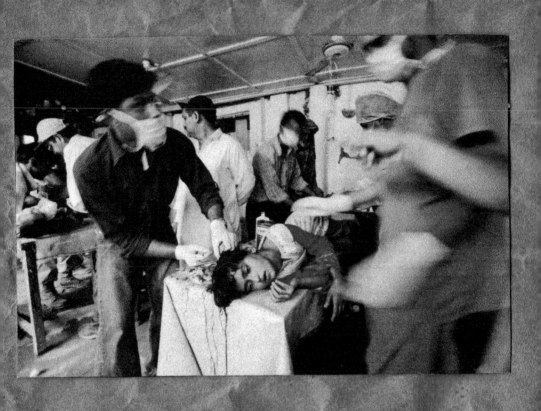

But lately you are beginning to wonder
if this is really how God intended things

to be.

And you question if God is really working through places of power.

Maybe, you wonder, God had a totally different idea in mind...

Jesus for President

Politics for Ordinary Radicals

Shane Claiborne
Chris Haw

Designed by SharpSeven

Jesus for President
Copyright © 2008 by The Simple Way

Requests for information should be addressed to:

Zondervan, *Grand Rapids, Michigan 49530*

Library of Congress Cataloging-in-Publication Data

Claiborne, Shane, 1975–
  Jesus for president : politics for ordinary radicals / Shane Claiborne and
  Chris Haw ; Designed by SharpSeven Design.
      p. cm.
    Includes bibliographical references.
    ISBN 978-0-310-27842-9
    1. Christianity and politics—United States. I. Haw, Chris, 1981–
  II. Title.
  BR526.C567   2008
  261.70973—dc22   2007029333

This book is printed on 100 percent postconsumer fiber which is certified
by credible, thorough environmental agencies.

All Scripture quotations, unless otherwise indicated, are taken from the *Holy
Bible, Today's New International Version*™. TNIV®. Copyright © 2001, 2005
by International Bible Society. Used by permission of Zondervan. All rights
reserved.

Internet addresses (websites, blogs, etc.) and telephone numbers printed in
this book are offered as a resource to you. These are not intended in any way
to be or imply an endorsement on the part of Zondervan, nor do we vouch for
the content of these sites and numbers for the life of this book.

All rights reserved. No part of this publication may be reproduced, stored in
a retrieval system, or transmitted in any form or by any means—electronic,
mechanical, photocopy, recording, or any other—except for brief quotations
in printed reviews, without the prior permission of the publisher.

Cover art by Chico and Tatiana Fajardo-Heflin
Art Direction and Interior Design by SharpSeven Design

Printed in the United States of America

08 09 10 11 12 13 • 18 17 16 15 14 13 12 11 10 9 8 7 6 5 4

A good creation of love and beauty takes a turn for the worse,
landing it in a murderous chaos. What to do? Flood it and start
fresh? Build a tower that reaches heaven? Appoint an adventurous
elderly couple to lead the people out of the nations to the Promised
Land?   Something has to save humanity from themselves...

The construction of a set-apart people into a living temple
of blessing is going so-so.   The solution:God puts skin on
to show the world what love looks like. But here's the catch:
the Prince of Peace isborn as a refugee in the middle of a
genocide and is rescued from the trash bin of imperial
executions to stand at the pinnacle of this peculiar people.
A strange way to start a revolution...

Flags on altars, images of the gods on money...Caesar
is colonizing our imaginations. What happened to the
slaughtered Lamb, the Prince of Peace??? There seems
to be another gospel spreading across the empire...
Two kingdoms are colliding.   What is a Jesus-follower
to do when the empire gets baptized?

Snapshots of the political imagination. The question is
not ARE WE POLITICAL? but HOW-- HOW ARE WE POLITICAL?
...not ARE WE RELEVANT? but ARE WE PECULIAR?   The answer
lies not just in what we believe but in how we embody
what we believe. Our greatest challenge is to maintain
the distinctiveness of our faith in a world gone mad.
All of creation waits, groans, for a people who live
GOD'S DREAM with fresh imagination.

INTRODUCTION

A Book to Provoke the

Christian Political Imagination

This book is a project in renewing the imagination of the church in the United States and of those who would seek to know Jesus. We are seeing more and more that the church has fallen in love with the state and that this love affair is killing the church's imagination. The powerful benefits and temptations of running the world's largest superpower have bent the church's identity. Having power at its fingertips, the church often finds "guiding the course of history" a more alluring goal than following the crucified Christ. Too often the patriotic values of pride and strength triumph over the spiritual virtues of humility, gentleness, and sacrificial love.

CHURCH (church), n.
By church, we mean
the body of people
who make the God of Jesus
visible in the world
(for better or worse).

STATE (steyt), n.

By state, we mean "a

country or nation with

a sovereign independent

government ruled by

kings, presidents, or

legislatures."

We in the church are schizophrenic: we want to be good Christians, but deep down we trust that only the power of the state and its militaries and markets can really make a difference in the world. And so we're hardly able to distinguish between what's American and what's Christian. As a result, power corrupts the church and its goals and practices. When Jesus said, "You cannot serve two masters," he meant that in serving one, you destroy your relationship to the other. Or as our brother and fellow activist Tony Campolo puts it, "Mixing the church and state is like mixing ice cream with cow manure. It may not do much to the manure, but it sure messes up the ice cream." As Jesus warned, what good is it to gain the whole world if we lose our soul?

So what we need is an exploration of the Bible's political imagination, a renovated Christian politics, a new set of hopes, goals, and practices. We believe the growing number of Christians who are transcending the rhetoric of lifeless presidential debates is a sign of this renovation. Amid all the buzz, we are ready to turn off our TVs, pick up our Bibles, and reimagine the world.

Over the last several years, the Christian relation to the state has become more dubious. The most prevalent example is the Christian language coming from the State Department of the United States. Professing Christians have been at the helm of the wars in Iraq and Afghanistan, implicitly or explicitly referencing faith in God as part of their leadership. Patriotic pastors insist that America is a Christian nation without questioning the places in distant and recent history where America has not looked like Christ. Rather than placing our hope in a transnational church that embodies God's kingdom, we assume America is God's hope for the world, even when it doesn't look like Christ. Dozens of soldiers who have contacted us confess a paralyzing identity crisis as they feel the collision of their allegiances. At the same time, many Christians are questioning whether God is blessing these wars and whether it's enough for our money to say "In God We Trust" while the daily reality of the global economy seems out of sync with God's concern for the poor.

We hope this book will broaden the definition of *political*. As you'll find in the following pages, political doesn't refer merely to legislation, parties, and governments. So while we will insist that the Christian faith be political, we also want to redefine what political means or looks like. We hope to redefine it simply as how we relate to the world.

This book doesn't presume to blaze new trails of scholarship. Also, readers hoping to find an exhaustive political account of every book in the Bible will feel we paint with too broad a brush. Rather, as we seek to understand Jesus, we'll attempt to distill the work of scholars and ordinary saints into an accessible read (while having a little fun along the way). The scholars we will cite have busied themselves for generations with finding the truest theological and historical nuances about Jesus. We are grateful for their work and hope to anchor it in poetry, real life, and images in a way that invites us into the story of the most creative king who ever lived.

We begin in the Hebrew Scriptures,[1] since this is where Jesus' story begins. While we may be tempted to jump to the good news and just write about Jesus, we must hear the Story from which he came and anchor his language, politics, and actions in that world. Just as America's narrative did not begin with America and will not end with America, Jesus' story did not begin in Matthew, nor does it end in Revelation.

1 We will use the term *Hebrew Scriptures* for the first thirty-nine books of the Bible, preferring it to *Old Testament*, which subtly implies that these books are outdated or invalidated by the New Testament, rather than seeing the New Testament as the fulfillment and continual unfolding of the biblical narrative.

SECTION ONE

Before There Were

Kings and Presidents

24

In the Beginning

Once upon a time there were no kings or presidents. Only God was king. The Bible is the story of a God who is continually rescuing humanity from the messes we make of the world. God is bringing the kingdom of heaven to earth. God is leading humans on an exodus adventure out of the land of emperors and kings and into the Promised Land. Out of Egypt, God first saves a group of slaves from the tyranny of Pharaoh. God is their deliverer, the one who saves them from their tears and sweat and points them toward something better than the empire that they have known. Out of the nations, God is forming a new kind of people—a "holy nation" that will light up the world. But let's not get ahead of ourselves.

This story begins in a garden.

In the garden, there were no wars, no poverty, no pollution or pandemics. There were no fast-food joints or sweatshops. Neither Republicans nor Democrats were to be found, not even the Green Party. Things were perfect. But amid all the organic, nongenetically modified or artificially pesticided trees full of fruit, there was one tree that the first humans were not supposed to touch—the tree of the knowledge of good and evil. God warned Adam and Eve[2] that if they ate of its fruit, they would discover something called "death." God warned them that they could not be both immortal and know both good and evil. But they decided they couldn't live without it—death, that is. Apparently death was a small price to pay for the possibility of Godlike knowledge.

Its the beautiful things that get us. Perhaps the greatest seduction is not the ANTI-GOD, but the ALMOST*GOD. Poisonous fruit can look pretty tasty. Thats *what is* so dangerous about ideas like FREEDOM, PEACE AND JUSTICE. They are all seductive qualities, close to the heart of GOD. After all, its the beautiful things we kill anddie for. And it's the beautiful we market, exploit, brnad, and counterfeit.

WE FIND OURSELVES POSSESSED BY OUR POSSESSIONS...
and enslaved by the pursuit of freedom. Nations fighting for peace end up perpetuating the very violence they seek to destroy. Serpents are slippery and slimy things.

MOST of the ugliness in the human narrative comes from a distorted quest to possess beauty. COVETING begins with appreciating blessings. MURDER begins with a hunger for justice. LUST begins with a recognition of beauty. GLUTTONY begins when our enjoyment of the delectable gifts of GOD starts to consume us. IDOLATRY begins when our seeing a reflection of God in something beautiful leads to our thinking that the beautiful image bearer is worthy of WORSHIP.

Along came a slick little serpent who convinced them that if they ate the forbidden fruit, they would be like God—quite an alluring proposition. They'd be the judges of good and evil, of what is beautiful and what is ugly. They would rule themselves and control their own destinies. We all want to be like God, right? And so they ate.

2 Adam in Hebrew means "human being made from the humus (soil)," and Eve means "living being" or "mother of the living." This couple represents the earthy origins of humanity.

It wasn't long before all sorts of ugliness emerged. The inaugural act of civilization, of life outside the garden, was murder. Adam and Eve ate of the fruit, and Eden's children tasted its bitter aftertaste, this thing called death. In Genesis 4, we read the story: Abel was a keeper of the sheep, and Cain a tiller of the ground. This first fratricide was the murder of a shepherd by a farmer on his own farm (a struggle for the land that migrant workers and peasants have always known to this day).

And God said something incredible: "Your brother's blood cries out to me from the ground." The next act of Cain's self-created chaos was to build a city that he named Enoch, after his son, and on goes the story of civilization. If the tree of the knowledge of good and evil had acted as a levee of protection for humanity, then eating its fruit broke that levee and released a flood of violence into the world. Before long, people were slaughtering one another in the pursuit of power and riches.

The Flood

So by the sixth chapter of the Bible, things had already gotten really ugly. We read, "Now the earth was corrupt in God's sight and was full of violence" (Gen. 6:11). Violence infected the earth like a disease. What was God to do?

At first glance, the flood might seem to us like the most violent thing that has ever happened, especially in the wake of contemporary storms and tsunamis. But the biblical narrative treats it as an act of protection from the corruption and violence that plagued the creation. It's like a divine chemotherapy, or the pruning of a diseased plant to save its life. God loves humanity so much that watching us kill ourselves is absolutely intolerable. So God saved humanity through the flood.

"And God said, 'This is the sign of the covenant I am making between me and you and every living creature with you, a covenant for all generations to come: I have set my rainbow in the clouds, and it will be the sign of the covenant between me and the earth. Whenever I bring clouds over the earth and the rainbow appears in the clouds, I will remember my covenant between me and you and all living creatures of every kind. Never again will the waters become a flood to destroy all life. Whenever the rainbow appears in the clouds, I will see it and remember the everlasting covenant between God and all living creatures of every kind on the earth.' So God said to Noah, 'This is the sign of the covenant I have established between me and all life on the earth'" (Gen. 9:12–17).

The Tower

From civilization's inception, humankind has had an insatiable hunger to reach the heavens, to pave the way to God. We build towers that stretch into the skies, whether in New York or Babel. You may remember the old story of Babel's tower from Sunday school, or maybe you can hear the distant tunes of Bob Marley preaching about Babylon.

God's people decided to build a sky-scraping tower (Genesis 11). Scripture says "the whole world had one language," and the people seemed quite impressed by their limitless power. So they began erecting an idol of human ingenuity to "make a name" for themselves. They hoped to attain the beauty of the heavens, only to find themselves growing farther and farther from the God who dwelt with them in the garden of Eden. During the project, God noted that "nothing they plan to do will be impossible for them" (Gen. 11:6). You can almost hear the echoes of Hiroshima and Nagasaki here. It seems that God has an aversion for limitless power. It's not that they were a threat to God but that they were a threat to themselves. This type of grand collaboration wouldn't be God's solution to a world "full of violence." Instead of letting them build a bridge to the heavens, God came "down" from the lofty heights and scattered the people across the land, confusing their languages and bringing them back down to earth. They became babblers. God confused the language of the whole human family, and any hope for harmony, communication, and reconciliation now lay only in God's hands.

This tale is less a tragedy of divine punishment and more an act of divine liberation of humankind from an imperial project that would lead to death. The land around the tower became known as Babylon, which will rise as the quintessential symbol of empire. The Bible ends with the depiction of counterfeit beauty personified by "the Great Prostitute" named Babylon, with whom the kings of the earth, the merchants, and the nations commit a naughty romance. They are dazzled by her splendor, transfixed by all she has to offer. The whole world stands in awe of her beauty … before she falls. It is no coincidence that what is written immediately after the scattering at Babel is the calling of Abram and Sarai (Genesis 12). Homeless, small, and powerless, they were the antithesis of the Babel project. God called them out of the babbling confusion to become a peculiar new people whom God entrusted to bless the world. God set them apart with a new law, a new culture, a new destiny that was nothing short of the redemption of the human race.

(handwritten margin note: ← NOT 'RID THE WORLD OF EVIL')

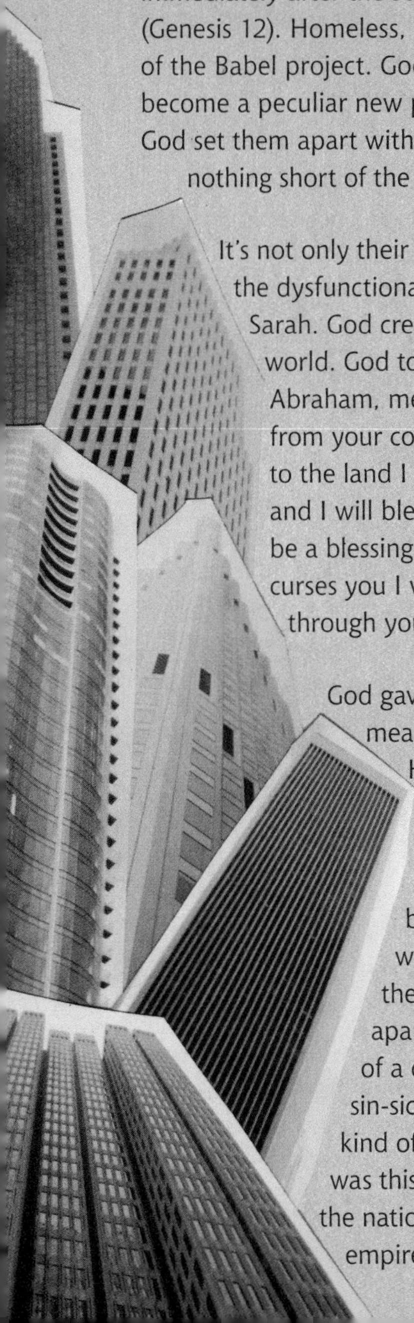

It's not only their story; it's our story. It's the story of our ancestors, the dysfunctional family of our father Abraham and mother Sarah. God created this family for the sake of redeeming the world. God told Abram, just before he was given the name Abraham, meaning "father of many nations" (Gen. 17:5), "Go from your country, your people and your father's household to the land I will show you. I will make you into a great nation, and I will bless you; I will make your name great, and you will be a blessing. I will bless those who bless you, and whoever curses you I will curse; and all peoples on earth will be blessed through you" (Gen. 12:1–3).

God gave these refugees new names, names filled with meaning: Deborah, Elijah, Miriam, Isaac, Rahab, Hannah, Aaron. They are heroic men and women who no longer belong to the empire. They are the characters of a new story. And in this story, Pharaoh, whose name everyone in the land had bowed down to worship, is nameless. For Pharaoh wasn't just a person; he was an icon of the world they came from. This new family, however, was set apart not just for the sake of being special but as part of a divine conspiracy to bless and heal the violent, sin-sick world. What is meant by "blessing," and what kind of people will they be? We will see. Nevertheless, it was this peculiar community that was set apart to redeem the nations, which continued to flounder in the messes of empire.

Exodus

The Hebrews were a people who found themselves suffering deeply from the ugliness of the empire they lived in. They were making bricks for Pharaoh's banks while they had no money for themselves. They were building storehouses of food for Pharaoh's family while their own families went hungry. They were midwiving the babies of the rich while their own suffered in poverty. They were catering banquets they could never afford to eat at, cleaning palaces they would never be able to sleep in, dying in wars to protect luxuries they would never afford. They were slaves.

God seems to have a knack for hearing the cry of oppressed people. Over and over the Hebrew Scriptures say that the people "cried out to God" and that "God heard their cry." And so God led them on an exodus, on a journey out of the land of empires and slaves and into the Promised Land of abundance, a land flowing with milk and honey.

God didn't choose just anybody to lead them. In the midst of imperially sanctioned genocide, a shrewd and courageous woman placed her little baby boy in a basket and floated him down the river. Another bold daughter, this one of the royal court, found his basket and took him in. That little baby was named Moses, an orphaned refugee who would lead God's people to the Promised Land—a land beyond empires and genocides. Moses, from the moment he was born, quivered under the shadow of an oppressive regime. It was from the water that God rescued Moses, and he would be rescued again when the waters swallowed up the armies of Pharaoh.

Moses led the people out of the land of Pharaoh, but he was no king. He was more of a prophet, one who is the "mouthpiece of God." As Moses led, kings fell—king after king was toppled from his throne. God fought for the people, protecting them, swallowing up armies and chariots. God instructed them that vengeance belongs only to God, which is a good way of saying, "Vengeance is not for you." It's the forbidden fruit. God scolded the people over and over for taking things into their own hands. The Israelites established an independent life in the hill country of Palestine, led by "liberators" (shophetim) and "prophets" (nebi'im) such as Deborah and Samuel, far from the land of kings and pharaohs. It is clear that God was reclaiming kingship over this peculiar nation of people, that they were not to trust in kings anymore. God was their only King.

It wasn't long, though, before the Hebrew people were tempted to be like those other nations and wanted a human king, one they could see and touch and worship. With growing fear of neighboring empires like Assyria and Babylon, they succumbed to the empty dream of domination. The very people who suffered so deeply from the things kings do demanded another king. Something whispered inside the Israelites that they needed a king "to be like the other nations"—a paralysis of faith and imagination. They still didn't get that they were to be a people "set apart" from the nations and from the patterns destroying them. Moses may have freed their bodies, but Pharaoh still colonized their conscience.

Nostalgic memories of home tempted them to turn back from their lonely desert journey and settle for Pharaoh's plantation. The taste of empire lingered in their mouths. And on weary days, their bellies cried for the

King of Jericho
King of Ai
King of Jerusalem
King of Jarmuth
King of Lachish
King of Eglon
" Gezer
" Debir
" Geder
" Hormah
" Arad
" Libnah
" Adullam
Kings of Makkedah,
Bethel, Tappuah,
Hepher, Aphek,
Lasharon, Madon,
Hazor, Shimron Meron,
Acshaph, Taanach,
Megiddo, Kedesh, Jokneam
in Carmel, Dor, Goyim in Gilgal,
Tirzah... 31 in all.

empire's meat and fast food. The enticements of Egypt tempted them to settle for the imperial dream.

Apparently, even being slaves of the empire was more comfortable and enticing than wandering with God in the desert. Aching for civilization, the Hebrews cried, "If only we had died by the LORD's hand in Egypt! There we sat around pots of meat and ate all the food we wanted, but you have brought us out into this desert to starve this entire assembly to death" (Exod. 16:3). As is often still the case with us, it may take only a few days to get out of the empire, but it takes an entire lifetime to get the empire out of us.

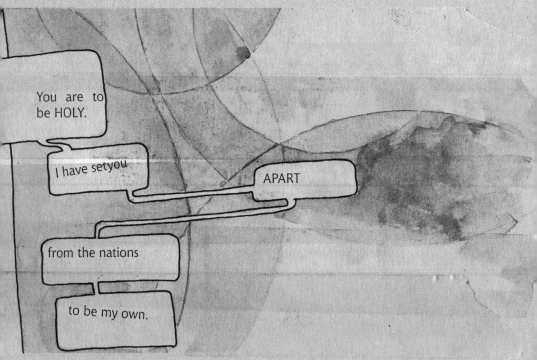

Maybe they wanted a king because it's hard to have faith in a King you can't see. Of course, they didn't know it would be even harder to keep faith in kings they can see. It's hard to wrap your hands around a God who, when asked for a name, says "I AM." But let's not forget that this is the same King who would rather stoop to camping out in the wilderness with the refugee people than get shut up in palaces or megachurches or oval offices.

Despite the fact that the Bible insists "God does not dwell in temples built by hands," we, in our hunger for power, credibility, and glamour, insist that God should. In 2 Samuel 7, King David found himself in a supersized mansion, living in a "palace of cedar," and started to think that maybe God needed a fancier place to dwell. But God rebuked David: "Are you the one to build me a house to dwell in? I have not dwelt in a house from the day I brought the Israelites up out of Egypt to this day. I have been moving from place to place with a tent as my dwelling" (2 Sam. 7:5–6). Instead of dwelling in what at that time symbolized a centralized political power—a temple—God likes camping. God likes pitching a tent with the people of struggle. God is close to the tears of the poor, and those tears are often a long way from the centers of power.

So the story continues. The people demanded a king so that they would "be like the nations." And God reminded them of the things kings do, warning them with these words:

This is what the king who will reign over you will claim as his rights: He will take your sons and make them serve with his chariots and horses, and they will run in front of his chariots. Some he will assign to be commanders of thousands and commanders of fifties, and others to plow his ground and reap his harvest, and still others to make weapons of war and equipment for his chariots. He will take your daughters to be perfumers and cooks and bakers. He will take the best of your fields and vineyards and olive groves and give them to his attendants. He will take a tenth of your grain and of your vintage and give it to his officials and attendants. Your male and female servants and the best of your cattle and donkeys he will take for his own use. He will take a tenth of your flocks, and you yourselves will become his slaves. When that day comes, you

When that day comes,
you will cry out for
relief from the king you
have chosen, but the
Lord will not answer
you in that day.

I SAM 8:11–18

God reminded them that the king would make them his slaves and soldiers to serve his palaces and wars. God reminded them of the things kings do, that they are a compromise to the very identity God was forming in them. How could they be set apart if they looked like the rest of the world?

But the people *continued* to demand a king. Brokenhearted, betrayed, sickened, God said to Samuel, "Listen to all that the people are saying to you; it is not you they have rejected, but they have rejected me as their king. As they have done from the day I brought them up out of Egypt until this day, forsaking me and serving other gods, so they are doing to you. Now listen to them; but warn them solemnly and let them know what the king who will reign over them will claim as his rights" (1 Sam. 8:6–9).

You can imagine the rest of the story even if you haven't read the Bible. Kings, kings, and more kings. Some good, some bad, but always making messes. Things aren't always predictable: it was often the good kings that were wiped out by Israel's enemies and the bad ones who did some serious border expansion and building projects. And it's not that they were inherently evil. People just aren't meant to have that much power. It tempts us beyond what we can bear. Even David, known to be the perfect king, "a man after God's own heart," soon forgot his story, betrayed the one who is King of Kings, and broke nearly every one of God's commands in two chapters of the Bible. (Makes even the sins of some presidents look mild.) Solomon, his son of adultery, took it a step farther. He imposed crushing taxes, built ruinous palaces, and took seven hundred wives and three hundred concubines … a little excessive. Can you imagine coming home to seven hundred spouses?

And it's not surprising that Solomon forgot the story of his faith, worshiped other gods, and built fortresses over the whole land. His son Rehoboam, drunk on power, inherited the corruption. No longer viewing Israel as a community but as subjects to be subdued, Rehoboam ruled with a heavy yoke, saying, "my father scourged you with whips; I will scourge you with scorpions" (1 Kings 12:11). And the people revolted.

They stoned the finance minister and rejected the house of David. No doubt few in the land were happy with their kings. When Solomon died, everyone hated him.

One king named Abimelek ended up killing his entire family (seventy brothers) to ensure his place on the throne of power. But there was one brother, Jotham (Jonathan), who survived the massacre and had a vision from God that even the trees were arguing over who would be king among them. The olive, the fig, and the vine all decided that they, beautiful as they were, bearing fruit for the world, were too precious to be tainted by kingship, so the throne was left to a thornbush! After he shared this vision, Jotham fled to the hills, lest he get killed,

> One day the trees went out to anoint a king for themselves. They said to the olive tree, 'Be our king.'
> But the olive tree answered, 'Should I give up my oil, by which both gods and men are honored, to hold sway over the trees?'
> Next, the trees said to the fig tree, 'Come and be our king.'
> But the fig tree replied, 'Should I give up my fruit, so good and sweet, to hold sway over the trees?'
> Then the trees said to the vine, 'Come and be our king.'
> But the vine answered, 'Should I give up my wine, which cheers both gods and men, to hold sway over the trees?'
> Finally all the trees said to the thornbush, 'Come and be our king.'
> Judges 9:8–14

for "he was afraid of his brother Abimelek." But God was King even over Abimelek, and God sent "an evil spirit" between Abimelek and his citizens. The text says that God did this in order that the crime against his brothers, the shedding of their blood, "might be avenged on their brother Abimelek and on the citizens of Shechem, who had helped him murder his brothers" (Judg. 9:24). One thing that is consistent throughout the Hebrew Scriptures is that God was deconstructing, redefining, and reclaiming kingship.

Through the voice of the prophets, God decried the people for thinking with the logic of empire, for depending on horses and chariots, for pledging allegiance to any other kings or idols, and God promised them more than the nations could ever offer. Over and over, the people settled for the empty promises of empire over the eternal dreams of God. But God is relentless.

God pursued, forgave, wooed them back, as a Lover.

Eventually, the people cried out to God ... again. And you can imagine what God said, sort of a gentle "told you so": "Where is your king, that he may save you? Where are your rulers in all your towns, of whom you said, 'Give me a king and princes'? ... In my anger I gave you a king" (Hos. 13:10).

But of course,

with God,

that's not the

end of the story...

GRACE ALWAYS

TRIUMPHS OVER

JUDGMENT.

For Every King There Is a Prophet

It's a miracle that the Hebrew people even survived, much less that they were able to pass on their story and preserve the harmony of voices that created it. There are many different perspectives on what makes a good king, and many contradictions. For instance, 2 Kings 15 says that Uzziah was a good king and "did what was right in the eyes of the LORD." But flip a few pages to 2 Chronicles 26 and we hear that Uzziah was a horrible king and that the Lord struck him with leprosy, which he had "until the day he died"!

It's great. It makes you rest in the assurance that everyone's voice, whether "conservative" or "liberal," is being brought to the table. It is sort of like if Christians were to write some books today on whether Bill Clinton was a good president. Some would say, "No, not at all; he committed adultery." Others might say, "No, he was a horrible president; he passed the welfare reform bill that cut federal assistance to thousands of our most vulnerable citizens." And still others might say, "Yes, he was a great president, doing many positive things in foreign relations and bringing peace in the Middle East." And maybe they are all a little right.

Every king had a prophet, a critic on the margins, a little thorn in their side. The prophets cleaned up the messes of kings, and even tried to prevent their messes. They helped tell the truth that nobody wanted to hear. King David had Nathan. King Nebuchadnezzar had Daniel. King Jeroboam had Hosea (and Amos ... bonus prophet). King Josiah had Jeremiah. King Herod had John the Baptist. You can often tell the true prophets because they usually end up getting killed (though they might get a national holiday in their honor).

When King Ahab tried to scheme up a lucrative but unethical business deal, Naboth gave him a little prophetic rebuke. (Of course, it cost him his life at the hands of ole Queen Jezebel.) David was scolded by Nathan for his adulterous and murderous affairs and for wanting to build a fancy dwelling place for God. He relayed God's message to David: "You are not to build a house for my Name, because you are a warrior and have shed blood" (1 Chron. 28:3; see also 1 Chron. 17:4; 1 Kings 5:3). Later, Herod got similar rebukes from John the Baptizer, which cost John his head. And other times, if the rulers were scared to kill the prophets, they invited them to dinner and tried to keep them in the royal court. (If you can't beat 'em, hire 'em!)

Most kings also had a false prophet or two. (You can often tell the false prophets by looking at their pay stubs; they're probably on the king's payroll.) There was Hananiah, who assured the masses that everything was all right when, really, things were in all kinds of a mess. Today we've got some false prophets too; we won't mention any names. (The list is too long, eh?) But the true heart of God is revealed through prophets who tell it like it is and who take on the false prophets, like when Jeremiah told Hananiah not to keep saying everything is at peace when things were not (Jeremiah 28).

While we are taught history mostly through the lives of kings and presidents, God tells history through the lives of the prophets. The prophets can make and unmake kings. Sometimes they have enormous popular support, and sometimes they are voices in the wilderness. But they are the voice of God whether or not the people listen. They speak regardless. And they speak recklessly. They have a profound sensitivity to evil as well as to good. God's fire and love rage through the lips of the prophets. Rabbi Abraham Heschel puts it like this: "To us a single act of injustice—cheating in business, exploitation of the poor—is slight; to the prophets, a disaster. To us injustice is injurious to the welfare of the people; to the prophets it is a deathblow to existence; to us, an episode; to them, a catastrophe, a threat to the world."[3] After all, a lot is at stake. And sometimes it takes just one voice to interrupt the pattern of injustice.

3 Abraham Heschel, *The Prophets*, 5th ed. (Peabody, MA: Prince Press, 2003), 4.

The prophets are weird. They set themselves apart from the normalcy of civilization and its pattern of destruction and war. Their vocation is to interrupt the status quo. They are set apart as a sign for all of Israel that they too are to be unlike the nations. The biblical prophets were always doing wild things—stunts, pranks, and miracles that exposed and unveiled truth. Moses turned a staff into a snake. Elijah hit a rock and fire came out of it, and he brought down fire on an altar. Jeremiah wore a yoke to symbolize imperial captivity. (He was eventually arrested.) John the Baptist ate locusts and made clothes out of camel skin. They stripped naked, ate scrolls, wore sackcloth, and lay on the ground outside of city gates. Ezekiel pulled off a protest in the nude and staged a prophetic stunt that involved cooking with poop (and not to win money on a reality show). Yes, the prophets are weird. It can embarrass us to read of their antics, but what they do is not nearly as embarrassing as the things we do, which their actions expose so we can see that another future is possible.

Big Beasts and Little Prophets

Daniel is one of the prophets known for their encounters with beasts. He's the one who was thrown into the den of lions by King Darius (because he bowed to worship God rather than the emperor, violating an official decree) only to find that God had shut the mouths of those imperial lions. Daniel was never scared to speak truth to power, even inside the royal court. On one occasion, he was offered fancy foods at the royal banquet and decided to fast. (This reminds us of when Mother Teresa would sneak out of fancy banquets where she was speaking to eat with the beggars.) Daniel had some wild visions of kings cast from their thrones and empires collapsing. He often talked about visions of beasts, not just wild animals but crazy horned, fire-breathing-dragon beasts like those in horror flicks. Daniel and some of the other prophets like John of Patmos (author of the book of Revelation) spoke about these apocalyptic monsters. They often used these images to represent empires and evil. We hear people talk about "the man" or "the system," but the prophets talked about "the beast."

In my vision...there before me was a fourth beast—terrifying and frightening and very powerful. It had large iron teeth; it crushed and devoured its victims and trampled underfoot whatever was left.
Dan. 7:7

Then another sign appeared in heaven: an enormous red dragon with seven heads and ten horns and seven crowns on its heads.
Rev. 12:3

The images of the beasts remind us that these creatures have mutated far from what God intended, even compared with the most savage of wild animals. These aren't snakes or scary grizzlies; these are demonic monsters of terror. The beasts are the manifestation of those systems of imperial power that had become so corrupt that they were only mutations of things made by God. The beasts of the prophets were not animals but fantastic horned, flying, fire-breathing monsters, as if to say that these powers and empires had grown so far from God's original creation that they had ceased to be human, natural, or a part of the divine order. They no longer reflected God's image or goodness. They were dehumanized systems that no longer had life or love or beauty in them and no longer did anything that humans were created to do, like love and be loved.

But there is a beautiful image in the book of Daniel amid the visions of beasts. Daniel's apocalyptic vision is a reassurance to faithful Jews being persecuted by Syrian monarch Antiochus IV Epiphanies that, just as Babylonians, Medes, Persians, and Greeks had come and gone, so this evil Syrian empire would pass—and God's kingdom would remain.[4] In his vision, Daniel saw four beasts. One was like a lion with wings. The second was like a bear, and the third like a leopard with four wings. The fourth came with iron teeth, like a tank devouring victims and running over everything in its path. And then (this is the beautiful part): "In my vision ... there before me was one like a son of man, coming with clouds of heaven" (7:13). He was led into the presence of the Ancient of Days as the beasts lay slain. And all the nations worshiped the son of man, or "the human one," who rose above the fallen beasts and ascended to the throne of the Ancient of Days, whose dominion "will not pass away, and his kingdom is one that will never be destroyed" (v. 14). The image is of the Son of Man[5] walking amid the slain beasts, whose fire and rage God has forever snuffed out. Long live the human one, the King who cries and laughs.

4 See Gerhard Lohfink, *Does God Need the Church?* (Collegeville, MN: Liturgical Press, 1998), 178.

5 Just like Adam, the Son of Man, in Hebrew, evokes an earthy sense. "Man" or humanity is linkable to dirt, humus, and soil (*'adama*).

Similar to the way the evil empires are likened to beasts—"like a lion ... like a bear ... like a leopard ..."—the holy kingdom is likened to "a son of man." But the old order is bestial, while the new is truly human. It is the human kingdom, where people learn to feel again, to laugh, to play, where the lion and the lamb lie down together, and a child cuddles with a bear (Isaiah 11). When humans start to act like beasts, God becomes a little baby. And the baby is given all the power in the world.

Daniel isn't the only one who spoke of beasts

Can you hear the chorus of THE BEAST?

"WARN THE TOWN THE BEAST IS LOOSE"

...the eerie warning of corporate and ~~polit-~~

political powers on the prowl for blood?

The song was written by a band who named themselves FUGEES,

short for Refugees.

When Kings Cry

Of course, not all prophets were men. There is the powerful, hidden biblical story of a heroic woman named Rizpah, whose tears stirred the humanity of King David during a time when blood stained the land (2 Samuel 21). Rizpah lived in a time like ours. Kings were making treaties and breaking them (v. 2). The land was stained with the blood of war. To try to make amends and heal the famine that cursed Israel, David made a deal with the Gibeonites. He used the currency of human lives. He handed human beings over to the Gibeonites to be massacred. It was promised in 1 Samuel 8 that kings and thrones would bring destruction, and this sad curse is displayed here. He took the sons of a poor concubine named Rizpah, and five others, and the children were "killed and exposed before the LORD." Not only were they killed, but they were left on the hill without proper burial, left to be devoured by wild animals. However, despite David's effort, God did not heal the land ... yet.

With the reckless love only a grieving mother has, Rizpah took sackcloth and spread it out on a rock beside the bodies. She set up camp. The text says she stayed from the "beginning of the harvest till the rains poured" (v. 10), implying that she was there for the season. Day after day, week after week, she protected the bodies from the animals. And word of her encampment spread across the land, making it all the way to the ears of King David. When he heard of her courage, he remembered Saul, and his friend Jonathan—harsh memories of violence in his past. An incredible thing happens next: he was moved to gather up the bones of all the dead.

Human suffering has the power to move even kings to feel again. Rizpah pricked the humanity of a king who had become so dehumanized that he could exchange children like currency and see them die without remorse. True liberation can set even kings free. True revolution is when, as anti-apartheid leader and Nobel Peace Prize–winner Bishop Desmond Tutu says (with a huge smile), "The oppressed are freed from being oppressed and the oppressors are freed from being oppressors." And this is when God heals the land (v. 14).

During a peacemaking trip to Iraq, during the 2003 bombardment, a bunch of us read this story and prayed that once again mothers would set up camp beside the bodies of their dead and wail so loudly that word of the travesty would spread throughout the earth. Maybe people from around the world would hear and come out with them on the rock beside the bodies. And we would groan together so loudly that even the kings would hear. Perhaps the kings would be moved to be human again, and then God would heal our land.

The prophets point us to what is ahead—the fulfillment of God's dream for creation. And they invite us not simply to wait but to begin enacting that dream—now.

Power in Weakness

Yahweh continues to be careful to choose the weakest, most unlikely characters to be the heroes of the liberation story, lest we be tempted to think we did it ourselves, with our own power or might or ingenuity. It is clear that God was the one fighting for these people whom no one else would fight for. God can use the sea to swallow up armies, and God can use music, worship, and dance to topple the walls of fortified cities like Jericho. As the people marched and the trumpets blew, the walls fell down (Joshua 6). And, of course, God saved the prostitute Rahab and her "inn" there in Jericho, for they were a beautiful part of the divine conspiracy, taking in the Israelite spies. Rahab would go on to join the lineage of Jesus (Matthew 1). God is good, and very unpredictable.

There is the brilliant story of Gideon, who went forth to fight the Midianites (Judges 7). Like any good commander in chief, he rallied the troops, 32,000 of them, to be exact. But then the Lord said, "You have too many men," and ordered that he send some away so that Israel couldn't boast that her own strength saved her. So 22,000 headed off, leaving him with 10,000. And then the Lord spoke again, telling him there were still too many, and shook it down to 300. From an army of over 30,000 to 300—not exactly a force to be reckoned with. But this is precisely the point. Only God can be trusted with power and strength, lest Israel think too highly of herself or depend on her military might rather than the miraculous God who can split oceans open to protect them.[6]

Think about the other folks God appointed to lead. Consider the fact that God chose a shepherd boy to be king. It's like picking a kid from the

6 Ironically, it was Gideon's son Abimelek who later took everything into his own hands, killing his entire family to ensure his kingship. But in a further irony, Abimelek was injured in a battle at the hands of a woman (who dropped a brick on him), and he was so ashamed in his weakness that he ordered his armor-bearer to kill him "so they can't say, 'A woman killed him.'" Strength and pride, men and swords ... dangerous things, aren't they?

sweatshops to lead a corporation. It's like choosing a politically powerless carpenter as God's Son. (Uh ... hold that thought.) Granted, shepherds did know a thing or two about God's protection. After all, some of their main clientele were families buying lambs for the Passover festival. During the festival, each family would slay a lamb to remember the blood that protected them during one of the imperial plagues in Egypt, when they wiped it on their homes to mark them as set apart. But they didn't know battle. Shepherding was not a very dignified job. It was more like the bottom rung of the chores list, and it was usually reserved for kids (not old guys in bathrobes like in the live nativity scenes). It was a life much like that lived by Bedouin children and peasants around the world. Shepherds were not necessarily the sharpest and brightest, and they weren't the most logical choice for a king. When Samuel was on his quest to find the one who was to be king of Israel, Jesse brought out his sons, all except David, whom he didn't even consider a candidate. Samuel said to him, "Are these all the sons you have?" And Jesse replied, "There is still the youngest, but he is tending the sheep." Jesse brought him in from the field. Upon his arrival, the voice of the Lord said, "Anoint him; this is the one" (1 Sam. 16:12). The anointed David would go on to be the little kid who killed the giant Goliath—who was not only a big dude but an "uncircumcised Philistine," the enemy of God's people. But if you know the story, you'll recall he didn't do it with mighty weapons. The Scriptures say that even as everyone was preparing for the big fight, David was going back and forth to care for the sheep. And he couldn't even walk with the armor they tried to put on him. Saul, familiar with violence (an understatement), loaded David up with armor and a sword, ready for battle. But David said, just like a child, "I cannot go in these" (17:39). He took them off, grabbed a few stones, and headed into battle to face the nine-foot embodiment of power. He looked into the face of Goliath with his five thousand shekel armor and his spear whose "iron point weighed six hundred shekels" (17:5). (If Goliath lived today, he definitely would have his own humvee and helmet.) But little David toppled the giant with a slingshot. Now that's humor. That's like a few campañeros in Latin America toppling a multinational corporation with a few fair-trade coffee beans. That lampoons power, like a kid with a supersoaker taking on Osama bin Laden. Which does seem to hold promise for a better world. What would the world look like if all the child soldiers were playing with supersoakers instead of US-made AK-47s?

Back in Egypt, God had charged Moses not to act pompous and powerful but to assert his low stature when confronting the powers. "When Pharaoh calls you in and asks, 'What is your occupation?' you should answer, 'Your servants have tended livestock from our boyhood on, just as our fathers did.' Then you will be allowed to settle in the region of Goshen, for all shepherds are detestable to the Egyptians" (Gen. 46:33–34).

The great paradox and humor of God's audacious power:
a stuttering prophet will be the voice of God ,
a barren old lady will become the mother of a nation,

a shepherd boy will become their king,
and a homeless baby will lead them home.

If the people of Abraham were called out to be "set apart," what did that look like in practice? How were they different? Much of the Hebrews' practices and rules are given in the cryptic and weird "purity code" found in Leviticus and other books. They are the source of great misunderstanding for us today. One writer expresses his confusion on the subject:

SET APART?

Thank you for doing so much to educate people regarding God's law. I have learned a great deal from you, and try to share that knowledge with as many people as I can. When someone tries to defend the homosexual lifestyle, for example, I simply remind them that Leviticus 18:22 clearly states it to be an abomination—end of debate. I do need some advice from you, however, regarding some other elements of God's laws and how to follow them.

1. Leviticus 25:44 states that I may possess slaves, both male and female, provided they are purchased from neighboring nations. A friend of mine claims that this applies to Mexicans but not Canadians. Can you clarify? Why can't I own Canadians?

2. I would like to sell my daughter into slavery, as sanctioned in Exodus 21:7. In this day and age, what do you think would be fair price for her?

3. I know that I am allowed no contact with a woman while she is in her period of menstrual uncleanliness (Lev. 15:19–24). The problem is: how do I tell? I have tried asking, but most women take offense.

4. When I burn a bull on the altar as a sacrifice, I know it creates a pleasing odor to the Lord (Lev. 1:9). The problem is my neighbors. They claim the odor is not pleasing to them. Should I smite them?

5. I have a neighbor who insists on working on the Sabbath. Exodus 35:2 clearly states he should be put to death. Am I morally obligated to kill him myself, or should I ask the police to do it?

6. A friend of mine feels that even though eating shellfish is an abomination (Lev. 11:10), it is a lesser abomination than homosexuality. I don't agree. Can you settle this? Are there degrees of abomination?

7. Leviticus 21:20 states that I may not approach the altar of God if I have a defect in my sight. I have to admit that I wear reading glasses. Does my vision have to be 20/20, or is there some wiggle room here?

8. Most of my male friends get their hair trimmed, including the hair around their temples, even though this is expressly forbidden by Leviticus 19:27. How should they die?

9. I know from Leviticus 11:6–8 that touching the skin of a dead pig makes me unclean, but may I still play football if I wear gloves?

10. My uncle has a farm. He violates Leviticus 19:19 by planting two different crops in the same field, as does his wife by wearing garments made of two different kinds of thread (cotton-polyester blend). He also tends to curse and blaspheme a lot. Is it really necessary that we go to all the trouble of getting the whole town together to stone them (Lev. 24:10–16)? Couldn't we just burn them to death at a private family affair, like we do with people who sleep with their in-laws (Lev. 20:14)?

I know you have studied these things extensively and thus enjoy considerable expertise in such matters, so I am confident you can help. Thank you again for reminding us that God's word is eternal and unchanging.[7]

7 Garry Wills, *What Jesus Meant* (New York: Penguin, 2006), 34–35.

Set Apart for Something Better

Significant dates and events led to Jewish holidays and rituals, all of which were put in place to remind the Hebrews of their story and to continue to form them into a new kind of people. Some of them may seem extreme, like slaughtering a lamb and wiping its blood on the doorframes of their houses, but so was their liberation story. The times in which they lived demanded extreme measures to set them apart. All of these were ways

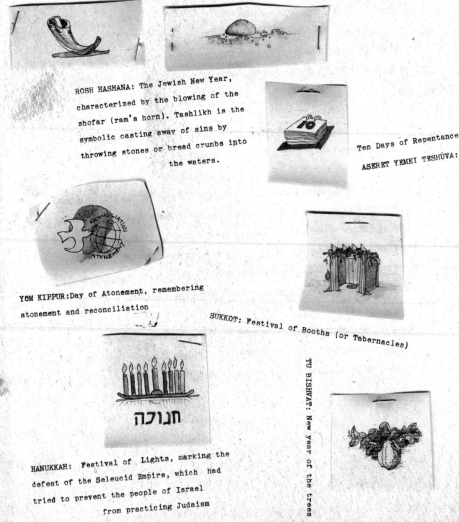

ROSH HASHANA: The Jewish New Year, characterized by the blowing of the shofar (ram's horn). Tashlikh is the symbolic casting away of sins by throwing stones or bread crumbs into the waters.

ASERET YEMEI TESHUVA: Ten Days of Repentance

YOM KIPPUR: Day of Atonement, remembering atonement and reconciliation

SUKKOT: Festival of Booths (or Tabernacles)

HANUKKAH: Festival of Lights, marking the defeat of the Seleucid Empire, which had tried to prevent the people of Israel from practicing Judaism

חנוכה

TU BISHVAT: New year of the trees

of remembering their identity as a people whom God was protecting and redeeming. Part of that process was creating their own culture, with their own customs and holidays.

Consider the Jewish holidays celebrated to this day and how they remind us of this peculiar group of people that is different from the nations. The Jewish calendar is not the same as the calendar of the empire from which they came.

SHEMINI ATZERET & SIMCHAT TORAH

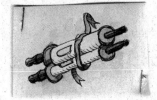

TISHA B'AV: a fasting day that commemorates two of the saddest days in Jewish history--the destruction of both the first temple in 587BC, originally built by King Solomon, and the second temple on the same date in AD 70.

TENTH OF TEVET: marks the beginning of the siege if Jerusalem

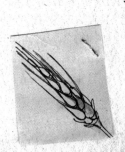

PURIM: Festival of Lots, commemorating the events that took place in the book of Esther

PESACH: Passover, commemorating the liberation of the Israelite slaves fro Egypt

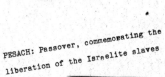

SEFIRAH: Counting the Omer

In forming a people who were set apart from their messed up world, God put some things in place to ensure and preserve that "set-apartness." Moses received the Law or Torah, a wise guide for life outside the empire[8] that included ways that God was shaping the Israelites individually and as a community, restoring their dignity so that they could rise from slavery's degradation and fulfill their original purpose in healing the creation. Some of the things in the Law were very overt ways God marked or branded them, like circumcision. And some were subtler, like eating kosher. Let's think about circumcision for a minute. Circumcision was one of the clear external marks of God on this new community (at least for half of them). At ninety-nine years old, Abraham was ordered to undergo circumcision. (Ouch ... no wonder he was called a man of great faith.) He did so, along with all the boys eight days old, as a "sign of the covenant," a covenant in their flesh, marking them as God's new humanity. The Bible speaks of the Law as a way that God was "circumcising the hearts" of Israel, cutting away the stuff of earth to set them apart for the things of God. It was sort of a blood rite into the counterculture of God.

This is all, of course, before you could get bumper stickers, T-shirts, or tattoos to mark yourself for God. And the question that will arise in the early church with Gentile converts is, "Do they have to get circumcised?" If they don't follow all the Hebrew laws concerning how to eat, dress, and live (and for those who don't have penises at all), then what will set them apart? It's a question we will turn to near the end of this book: What is

8 Lohfink (*Does God Need the Church?* 114) notes that the biblical authors intentionally excluded the period of statehood, starting under David, from this fundamental text. Statehood and kingship, as we have shown, are written into their later history as a compromise and an affront to God.

it that sets the people of God apart as a "holy nation" for God? How has God branded and marked our lives and communities?

As you read the purity laws in books like Leviticus and Deuteronomy, some of the laws make a lot of sense. For example, we can think of health reasons that might justify circumcision. Others are a little trickier to figure out. For instance, the Israelites weren't to touch the skin of a pig ... not great for football fans, but arguably a healthy corrective for our obsession with contemporary imperial games. They weren't to mix two kinds of thread, which would cramp our style a bit. But with a closer look, we can see that many of these laws were intended to create a new culture free of the unhealthy patterns and branding of empire. If we imagine putting those laws in contemporary terms, we can see the subtle critique of culture implicit in them: "Thou shalt not have in thy home the electric box with the talking screen," or, "Thou shalt not wear clothing marked with a swoosh or any other image that requires the blood of sweatshop children." We'll get back to that later.

We can start to see how these peculiar people came to see themselves as resident aliens on this earth and how they often found themselves at odds with the culture of empires and markets. Emperors such as Antiochus IV Epiphanies even forbade circumcision, as an attack on the set-apartness of God's people and to force assimilation. Many of the Israelites' laws were, after all, a direct confrontation with those of the world they knew. They were ways of driving a wedge into the wheels of injustice and interrupting cycles of oppression.

Consider the "eye for eye, tooth for tooth" laws written in the Hebrew constitution (Exod. 21:24; Lev. 24:20; Deut. 19:21). These commands were put in place not to promote retaliation but rather to *limit* it. The young exodus people were being led to discover a new way of living outside the empire. God made sure there were some boundaries—like if someone pokes out your eye, you can't poke out both of their eyes. If someone breaks your arm, you cannot go and break their arm *and* a leg. And as we will see, Jesus later takes this command to its fullest spirit and intent by saying, "You have heard that it was said, 'Eye for eye, and tooth for tooth.' But I tell you …" These limits ensured that the Israelites might avoid the ugly blowbacks of the myth of redemptive violence that nations know so well. These laws were ways of interrupting the pattern of violence escalating violence, as in the case of feudal wars, urban gang wars, or the war in Iraq.

God put in place other beautiful initiatives to awaken the Israelites' political imagination and ensure that they didn't default to old ways of living. One of the first stories of the Israelites' exodus adventure is the famous feeding in the wilderness, when God heard their groaning from hunger and rained down manna from heaven. And in that story, we hear one of God's first commandments (even before he gave them the Big 10) when they were stuck in the middle of the wilderness somewhere between Pharaoh's empire and the Promised Land: each one was to gather only as much as they needed (Exodus 16). In the exodus story, God poured food from the sky and assured them if they would not take extra, there would be enough. When they did take extra, God sent maggots to destroy their stockpile. (Maybe we need some maggots today.) They were ordered to carry with them one "omer" of manna, which was symbolic of their daily providence of bread.

SABBATH

And when they finally did reach the Promised Land,[9] they had what biblical scholar Ched Myers calls "the Sabbath laws."[10] The Sabbath laws were put in place not just so people could go to worship services on Sunday (or Saturday) mornings but to make sure that the Hebrew people didn't revert to the exploitative economy of the empire from which they were saved. If they were going to be a peculiar people, then they needed a peculiar kind of economy. Instead of trying to reform the empire's economy when they were in Egypt, God brought them out to this new place so that they could cultivate an entirely new economy, Yahweh's economy of life rather than the imperial economy of death.

The Sabbath laws were sort of like God's system of checks and balances on Israel's economy to make sure that no one got too rich and no one got too poor. God knew the painful reality of human sin all to well and the probability that the Hebrew people might drift back into a society of haves and have-nots. To prevent this distorted economy from developing, God got creative and came up with these Sabbath laws.

We catch a glimpse of these laws in those books of the Bible that most of us hardly ever read. Growing up, we were taught to sing the exciting songs

9 Again, it is noteworthy to see that entering the Promised Land was intentionally not included in the Torah. The Hebrews were to retain a sense that they had not "arrived." Lohfink writes that at the end of Deuteronomy, "the people stand on the threshold of the land of promise, but they are not yet in the land itself. Everything remains open. The threshold has not yet been crossed" (ibid., 125).

10 Check out brother Myers' little booklet on the Sabbath laws: Ched Myers, *The Biblical Vision of Sabbath Economics*, Tell the Word series (Washington, D.C.: Church of the Saviour, 2001).

of Noah and Abraham and little David and Goliath. But never were we taught songs about debt cancellation, land reforms, food redistribution, and slave amnesty. We don't know if it was just hard to come up with words that rhyme with "debt cancellation" or if folks were hesitant about venturing into the ancient (and sometimes boring) world of Exodus, Leviticus, and Deuteronomy (in which case, we wouldn't blame them). Whatever the case, those books are where some of God's most creative and exciting ideas come alive.

There were laws for welcoming strangers and illegal immigrants and for practices like gleaning, which allowed the poor to take leftovers from the fields. (God would have some harsh things to say about laws prohibiting dumpster diving for food.) The Sabbath laws made sure that the most vulnerable of society (usually widows, orphans, and the elderly) were looked after. And there were clear warnings against taking financial interest or creating debt. (So you can see where we're headed. If we applied Sabbath law today, the bank owner would be as much of a criminal as the bank robber. And a

For the LORD your God is God of gods and Lord of lords, the great God, mighty and awesome, who shows no partiality and accepts no bribes. He defends the cause of the fatherless and the widow, and loves the alien, giving him food and clothing.
Deut. 10:17–18

lot of credit card companies and international organizations would be in really big trouble.)

One of the most exciting of the Sabbath laws was applied every seven years. Just like the Hebrew people were supposed to refrain from working every seventh day so that their land, animals, and servants could rest (a marked contrast to their overworked life in Egypt), every seventh year, the Hebrew people had a celebration called the Jubilee (named after the *jovel*, a ram's horn that sounded to herald the remission), during which they would *take the whole year off* from work. During this one-year break, all the food that continued to grow in their fields was free for the taking for families who were struggling to get by (Exod. 23:10). And any debt that folks had incurred during the past six years was erased. These laws ensured that those in society who were intent on getting ahead had to take a break so that the gap between the rich and the poor would be kept to a minimum. It is almost impossible for us to grasp how wildly countercultural (and difficult) this economic practice really was. God's idea for this peculiar people was that there be "no poor people among you" (Deut. 15:4), which was a very different way of life for these former slaves.

And as if that weren't enough to keep society from going off-kilter, God threw in one more practice—one giant celebration to be celebrated every 49th/50th year (seven times seven). It was called the Jubilee of Jubilee—God's comprehensive unilateral restructuring of the community's assets to remind Israel that all property and land belonged to God, and that they must never return to a system of slavery (Lev. 25:42). The Jubilee of Jubilee aimed to dismantle structures of social-economic inequality by releasing each community member from debt (Lev. 25:35–42), returning encumbered or forfeited land to its original owners (25:13, 25–28), and freeing slaves (25:47–55). Some might call it a regularly scheduled revolution.

God had seen how these people had suffered under empire in Egypt and had hoped that these initiatives would prevent that from happening ever again.

For the sake of a watching world, God systematically interrupted the human systems that created poverty—releasing debt, setting slaves free, prohibiting usury, and redistributing property. Sounds like a pretty good kingdom, especially compared with the one from which they came and all the surrounding Canaanite powers. Sounds like a platform even we could vote for.

Some folks say dismissively that the Israelites never fully lived out the Jubilee. But folks could also say that Christians don't live out the teachings of Jesus. These are still God's commands and dreams for the world. At their core, these Hebrew laws were ways God was protecting the integrity of a new humanity. It was not simply for their sake but for the sake of creation. For the original plan of God was that Israel would be set apart to redeem the nations. This was not a plan to reform the pagan nations around it—like making the neighboring Assyrian empire better at doing empire. Rather, God would save the world through fascination, by setting up an alternative society on the margins of empire for the world to come and see what a society of love looks like. It would be the city on a hill that God would use to light up the world, drawing the world back to God. Their light dimmed (at times, almost snuffed out) with Israel's unfaithfulness and would require a new strategy—but not another flood. Death would be defeated by love. In the story of Noah, God exterminates the many to save the few, and in the story of Abraham, God sets apart the few to save the many.

This little group continued to return to the patterns of the nations and fall short of the dream of God. They never fully entered the Promised Land. But God didn't give up. God will give them a fresh vision of the Promised Land, which they will come to know as the kingdom of God on earth. God's Son will embody all that Israel was meant to be. He will gather a people who will embody that hope for the world. God has had enough of the messes of empires and kings. Indeed, it's time for a different kind of king and a different kind of empire. The Prince of Peace, the royal Son comes to earth. To triumph?

We'll see....................

SECTION TWO

A New Kind of Commander-in-Chief

As Israel continued to break the covenant and failed to be distinctive, God came to show us in one person all that Israel was meant to be. After over and over seeing God's people fail to live up to the law of love, it seems God could not watch humanity continue to destroy herself. Amid the many unresolved questions in the Hebrews' story, one thing seems clear: Jesus came to fulfill the story begun in Abraham and Sarah.

"In those days Caesar Augustus issued a decree that a census should be taken of the entire Roman world. ... An angel of the Lord appeared to them, and the glory of the Lord shone around them, and they were terrified. But the angel said to them, 'Do not be afraid. I bring you good news [*evangelion*] of great joy that will be for all the people. Today in the town of David a Savior has been born to you; he is the Messiah, the Lord'" (Luke 2:1, 9–11).

Ah, the good old Christmas story. Conjures up warm feelings of Christmas pageants, eggnog by the fire, and that shimmering Christmas tree we have all grown to love. The opening words of Luke's gospel have become a fixture in the liturgy of American cultural Christianity. Rather than shaking us to the core (as it did to those poor shepherds), the story of Jesus' birth has been tamed and now sits nicely on the front of cheesy Hallmark cards (which, admit it, you eventually just throw away).

But Luke's words instilled much courage and hope in Jesus' first followers. To those managing the affairs of the state, they were grounds for arrest. So many of the words we just throw around in Christian circles today were loaded with political meaning for Jesus and his contemporaries. Many were words Jesus swiped from the imperial lexicon and spun on their heads in beautiful political satire.

Consider these words:

gospel
faith

kingdom

throne

savior
banner

Lord

Messiah

All of these were words that Rome knew well.

Imperial Language

Jesus' Language

Basilea ("empire" or "kingdom"): Term used for the Roman Empire. At the head: Caesar.

Basilea: Jesus' most common topic of conversation: the kingdom of God or the kingdom of the heavens. At the head: YHWH, who liberated the Israelites from Egyptian slavery.

Gospel (*evangelion*: "good news"): An imperial pronouncement, usually accompanied by flags and political ceremony, that an heir to the empire's throne had been born or that a distant battle had been won.

Gospel: Jesus' good news that the kingdom of God is at hand.

Christ (Greek translation of Hebrew *messiah*): Known by the Romans as the name Jews used for their ruler, anointed by God and the people. The King of the Jews job title had already been granted to Herod, hence the problem when Jesus was also considered to be a King of the Jews. Only one person at a time can fit on a throne.

Expression of being commissioned or appointed, especially by divine authority—precisely how folks thought of the Roman emperors (literally means "dripped on by the gods," as in anointed with oil).

Messiah: Divinely anointed ruler over Israel who would fulfill the scriptural promises of saving the Israelites from oppression (and from themselves). While a primary title for Jesus, this is also the name used for David and other rulers. Messiah does not mean, as it is commonly mistaken to mean, that God beamed down to earth and squeezed into human flesh, but a "divinely mandated royal man." (We might understand Jesus as the incarnate deity, but *Messiah* had a very different political connotation and historical role.)[1]

1 It's not that divinity and politics were two separate things to be combined but that they were, to a great extent, the same thing.

Son of God: A popular title for kings and emperors.

Name taken up by Alexander the Great (also used King of Kings) and Octavian, later known as Augustus, in the lineage of Julius Caesar.

Ekklesia: A local public assembly within the greater Roman Empire, much like a town meeting. These assemblies bestowed citizenship,[3] discussed local political concerns, assigned "elders," and offered prayer and worship to Caesar. There was no separation of religion (cultic sacrifices, etc.) and secular political business.

Son of God: Name given to Jesus,

though he more commonly spoke of himself as the Son of Man (or "the human one," a term borrowed from the prophet Daniel). Used by the Tempter in the desert in reference to tempting a king.[2]

Ekklesia: Word used for the early church. "Emphasizes that the followers of Jesus were called to participate in their world as 'local communities of an alternative society to the Roman imperial order.'"[4] Bestowed alternative citizenship and assigned elders. Though it discussed its own political and religious concerns, it was understood as separate from, and in contrast to, the state and the other *ekklesiai*, their politics, and their religion.

2 Concerning the political name the Tempter calls Jesus in the desert, John Howard Yoder writes, "'Son of God' cannot very well in Aramaic have pointed to the ontological coessentiality [meaning: "having the same being"] of the Son with the Father. ... The 'Son of God' in Psalm 2:7 is the King; all the options laid before Jesus by the tempter are ways of being king ... the title is meant messianically and not metaphysically ... Luke 22:76–23:21 (substantially the same in the parallels) equates 'Messiah' and 'Son of God' (in a Jewish context) with 'King of the Jews' (before Pilate). All three titles in standard usage referred not to incarnate deity but to a divinely mandated royal man" (John Howard Yoder, *The Politics of Jesus* [Grand Rapids: Eerdmans, 1994], 24–25).

3 Ekkehard W. Stegemann and Wolfgang Stegemann, *The Jesus Movement: A Social History of Its First Century* (Minneapolis: Fortress, 1999), 275.

4 Wes Howard-Brook and Anthony Gwyther, *Unveiling Empire: Reading Revelation Then and Now* (Maryknoll, NY: Orbis, 1999), 117.

Parousia (literally "presence"): The return of of Caesar to visit a town.

Parousia: The second coming of Jesus, seen in contrast to the *parousia* of Caesar.[5]

Savior (*soter*: literally "healer" or "preserver"): Caesar Augustus, as Savior, was seen as the one who healed the chaos of Rome and brought it into a new golden age.[6]

Savior: A title for Jesus.

Faith: A term used for trust in, allegiance to, and hope in Jesus.

Faith: A term used for trust in, allegiance to, and hope in the *Pax Romana*. It had much to do with loyalty, as with a faithful husband.[7]

Lord: A much more international acclamation for Jesus than the term Christ/Messiah.

Lord (*kyrios*): Name for a ruler, particularly a supreme ruler.

Emmanuel (*dues praesens*): The manifestation of the presence and will of the gods; a title claimed by emperors like Antiochus IV Epiphanes and Domitian.

Emmanuel: Means "God with us" and is the name prophesied in Hebrew Scripture for the Messiah, later proclaimed by the angel to Mary as one of the names for Jesus (Matt. 1:22–23; see also Isa. 7:14).

Worship (*proskynesis*): A practice involving the act of prostration or bowing in submission before a ruler or emperor; an act of submission.

Worship (*proskyneo*): Bowing before God in praise and adoration. For example, this word is used when the magi bowed down before the baby Jesus in the manger.

5 N. T. Wright, *The Resurrection of the Son of God* (Minneapolis: Augsburg Fortress, 2003), 231ff.

6 Cf. Richard A. Horsley, *Jesus and Empire* (Minneapolis: Augsburg Fortress, 2002), 23–24.

7 *Fides/pistis* = "loyalty" (i.e., submission and deference). Ibid.,.27.

You can find this language woven in political poetry throughout the empire. The following was found chiseled on the ruins of an old government building in Asia Minor, dated 6 BC:

The most divine Caesar ... we should consider equal to the Beginning of all things ... for when everything was falling (into disorder) and tending toward dissolution, he restored it once more and gave the whole world a new aura; Caesar ... the common good Fortune of all ... The beginning of life and vitality ... All the cities unanimously adopt the birthday of the divine Caesar as the new beginning of the year ... Whereas the Providence which has regulated our whle existence ... has brought our life to the climax of perfection in giving to us (the emperor) Augustus ... who being sent to us and our descendents as Savior, has put an end to war and has set all things in order; and (whereas,) having become (god) manifest /PHANEIS/, Caesar has fulfilled all the hopes of earlier times ... the birthday of the god (Augustus) has been for the whole world the beginning of good news /EVANGELION/ concerning him. ...[8]

8 Cf. Horsley, *Jesus and Empire*, 23–24. See also, *Orientis graeci inscriptiones selectae*, W. Dittenberger ed., vol. 2 (Leipzig, 1903–5), 458.

Now read that quaint Christmas story again, but this time with first-century eyes. Rome already had a Savior. His name was Caesar. And Caesar had a gospel. But now in Jesus a different kind of Savior was being proclaimed—and he had a different kind of gospel and a different kind of kingdom.

Some of us may remember a Sunday school tune: "His banner over me, his banner over you, is love, love, love." This is another way of saying *his* banner, and not Rome's banner, is over me. And his banner means "love, love, love," not Rome's "freedom, peace, and security." We wave the banner for Jesus and not for Rome, the United States of America, or any other nation or empire that vies for our allegiance.

But it wasn't as if Jesus, in using such language, wanted Rome's power or wanted to gain a foothold in the culture wars of his time. He didn't want to climb Caesar's throne. This political language doesn't harmonize with the contemporary church project of "reclaiming America for God." Precisely the opposite: Jesus was urging his followers to be the unique, peculiar, and set-apart people that began with Abraham. He didn't pray for the world in order to make governments more religious; he called Israel to be the light of the world—to abandon the way of the world and cultivate an alternative society in the shell of the old, not merely to be a better version of the kingdom of this world.

A Little Political Backdrop

Just as a light reading can cause us to miss much of Scripture's political jargon, it is also easy for us to overlook biblical names and proper nouns as if they had no contemporary significance. But each name or place had critical meaning for first-century Mediterraneans that we might miss. Just as we have all kinds of thoughts when we hear Rumsfeld or Capitol Hill or Obama or the Oval Office, names like the Praetorium or Golgotha or Antipas or Pilate or the Decapolis were loaded with meaning in Jesus' time.

BETHSAIDA

JORDAN RIVER

For generations both before and after Jesus' birth, the Galilean and Judean people repeatedly protested and revolted against the Romans and their client rulers—the Herodian kings and the high priests in Jerusalem. It was an age filled with popular unrest, suppression, and protests, movements, and riots. Uprisings and slaughter plagued entire cities. In the decades before Jesus was born, Roman armies marched through the area burning villages, enslaving entire towns, and killing all who resisted.

Let's take a look at the town of Sepphoris.[9] Herod Antipas built Sepphoris on the backs of the Galileans, with their taxes and sweat. Joseph, who was a carpenter, and Jesus may have worked there on the building projects as Jesus grew up.[10]

9 Much of the following section is inspired by the teaching of Rob Bell.

10 There is even a story in which a family in Nazareth, perhaps some of Jesus' relatives, was dragged before Caesar and interrogated "as descendants of David." The emperor (Domitian) asked how much money they had. And the couple replied that they were poor people of the land and had little money. They showed the emperor the calluses on their hands and the hardness of their bodies to prove it. Theirs was the life of incessant hard work in Nazareth. How could a king come from such a place? Only Caesar's carpenters, farmers, and janitors lived there (Eusebius, *Ecclesiastical History* 3.19.1–3.20.7; 3.32.5–6).

Emmaus, where Jesus made his famous last walk, was destroyed in this political chaos. An entire city called Magdala, a few miles from Nazareth, was destroyed a generation before Jesus was born (52 BC), and tens of thousands of its people were taken as slaves. Scholars believe that Mary Magdalene was likely from this town (hence her name). Her ancestors may have even been killed, raped, or enslaved during that horror. No doubt, with the ruins of the empire on all sides, Jesus walked through these areas of mass trauma and heard their stories.

LAKE OF GALILEE

TIBERIAS

MAGDALA

NAZARETH

SEPPHORIS

EMMAUS

Jewish historian Josephus records that in Roman retaliation for a widespread revolt in 4 BC, General Varus burned towns and scoured the hills for rebels, crucifying two thousand of them at one time. General Titus rounded up rebels and ended up killing up to five hundred folks daily, and "space could not be found for the crosses nor crosses for the bodies."[11] Josephus goes on to say that the soldiers amused themselves by nailing them up in different postures. It was a brutal age. And, of course, the men killed on crosses next to Jesus were labeled "bandits" (*lestes*), a word the Romans used for everyone from protestors to insurgents.

11 Josephus, *Jewish War* 5.449–51.

Riots and Revolutions

Trying to understand Jesus and his execution without understanding his context is like trying to understand Martin Luther King without learning about the Montgomery bus boycott, Jim Crow laws, and the war in Vietnam. The area where Jesus was born—the northern region of Galilee—was the hub of many of anti-imperial uprisings. This could be why some were skeptical that the Messiah could come from such a place and asked sarcastically, "Nazareth! Can anything good come from there?" (John 1:46).

There were all sorts of countercultures and underground movements trying to create a world better than what Rome had in mind. Some got ugly. The Zealot movement was made up of violent revolutionaries who were ready to overthrow Rome and even marched in legions with hundreds of militiamen. (A few of them would later convert to Jesus' vision.) The Sicarii[12] (named after the curved blade of their daggers) was another extremist group. Scholars say they kidnapped prominent

12 Because of the similarity of his name with Sicarii, Judas Iscariot is considered to be a likely sympathizer with, if not participant in, this movement. Scholar Oscar Cullman suggests that "perhaps as many as half of the twelve were recruited from among the ranks of the Zealots" (Oscar Cullman, *The State in the New Testament* [New York: Charles Scribner's Sons, 1956], 8ff; cf. Yoder, *Politics of Jesus*, 39).

authorities and tried to negotiate the release of their fellow rebels. Led by many intellectuals and teachers, the Sicarii assassinated those who were symbols of power, such as high-profile Jewish collaborators with the Roman occupation (much like some Iraqi resistance fighters do today).

Other groups, such as the Essenes and the Qumran communities, decided to withdraw altogether from such a polluted society and take to the hills, caves, or the desert to set up little utopian villages far away from the struggles between the peasants and the powers. Jesus' cousin John seems to have been inspired by some of their spirit. One community had entirely rejected the temple system of Jerusalem, considering it a compromise of their history. In a dramatic embodiment of Israel's pre-king history (told in the Torah), this group wandered around the desert lands, considering themselves to be the temple.[13] One could argue that John, sympathetic to this radical movement, was enacting alternative washing rituals to those at the Jerusalem temple when he baptized in the desert.

And there were nonviolent mass demonstrations against the empires' antics, like the occasion just before Jesus was born (which his parents probably remembered the way many today recall the 1960s). Imperial

13 Horsley, *Jesus and Empire*, 96.

authorities were trying to import Roman coins with Caesar's image on them into Jerusalem. But "a vast number" of Jews went to appeal to Pilate in Caesarea, which led to a five-day standoff. These Jews were invoking their ancient and subversive belief in "no king but God."[14] Pilate sent in a huge force of soldiers in riot gear. The troops formed a giant ring three layers thick around the protest. Undeterred, the Jewish peasants did not fight but laid down and exposed their necks, saying they would rather have their throats sliced than have their land and convictions defiled. The troops had no idea what to do with that,[15] and they eventually left.[16]

In another conflict, a statue of Caesar was to be placed at the temple in Jerusalem.[17] In a nonviolent manner, "many ten thousands" of Jews lay in protest for forty days. They proclaimed, "We will not by any means make war with [Caesar], but still we will die before we see our laws transgressed." Apparently these farmers were very committed, for they went poor and hungry during this protest, leaving their fields untilled.

These are some of the stories Jesus probably grew up hearing. No wonder he told such good stories with a revolutionary edge. And into the culture, with of all its popular movements of resistance—Zealots, terrorists, hermits—Jesus breathed fresh life and imagination. People were hungry for a revolution, as we can see by their choosing the insurrectionist Barabbas over Jesus when Pilate offered to free one political prisoner to appease the mob outside his palace.

---

14 It's striking to find in Josephus random clauses that refer to "God, who was their Governor" (*Jewish Antiquities* 18.8.6). Apparently the "aversion to monarchy" written about in 1 Samuel 8 was still alive and well.

15 Emperor Caligula ordered the military commander to attack them, but Petronius refused, risking death. The emperor then ordered Petronius to kill himself, but Caligula died before the message was delivered!

16 Josephus, *Jewish War* 2.9.2–3; *Jewish Antiquities* 18.3.1.

17 Josephus, *Jewish Antiquities* 18.8.1–3.

Herod the Not So Great

The political tumult in Palestine[18] dates back hundreds of years before Jesus, and without coming to understand some of this history, it's easy to treat Jesus as just some iconic figure and not a real human with teachings and politics for us all. Jesus' homeland was right in the middle of an ancient trade route between Asia Minor, Africa, and the East, so it had been fought over for centuries. Around the 300s BC, Alexander the Great began history's first globalization effort. He conquered countless regions and tried to glue them all together with a Greek monoculture—Hellenism. After Alexander's conquest, Palestine passed through the hands of many rulers who attempted to keep hold of this strategic region. After Alexander came the Seleucids. Then came the Hasmoneans—a Jewish revolution to "take back the power." Next came the Romans. They, governed by the popular Julius Caesar, passed rule to a man named Antipater, father of Herod the Great. Herod's family descended from the Idumeans, "a mixed population of Jews and Arabs who lived south of Jerusalem between the Judean hills and the Negev desert."[19]

Herod the Great, who eventually gained the title King of the Jews, was a half-Jewish hybrid king who had spilled blood all over the land through slavery, slaughter, and war. He wasn't well-loved, especially by the Jews. Feeling continually threatened by his sons' insatiable appetite for wealth and power and jealous pursuit of the throne, Herod killed his own kids. He even had one of them drowned in the royal pool. He died just after Jesus was born, around 4 BC. After his death, three of Herod's surviving sons—Archelaus, Antipas, and Philip—fought for the throne, and the

18 A name derived from *Philistines*. Depending on your perspective, time frame, and agenda, Canaan and Judea are other names for this land.

19 Thomas Cahill, *Desire of the Everlasting Hills* (New York: Doubleday, 1999), 54.

Jewish people were once again stuck in a royal mess. When the boys took their case to Rome, the Jews sent a delegation to protest, declaring that they had had enough of the Herod clan and didn't want any of these boys as their king. (Archelaus later hunted down and slaughtered this group of Jews.)[20] The Roman emperor didn't listen to the protest and instead divided the kingdom among the Herod family, giving them less to botch up. Philip got the East, Archelaus got Judea and Jerusalem, and Antipas got Galilee.

We don't hear much more about Philip in the Gospels. But we do hear all about the other two brothers, the pseudo-kings with little to rule over. And they did a dreadful job even with that. One of the first things Archelaus did was to send soldiers into the volatile Passover celebration in Jerusalem, where tens of thousands (some say even a couple of hundred thousand) Jews were celebrating their ancestors' deliverance from Egypt. Some of the protestors hurled stones at the soldiers. When word of this reached Archelaus, he was irate and sent in a thousand troops, who ended up massacring three thousand Jews.[21] That's the beginning of the reign of Archelaus.[22]

Squirmy King Antipas ended up ditching his wife and married his brother's wife Herodius. John the Baptizer, Jesus' cousin, had a few things to say

20 In light of this little fiasco in Rome, take a look at Jesus' political satire in Luke 19:11–27. The powerful figure in Jesus' parables doesn't always represent God or how the kingdom works but sometimes represents the way of the world, which is why Jesus doesn't begin this parable with the phrase "the kingdom of God is like ..."

As we begin to discuss and interpret the Gospels, keep in mind that we are taking a path different from most contemporary biblical scholarship. Instead of drawing from a specific gospel for historical or interpretive reasons, we are painting in broad strokes, reading from the four gospels to draw out themes and elements found in them all. Our limited effort is focused on themes that inspire the Christian imagination.

21 Josephus, *Jewish War* 2.1.2–3.

22 When we understand this context, we see Jesus' dad in a better light: "So he got up, took the child and his mother [from Egypt] and went to the land of Israel. But when he heard that Archelaus was reigning in Judea in place of his father Herod, he was afraid to go there. Having been warned in a dream, he withdrew to the district of Galilee, and he went and lived in a town called Nazareth" (Matt. 2:2–23).

about this—the Scriptures record his biting critique of Herod's flaunting of power.[23] John called the entire establishment into question, and folks flocked to hear him in the desert. John was the new exodus. He invited people from the centers of civilization to the desert, to the margins, to find God. All of Rome's dreams were made irrelevant as he ate locusts and made his clothes from camel skin. And folks didn't go to the desert simply to escape the world; they went to the desert to save the world.

Just as they were for John's ancestors in the wilderness outside Pharaoh's land, the margins of the empire were not only an in-between space but also the vortex of the kingdom of God. People went to the wilderness to get Rome out of them, purging themselves of empire and seeing the world stripped of the fabrications of civilization. Even the tax collectors and soldiers, the wealthy and powerful protectors of the empire, left the centers of civilization to find God in the margins. And John preached, "Repent," a message stronger than a neon sign outside a soup kitchen. It was a radical invitation to rethink the way we live,[24] affecting everything that we are and own. Along with this invitation, he told those who have two coats to share one with the cold stranger who has none (a message we're sure Antipas wasn't excited about, probably having more than one tunic in his palace and a fair amount

23 Matt. 14:3–5; Mark 6:17–20.

24 *Repent* (*metanoeite*) has nuanced meaning, translatable to "change your mind," "rethink your life," "think about the way you think," or "turn your life around." Consider the connected word *pensive* in English or *pensar* in Spanish, which both relate to thinking.

to repent of). John taught, "Don't extort money and don't accuse people falsely—be content with your pay" (Luke 3:14). And he spoke boldly of the unlawful marriage and womanizing of King Antipas until it got him in a heap of trouble. The Scriptures say that Herod wanted to kill John but was scared because the people "considered him a prophet" (Matt. 14:5). John had quite an underground movement of locust-eating, camel-skin-wearing revolutionaries out there in the desert. Josephus even says, "Herod, who feared lest the great influence John had over the people might put it into his power and inclination to raise a rebellion (for they seemed ready to do any thing he should advise), thought it best, by putting him to death, to prevent any mischief he might cause."[25]

But then on the big birthday of King Antipas, Herodius's daughter danced for him, and apparently he was quite moved by it all and offered her anything she wanted (as kings often do), frivolously flaunting a little power and wealth. But she didn't ask for fame or fortune. Prompted by her mom, she asked for the head of John the Baptizer on a platter. Ouch. A little distressed, Antipas granted the request and sent out the bounty hunters, who brought the head back on a platter for her. Talk about a birthday party gone bad. But the message was unmistakable: if you mess with the Herod, you'll find your head on a platter. Everything in Herod's world was about flaunting power and wealth and dominion—and crushing the enemies of the establishment. He would shock and awe people with his power, even at a birthday party. His kingdom was built around the principle "bow your head to us or lose it" (see Matt. 14:1–12).

25 Josephus, *Jewish Antiquities* 18.5.2.

The Royal Birth

But we are getting ahead of ourselves. It may be helpful to flash back a little, to remember that Jesus and John were cousins, both born around the same time. John was that voice in the wilderness paving the way for Jesus and colliding with powers until he was killed. Jesus would soon follow. Herod the Great had ruled the empire with an iron fist for forty years, and just before his death, Jesus entered the scene. For some reason, King Herod was not excited to hear all the buzz about the birth of a baby King of the Jews (go figure). Even royal wise folk were coming from afar to find the new king. So Herod gathered these magi and ordered them to report to him when they found Jesus. Herod said it was so he could "go and worship him." But they knew better (after all, they were wise folk) and defied the royal order. The Scriptures say that after they brought their presents to Jesus, they were "warned in a dream not to go back to Herod," so they returned to their country by another route. Jesus' birth was a divine conspiracy.

Then Jesus' family was warned in a dream that Herod was going to try to kill Jesus. The baby Messiah was only crying and pooping at this point, but already he was a threat to Caesar. So Jesus was born on the run. They fled to Egypt because Herod signed an edict to kill all the boys in Bethlehem and its vicinity who were two years old and younger. Jesus was born in the middle of Herod's genocide and stayed in Egypt until Herod died. After Herod's death, an angel told Jesus' parents they could return home.

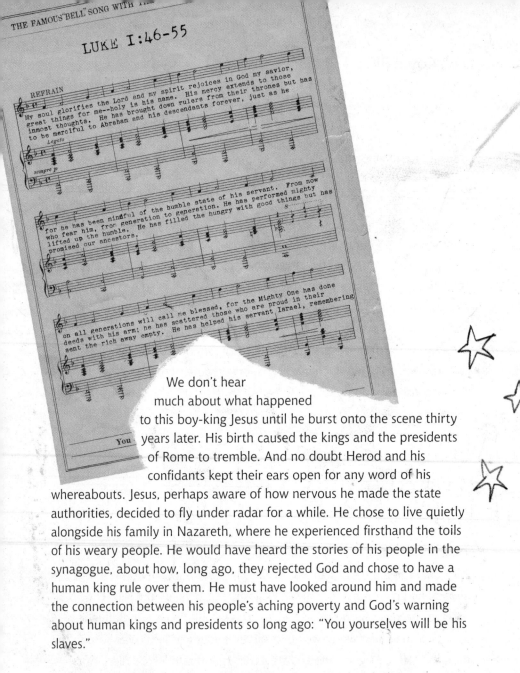

We don't hear much about what happened to this boy-king Jesus until he burst onto the scene thirty years later. His birth caused the kings and the presidents of Rome to tremble. And no doubt Herod and his confidants kept their ears open for any word of his whereabouts. Jesus, perhaps aware of how nervous he made the state authorities, decided to fly under radar for a while. He chose to live quietly alongside his family in Nazareth, where he experienced firsthand the toils of his weary people. He would have heard the stories of his people in the synagogue, about how, long ago, they rejected God and chose to have a human king rule over them. He must have looked around him and made the connection between his people's aching poverty and God's warning about human kings and presidents so long ago: "You yourselves will be his slaves."

We can only speculate about what the boy-king Jesus might have pondered during his life as a poor laborer, but we know for certain that he knew personally the awful consequences of the messes kings make. .

Political Seduction in the Desert

In one of those moments when he was uncomfortably honest in ways Christian artists are not supposed to be, late musician Rich Mullins talked about his vulnerabilities. He said usually he didn't really want to sin, but he just wanted to be "tempted real good" by all that the world had to offer. Then he could know what he was saying no to.

One of the first things Jesus did before starting his public ministry was to go to the desert, where he got tempted real good (Luke 4:1–13). After fasting forty days, he was tempted in ways Israel had been tempted throughout its long history.[26] The Scriptures say he was tempted in all the ways we are (Heb. 4:15), like settling for a better version of this world's kingdom (or just chewing on some magical desert cactus to escape the world's pain). As with most temptations (think back to the garden), the most enticing things are the sweetest fruits this world has to offer. The Tempter's best lie is 99 percent true, and his (or her) greatest strategy is getting us to settle for less than God's dream, or for a subtle distortion of it.

In the desert, praying and fasting, Jesus was "with the beasts." Perhaps the Devil came as the golden eagle of the empire with his offers. Perhaps he came as the Wall Street bull. Maybe the disguise was a presidential elephant or a royal blue donkey. Or maybe he came in a tux and a limo, or in the face of a hungry kid.

While we don't know what form the temptations came in, we do know the propositions. First came the temptation to turn stones into bread. The irony is thick—the Bread of Life starving in the desert. Jesus was tempted to end hunger through a miraculous technique. And he had

26 The biblical authors are here reminding us of the great forties in the Scriptures, such as the forty days of rain before God created a new world through Noah, and especially the Israelites' forty years in the wilderness. As many sages from other cultures have done, Jesus was reentering the story of his ancestors through a "vision quest," time traveling, so to speak, and reengaging the historical mistakes (or successes) of his people. We are indebted to Ched Meyers and Will O'Brian for this and other helpful insights in this section.

the power to turn water into wine or to rain down manna from heaven. Maybe he could see the faces of little peasant girls in his hometown who were starving even as they grew food for Herod. Maybe he could hear the groaning bellies of the Egyptian slaves in the wilderness as they longed for the imperial stew, wondering if God had brought them into the desert to starve them to death. Maybe he could hear the 35,000 children who will starve to death today because they don't have bread and clean water.

But Jesus resisted the temptation, saying, "People do not live on bread alone." Remembering the exodus people in the desert, Jesus knew that "bread from heaven" was not about miracles but was a test—to see whether Israel could resist the Egyptian imperial economics of hoarding.[27] The temptation to return to Pharaoh's economy is a wound in the Israelites' historical identity, and Jesus was trying to cure it. The seduction of the empire's markets of accumulation had enslaved Israel; it wasn't just "Rome's fault." The true Israelite mind must learn in the desert how to say "enough," how to pray simply "for daily bread." And it must be "our" daily bread, because God's economy is communal. Jesus was tempted to exploit the land for sustenance and security, but he resisted. He could

_To Do:_

- VOTE
- GIVE MONEY TO THE POOR
- BUY CHEAP CLOTHES
- BUY GROCERIES
- DIET
- DEMAND LOWER GAS PRICES FROM CONGRESSWOMAN
- GET BACK AT MY ENEMY
- RECYCLE

27 Everyone should gather only enough for their needs. "The one who gathered much did not have too much, and the one who gathered little did not have too little" (Exod. 16:18). This also implies keeping Sabbath, as opposed to the Egyptian slave work week.

have started a revolution to "win the masses" with "bread and circus," but he resisted.[28]

The second temptation in the desert was not a steamy love affair with Mary Magdalene but political power. The Tempter showed Jesus all the kingdoms of the world and said, "I will give you all their authority and their splendor; it has been given to me, and I can give it to anyone I want to. If you worship me, it will all be yours." Unsurprisingly, given the Jewish story, the temptation was to take power back from Rome. Just as Israel was tempted in 1 Samuel 8 to "become like the other nations" and install a king, Jesus was tempted with a throne. The Devil used the title Son of God, raising the question of what kind of king Jesus would be.[29] He could have been the one to overthrow Rome and knock Caesar off his throne. He could have been the one to punish all the enemies of the Jewish people. He could have "stuck it to the Man." He could have ended Herod's genocide and wars and instituted better foreign policies and social services to set all things right again. And the people were ready for it.

It's extraordinary that when the Devil said all political power in the world belongs to him and he can give it to whomever he wishes, Jesus didn't dispute the claim; he just flat out refused the offer. He knew well the bitter fruits of this world's power. He saw governmental power not as a coveted position to run after but rather as the Devil's playground. Jesus' ancestors had suffered from the bloodshed and hunger and pain inflicted by kings and empires. He knew how the powers had killed the prophets before him, and so he abandoned his self to the imperial cross. Instead of ascending the throne of power to establish God's society, he

---

28 Richard Horsley, in *Jesus and Empire* (24–25), describes how "bread and circus," a term popularized by Roman satirist Juvenal, was a major feeding system put in place by the Romans to feed the poor and win popular support. Though the empire was obviously culpable for creating the conditions of poverty in the first place, it could nevertheless garner favor by cleaning up the mess it had made. Giving bread to the masses was a kind of welfare system to placate people—sort of like granting tax exemptions to keep people happy.

29 Cf. Yoder, *Politics of Jesus*, 24–25.

would descend into the world as a slave. Jesus' rebuke was, "It is written: 'Worship the Lord your God and serve him only.'" To serve God alone is to refuse to take the reins of world power. Serving God alone is another way of praying, "Your kingdom come"—which is to say, "May your sovereignty be restored."[30] Jesus would enter his people's story, tears, sweat, and hunger and show them a way out that doesn't require the financial, military, and political power of kings and presidents and cabinets.

So can you pick up what we're putting down, smell what we are stepping in? Jesus would make for a bad president. It's hard to imagine Jesus wearing a "God Bless Rome" T-shirt and promoting his campaign with stickers and buttons and a hundred-million-dollar campaign. And he would be considerably uncomfortable as commander in chief of the largest military in the world. Nevertheless, he was political. All of his titles granted him political authority. Calling him Messiah or Lord is like acclaiming him—unlikely as it is—as president. He was the president who did not want to be president.[31] His politics aspired to something different from state power.

For the third temptation, the Devil, perhaps as a televangelist or a campaign organizer, suggested Jesus should stand on the pinnacle of the temple and throw himself off, knowing the angels would keep him from harm. The temptation was to do something spectacular so folks would believe—and, of all places, to do it in the center of the Jewish world. He

30 Meyers notes, "To pray this is to delegitimize every other jurisdiction—particularly those that claim sovereign authority. Otherwise would the disciples not simply have been instructed to ask God's blessing upon the king-of-the-moment? This is the real significance of Jesus' famous proclamations about the 'Kingdom of God'" (Ched Meyers, *Led by the Spirit into the Wilderness: Reflections on Lent, Jesus' Temptations, and Indigeneity*; see www.bcm-net.org).

31 We find this wisdom in places other than the Christian tradition. Consider Plato's theme of the philosopher-king in *The Republic*: the only person worthy of ruling is the person wise enough to resist becoming a ruler.

wasn't just overlooking a cliff to consider a stunt but was wrestling with the center of Israel's politics at the temple. Just like the throne is portrayed in Israel's history as a compromise to their allegiance to God alone, so too the temple needed to be tested and reconsidered: is it just a show, so Israel can look like the other nations? Certainly Jesus had the power to transcend nature's laws, as we see when he walked on water, and when he glowed like fire during the transfiguration, and when he rose through the clouds at the ascension. If Jesus had staged this stunt at the temple (which he would later call a "den of thieves"), he could have used his might to mesmerize the powerful and the elite, winning religious legitimization. But photo ops are out of the question for this king. Jesus resisted the spectacular.

And so the Devil departed from him "until an opportune time." No doubt Jesus was tested for the rest of his life.

Perhaps that opportune time was when the Devil later came in the guise of Peter, Jesus' key disciple to whom he hands the "keys of the kingdom of heaven." When Jesus predicted his death at the hands of the Romans and the religious elite, Peter wouldn't have it (Matt. 16:21–23). He said no to Operation Slaughtered Lamb. The Scriptures say Peter took Jesus aside and rejected the plan Jesus had laid out, saying, "Never, Lord! This shall never happen to you!" And Jesus turned to Peter and said, "Get behind me, Satan! You are a stumbling block to me; you do not have in mind the concerns of God, but merely human concerns." Funny that Jesus reserved such extreme language for the one closest to him, one in whom he had been placing much trust, and not for Judas or the authorities. Those were some harsh words, and they were well deserved. Peter just didn't get it. He couldn't imagine a president who dies on a cross. He would have rather had a Savior who glides into Jerusalem in a polished limousine than one who chooses to ride a lowly donkey. He still had in mind the things of kings, of Pharaoh, of Herod. He wanted to save the world through militaries and markets and foreign policies rather than through sacrificial love and grace.

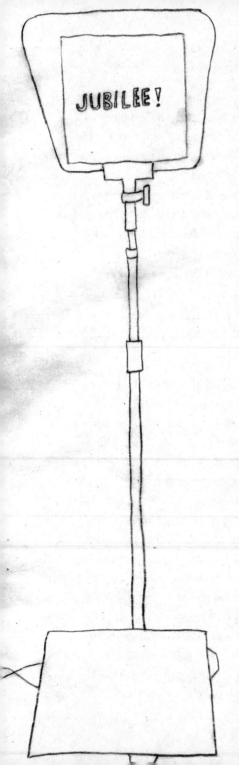

Commencement Speech

Leaving the desert, Jesus soon returned to his hometown, Nazareth. And he didn't preach the kingdom of Antipas; he proclaimed the good news of the kingdom of God, which could not have been more subversive. Jesus spoke about a throne, and Herod wasn't on it. This is where the kingdom of God originated—in an underground revolution. Jesus' formal entrance into this political scene, his "commencement address," was at a synagogue in his hometown. He read the following text from Isaiah: "The Spirit of the Lord is on me, because he has anointed me to proclaim good news to the poor. He has sent me to proclaim freedom for the prisoners and recovery of sight for the blind, to set the oppressed free, to proclaim the year of the Lord's favor" (Luke 4:18–19; see also Isa. 58:6; 61:1–2).

If we might call Jesus president, we could say that his campaign slogan was "Jubilee!" Just like Isaiah had done many years before, Jesus called upon the great economic tradition of the Torah, the counterimperial way of life we explored in section 1. To release the prisoners and the oppressed is to practice jubilee. It is to speak of debt cancellation and the dismantling of inequality. It is to consider Israel not as a fragmented society without an identity but as a community, maybe even a family, with cultural form and integrity, with a capacity to practice a unique economics.[32] Jesus invoked them as the people of God.

On the surface, the jubilee reading was a great slogan and an exciting proposition, for many of his listeners "spoke well of him and were amazed." But this wouldn't last long. Jesus wanted to take the discussion deeper. Maybe he understood that actually living out jubilee would turn the whole world upside down—and get them in serious trouble with the IRS.

It was one thing for Jesus to pronounce that the captives were going to go free and that the oppressed would be released, but what an ailing Jewish population wanted to know was, "How exactly is this going to be accomplished?" The Romans controlled large portions of the Israelites' land (for first-century peasants, as it is for much of the world today, having a portion of land on which to farm was the only way to be economically stable), and the burden of taxes, tithes, and tributes drove the people of Israel deep into debt, which resulted, of course, in widespread poverty. (Ever wonder why the Gospels are full of lepers, beggars, bleeding women, and sick children?)

32 While some have argued that globalization, whether it's at the hands of Alexander the Great or McDonald's, unifies cultures, the experience of the colonized and globalized is often one of cultural disintegration and devastation—hence the biblical criticism of the Tower of Babel archetype. Gerhard Lohfink writes that, because of the chaos of being enslaved and colonized by the powers, "at the time of Jesus, many of the twelve tribes had ceased to exist" (Gerhard Lohfink, *Does God Need the Church?* trans. Linda M. Maloney [Collegeville, MN: Liturgical Press, 1999], 162). The Jews had also abandoned their native Hebrew for the more common Aramaic and, in some places, Greek. The Romans, of course, continued the globalizing project and did their best to squeeze Hebrew culture into their acceptable mold. (For more on the effect of Alexander and ancient globalization on Jesus' context, see Cahill's *Desire of the Everlasting Hills*.)

Jesus' answer to this chronic situation of debt, slavery, and poverty was to remind the people of the way of life they lived back when they sought the Promised Land. In the Sermon on the Mount, Jesus urged his people to remember the Sabbath laws and their little alternative economic system of sharing, debt cancellation, and land redistribution. Jesus knew that the way out of Rome's grip lay not in appealing to Rome or in trying to overthrow Rome but in resurrecting Yahweh's alternative economy right under Caesar's nose. After the exodus, Israel had practiced God's anti-imperial economy out in the desert, but now Jesus was calling them to practice it right in the middle of Pharaoh's turf.

This is what Jesus had in mind: folks coming together, forming close-knit communities and meeting each other's needs—no kings, no major welfare systems, no presidents necessary. His is a theology and practice for the people of God, not a set of suggestions for empire.

But Jesus' vision of cultivating alternative communities of sharing, debt cancellation, and mutual aid didn't just end with the people of Israel. His jubilee was a liberation of all of the poor and broken peoples of the empire. Amid the amens in the crowd, the tide began to change. In this jubilee speech at the synagogue, he lamented that "prophets are not accepted in their hometowns"—in other words, "You are not going to like this." So he went on to recall for his listeners how the great prophet Elijah, in the trying times of famine, was sent not to Israel but to an *outsider*. And during Elisha's time, a great disease afflicted Israelites, but only a *Syrian* was healed. Not knowing Israelite history, it's difficult for most of us to understand how serious these statements were, but a drastic and violent shift quickly happened at this point in the conversation. "All the people in the synagogue were furious when they heard this. They got up, drove him out of the town, and took him to the brow of the hill on which the town was built, in order to throw him off the cliff" (Luke 4:28–29).

The commencement address had started off so well. Why were they so threatened? It's not just that Jesus proclaimed the jubilee but also that he radically redefined Israel's identity. Jesus reminded Israel that God's plan wasn't for them to be God's favorites or to be more blessed than others. Rather, they were blessed to be a blessing for the whole world. In this case of the jubilee, practicing economic justice was not just an ancient dream but was to be practiced among and for the poor and broken of the world. Was it also possible that the new king Jesus taught that Israel should practice jubilee, forgiveness of debts, and communal love toward *outsiders*? Should they love those vicious Romans, who pillaged their land? Should they include the non-Jewish poor and outsiders in their communities? Whatever we find in Jesus' opening statement in Nazareth, one thing is for sure: in the here and now, he was all about the economy of God, the forgiveness of debts, and the release of slaves, all in accordance with the jubilee economics of the ancient exodus desert tribes.

A Security Plan That Will Never Win an Election

After his speech in Nazareth, Jesus began a traveling ministry of teaching and healing. If you want to see Jesus' platform, the place to look is the Beatitudes and the Sermon on the Mount (Matthew 5–7). These teachings aren't election winners or great plans for leading an empire. But that's not the point. Something much more radical was going on.

"Whoever finds their life will lose it, and whoever loses their life for my sake will find it" (Matt. 10:39). Ever heard that from a president's mouth?

You gotta love Jesus' imagination. Author and professor Walter Wink does brilliant work exploring Jesus' creativity in his teaching in the Sermon on the Mount, especially in the familiar "turn the other cheek" verses (Matt. 5:38–42). Wink points out that Jesus was not suggesting that we let people sadistically step all over us. Jesus taught enemy love with imagination. He gave three real examples of how to interact with our adversaries. In each instance, Jesus points us toward disarming others. Jesus teaches us to refuse to oppose evil on its own terms. He invites us to transcend both passivity and violence through a third way.

When hit on the cheek, turn and look the person in the eye (v. 39). In the orderly Jewish culture, a person would hit someone only with the right hand. (It's sort of like how some cultures have a "wiping" hand and an "eating" hand, designated purposes with respective cultural taboos.) In some Jewish communities, if you hit someone with the left hand, you could be banished for ten days. So a person would have to use a backslap to hit someone on the right cheek with the right hand. It's clear that Jesus described a backhand, like an abusive husband to a wife or a master to a slave. It was a slap to insult, degrade, and humiliate, a slap meant not for an equal but for an inferior, to put someone in their place. But by turning the cheek, the person made the abuser look them in the eye, and the abuser could now only hit them with a fist, as an equal. By turning the cheek, the other person said, "I am a human being, made in the image of God, and you cannot destroy that." Do not cower and do not punch back. Make sure the person looks into your eyes and sees your sacred humanity, and it will become increasingly harder for that person to hurt you.

When someone drags you before the court to sue you for the coat off your back, take off all your clothes and hand them over, exposing the sickness of their greed (v. 40). Only the poor were subject to such abuse. A poor person, having nothing at all, could be taken to court for their outer garment (Deut. 24:10–13), which wasn't unusual for peasants who lost everything to wealthy landlords and tax collectors. So here Jesus is telling impoverished

debtors, who have nothing but the clothes on their backs, to strip naked and expose the greed of the repo man. Nakedness was taboo for Jews, but the shame fell less on the naked party and more on the person who looked on or caused the nakedness (Gen. 9:20–27). Brilliant. Following Jesus' suggestion would be a way of saying, "You want my coat. You can have it. You can even have my undies. But you cannot have my soul or my dignity."

When someone makes you walk a mile with them, go with them another mile (v. 41). This may seem like a strange scenario, but for first-century Jews, it was common to be asked to walk a mile with a soldier. With no Humvees or tanks, soldiers traveled on foot and carried large amounts of gear, so they depended on civilians to carry their supplies. I'm sure there were plenty of Zealots listening to Jesus who threw a fist in the air when they were asked to walk with a soldier. Roman law specified that civilians had to walk one mile, but that's all. (In fact, going a second mile was an infraction of the military code. It would be simply absurd for a Jew to befriend an occupying soldier and want to walk an extra mile with him.) It's a beautiful scene to imagine a soldier asking for his backpack but the person insists on another mile. When asked to carry a pack, don't spit in the person's face but walk with them, even two miles instead of one. Get to know them, not as an enemy but as a person. Talk with them and woo them into our movement by your love—that is, if they'll break their own law to walk two miles with you.

In each of these instances, Jesus taught the third way. Here we see a Jesus who abhors both passivity and violence, who carves out a third way that is neither submission nor assault, neither fight nor flight.[33] But all of this makes sense only if you realize that Jesus isn't talking about the best ways to successfully win the age-old battle to restrain evil. For Jesus redirects this urge by saying, "Do not resist an evil person." He has an entirely different way of viewing evil. This third way teaches that "evil can be opposed without being mirrored ... oppressors can be resisted without being emulated ... enemies can be neutralized without being destroyed."[34] We need more of the prophetic imagination that can interrupt violence

33 It can be argued, however, that Jesus' command for the disciples to *flee* the city and "run to the hills" (Matt. 24:15–21) on the day of Israel's disaster (AD 70) is a nonviolently prudent idea, lest they all be slaughtered in fighting against the Romans. Following Jesus' teachings, the Christians in the 60s and 70s indeed did not fight in the Jewish War but fled to cities like Pella.

34 Walter Wink, *The Powers That Be* (New York: Doubleday, 1998), 111.

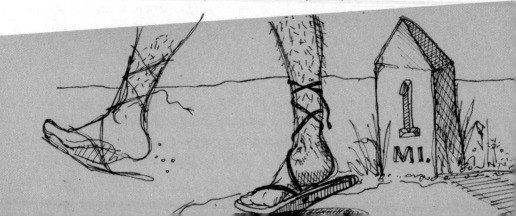

and oppression.[35] If the people of God were to transform the world through fascination, these amazing teachings had to work at the center of these peculiar people. Then we can look into the eyes of a centurion and see not a beast but a child of God, and then walk with that child a couple of miles. Look into the eyes of tax collectors as they sue you in court; see their poverty and give them your coat. Look into the eyes of the ones who are hardest for you to like, and see the One you love. For God loves good and bad people. Even God doesn't grasp for the knowledge of good and evil but sends rain to water the fields of both the just and the unjust. That's why enemy love is the only thing that Jesus says makes a person like God—perfect.[36]

The Sermon on the Mount and the Beatitudes just don't seem like the best tools with which to lead an empire or a superpower. Jesus' truth is that if you want to save your life, you will lose it. It's a whole new way to view the age-old quest for success in the world. Giving your life away doesn't sound like a good plan for national security. As old troubadour Woody Guthrie sang, "If Jesus preached in New York what he preached in Galilee, we'd lay him in his grave again" (especially if he did it on Wall Street). I guess that's why we hear a lot about God's blessing and God expanding our territory, but very little about a cross or love for enemies.

---

35 A phrase coined by Walter Bruggeman in his book *The Prophetic Imagination.*
36 Yoder notes that the word *perfect* here doesn't mean "without blemish," but means "unconditional" (*Politics of Jesus*, 117).

Jesus' Policy on the "War on Terror"

So how do Jesus' teachings about the third way and taking on his yoke play themselves out in the world? How do the people of God interact with the world powers, with tyranny and genocide—after all, what did Jesus know about tyranny and genocide? What if turning the other cheek doesn't work? And how many times do we turn the cheek before we revolt?

Jesus taught not only how to live in the kingdom of God but also how the kingdom of God lives in the empire of Herod. To do this, he gave us many snapshots in parables, often beginning with the phrase "the kingdom is like …"

The kingdom of heaven[37] is like a man who sowed good seed in his field. Butw while everyone was sleeping, his enemy came and sowed weeds among the wheat, and went away. When the wheat sprouted and formed heads the the weeds also ~~appeered~~ appeared.

The owner's servants ~~came~~ came to him and said, ~~"aSr"~~"Sir, didn't you sow good seed in your field? Where then did the weeds come from?"

"An enemy did this," he replied.

The servants asked him, "Do you ~~wants~~ us to go and pull them up?"

"No," he answered, "because ~~while you were~~ are pulling the weeds, you may uproot the wheat with them. Let both grow together until the (harves At that time I will tell the harvesters: First collect the weeds and tie them in bundles to be burned; then gather the wheat and bring it into my

barn." (Matt. 13:24-30, emphasis added)

37 Matthew, possibly more sensitive to the Jewish hesitance to compromise the mystery of God by using a name, may have preferred a word of separation, using "heaven" to signify God. In a similar manner, many today refer to God as "the Name," or "G-d," thinking that God, truly wild and mysterious, cannot be categorized by a name.

This parable shows what Jesus thinks of "ridding the world of evil." It harmonizes perfectly with the popularly ignored, "Do not resist the evil person," or Paul's command, "Do not take revenge, my dear friends, but leave room for God's wrath."

While this parable speaks to everybody, its primary audience likely wasn't those in power but Jesus' fellow oppressed Jews. Given the prevailing revolutionary mindset in Jesus' day, a prime temptation would have been to cut the throats of the Romans, outsiders, and collaborators with the occupation.[38] Jesus' listeners would have understood the Romans to be the weeds sown among the wheat.[39] How to rid the world of their evil? But Jesus redirected this and insisted that

1 you cannot easily distinguish the weeds from the wheat.[40] (It's not so easy to say, "We are all good and they are all evil." Sometimes only God can distinguish.)

2 destroying evil might destroy good.

38 At the time of this writing, this temptation faces thousands of Iraqis regarding their relationship to American occupiers. Many, obviously, are opting to "root out the weeds," resulting in an ever-tightening cycle of violence and revenge.

39 "In [these teachings] he does not take the path blazed by Jewish apocalyptic. That strain of thought was also deeply touched by the miserable condition of the people of God and the power of God's enemies in history, but the apocalypticists drew a different conclusion than Jesus did. For them it was no longer imaginable that God could still succeed in a world so damaged and depraved. In 'this world,' in 'this eon,' they said, the promises of God could no longer be fulfilled. God must intervene violently in history, destroy the old world with fire and create a new world, the 'new eon.' Only in it could God's promises come true" (Lohfink, *Does God Need the Church?* 45).

40 The word used for weeds here is *darnel*, which is a weed that suspiciously looks like wheat. See *Zondervan's Pictorial Encyclopedia of the Bible*.

Jesus practiced what he preached. He showed no sign of associating with so-called good people and leaving out the bad.[41] He reached out to the occupiers and the occupied, which is a *very* dangerous affair. Jesus not only cared for the poor, he cared for the powerful Roman centurion who was illegally policing his country. Imagine, for example, the risk an Iraqi would take bringing a U.S. soldier home for hospitality. Imagine, while neighbors suspiciously watch such hospitality, that the Iraqi cares for the needs of this occupying soldier.

Jesus' weeds-and-wheat parable was not meant for heaven; it was not a utopian dream. It invoked heaven onto earth. Jesus recognized the presence of evil but chose to deal with it through active nonresistance, patience, and hope. More on that later.

41 One could argue, What about Jesus' attempt to root out evil by cleansing the temple? It's worth noting that Jesus didn't kill or even hurt anybody in this action. He used his whip simply to drive animals out, not to smack people. Most important, his goal was not to rid the *world* of evil (he didn't cleanse Pilate's or Herod's palaces) but to cleanse his "Father's house," which is supposed to be a unique witness to the world. Though we won't treat this action in depth, there's no serious reason to think Jesus contradicted his stance of creative nonviolence. For more see Yoder, *Politics of Jesus*, 42–43.

The Way the Kingdom Grows (Or, Was Jesus Like Che?)

It would be easy to call Jesus' vision of the nonviolent kingdom naive. Who really thinks that loving your enemies works? Who ever heard of a society of people that doesn't use violence? But Jesus tells a parable: "A farmer went out to sow his seed. As he was scattering the seed, some fell along the path, and the birds came and ate it up. Some fell on rocky places, where it did not have much soil. It sprang up quickly, because the soil was shallow. But when the sun came up, the plants were scorched, and they withered because they had no root. Other seed fell among thorns, which grew up and choked the plants. Still other seed fell on good soil, where it produced a crop—a hundred, sixty or thirty times what was sown" (Matt. 13:3–8).

About this parable, German theologian Gerhard Lohfink writes, "Jesus is very aware of the 'impossibility' of the cause of God in the world. In his seed parables he depicts not only the unstoppable growth of the reign of God, but also the frightening smallness and hiddenness of its beginning; still more, he describes the superior power of the opponents who threaten the work of God from beginning to end."[42] The blessing of the world through the people of God is not like a violent, quick revolution that takes over power. It starts small, grows silently, faces setbacks, but nevertheless permeates the world with love. That's difficult for us in a world where we bounce between aggressive impatience and paralyzing cynicism. Without a doubt, Jesus portrays patience and perseverance as essential characteristics for dealing with this crazy world; his caution on ridding the world of evil makes no sense without them.

42 Lohfink, Does God Need the Church? 45.

While we can understand that Jesus might have been teaching his followers to be like the good soil and receive God's Word, there are other dimensions to this parable. Jesus did not think that *only he* sowed the Word of God. He was constantly sending people away, telling them also to sow the seed of the kingdom. With this in mind, we see that the parable encouraged his followers to continue sowing, saying, "In a distracting, violent, and tempting world, keep sowing the seed of love. Sow it everywhere, even when Herod cuts it down, and even when the world's riches try to choke it. You never know when it will spring up and make great fruit!"

Sowers must not become discouraged easily. The disciples were constantly butting up against Jesus' thoughts about the way God's reign comes on earth. "It will never work that way!" you can hear the disciples thinking at almost every encounter. They thought the kingdom would come quickly, like the apocalypse, as almost all revolutionaries from Marx to Guevara have insisted. But Jesus' revolutionary patience claimed that another kingdom is coming—one that you can participate in but cannot build, a seed you can plant and water but cannot make grow. You can't drag the kingdom of God into the world. But you can't stop sowing the seeds either. Sow them everywhere! This is where the fashionable language about "building the kingdom of God" gets dangerous; even in secular spheres people have similar aspirations to "build a global movement" to take the power back.

One might wonder if Jesus was tapping into Israel's memories of the recently attempted Maccabean revolution. Israel's divine patience had dried up, and they aimed to kill their oppressors. They succeeded, but within only a few years, those who had taken the power back became yet another regime of domination. So Jesus refocused their attention with more seed stories: "Then Jesus asked, 'What is the kingdom of God like? What shall I compare it to? It is like a mustard seed, which a man took and planted in his garden. It grew and became a tree, and the birds perched in its branches.' Again he asked, 'What shall I compare the kingdom of God to? It is like yeast that a woman took and mixed into about sixty pounds of flour until it worked all through the dough'" (Luke 13:18–21).

The kingdom starts small and then permeates and transforms the larger world. This is the heart of Jesus' political imagination. In these parables, Jesus echoed the vision of what Abraham and Sarah's descendants would do. They would become a small peculiar seed of God planted in the midst of the world. If we don't understand that Jesus' politics are rooted in that overarching historical biblical theme, his teachings will remain ambiguous to us. They will seem like a set of wise abstract truths that we can "apply" to America or any given empire. But his worldview is for the small people.

The Mustard Seed Revolution

Let's keep rolling with these ideas of how the kingdom spreads, because they fly in the face of how both empires and popular revolutions seem to grow. Yeast and mustard, both of which were known for their infectious spreading qualities, seem to be unlikely metaphors for God's kingdom.

Jews were not big fans of yeast, which is why Jesus used it to describe the infectious arrogance of the Pharisees that everyone was to beware of. So, then, for the folks not digging the yeast imagery, he said that God's kingdom is like mustard. Probably they didn't like that any better.

We've all heard plenty of cute sermons about the mustard seed parable, how God takes little seeds and makes big trees out of them, but there's much more going on here.

Matthew strategically placed the mustard parable in the middle of the story about the weeds and the wheat. He told his listeners that the kingdom of God is like mustard, which grows like a wild bush. Farmers say it's like kudzu, and a city preacher once compared it to the wild weeds that grow out of abandoned houses and crack the sidewalks.[43] The mustard seed's growth would have been familiar to first-century Jews, since many of them were farmers and peasants well acquainted with its way of taking over gardens. It might even have been growing in the wild around them where Jesus spoke.

Jews valued order and had very strict rules about how to keep a tidy garden, and one of the secrets was to keep out mustard. It was notorious for invading well-trimmed veggies and other plants and quickly taking over the entire garden. (Kind of like how yeast works its way through dough ... hmm.) Jewish law even forbade planting mustard in the garden (*m. Kil.* 3:2; *t. Kil.* 2:8). When those first-century peasants heard Jesus' images, they probably giggled, or maybe they told him to hush before he got himself killed for using this infamous plant to describe God's kingdom subtly taking over the world.

Plenty of people had lofty expectations of the kingdom coming in spectacular triumph and were familiar with the prophets' well-known "cedars of Lebanon" imagery, which described the kingdom as a giant redwood—the greatest of all trees. The cedars of Lebanon as a metaphor for the kingdom would have brought some enthusiastic amens from the crowd, gotten some people dancing. But Jesus ridiculed this triumphal expectation. After all, even mature mustard plants stand only a few feet high—modest little bushes.

43 Kudzu is a wild vine that vigorously but rather unassumingly takes over. It can blanket entire mountainsides, smother trees, and crack cement buildings.

What Jesus had in mind was not a frontal attack on the empires of this world. His revolution is a subtle contagion—one little life, one little hospitality house at a time. Isn't it interesting that Saul of Tarsus went door-to-door (Acts 8:3) trying to tear up the contagion, like it was a weed? But the harder people tried to eradicate it, the faster it spread. When mustard is crushed, its potency is released. As we say, "In the blood of the martyrs lies the seed of the church." Paul caught it—the mustard weed grabbed him. Another convert we love is Minucius Felix, who, as a persecutor of the early Christians, had this to say about the followers of the Way: "They form a profane conspiracy" infecting the Roman Empire, "and just like a rank growth of weeds ... it should at all costs be exterminated, root and branch."[44]

Mustard also has always been known for its fiery potency. In the days before the Roman Empire, it was a sign of power. Darius, King of the Persians, invaded Europe and was met by Alexander the Great. Darius sent Alexander a bag of sesame seeds as a taunt, indicating by the seeds the vast multitude of soldiers he had. Alexander sent back a bag of mustard seed with the message, "You may be many, but we are powerful. We can handle you." And they did.

So there goes Jesus spinning power on its head again. His power was not in crushing but in being crushed, triumphing over the empire's sword with his cross. Mustard must be crushed, ground, broken for its power to be released. John's gospel describes Jesus' death and resurrection as a seed that is broken: "Unless a kernel of wheat falls to the ground and dies, it remains only a single seed. But if it dies, it produces many seeds" (John 12:24). This is the crazy mystery that we celebrate, a Christ whose body is torn apart and whose blood is spilled like the grains and grapes of the Eucharist that gives us life. Mustard was also known for healing and was

44 Eberhard Arnold, ed., *The Early Christians: In Their Own Words* (Farmington, PA: Plough, 1998).

rubbed on the chest to help with breathing, sort of like Vicks vapor rub. Mustard, a wild contagion of a weed, a healing balm, a sign of upside-down power—official sponsor of the Jesus revolution.

As if that weren't enough (and we wonder why people were so angry!), Jesus added one more thing: "The birds of the air can rest here." There was another popular Hebrew image of the cedars, that the nations can build nests in the branches. But Jesus put an interesting spin on it, as he said the "fowls" can come and rest in the branches of the mustard bush. The fowls are not the mighty eagles that would dwell in the cedar but the detestable birds, the ones that ate animal carcasses (Gen. 15:11; Deut. 28:26). Farmers didn't want fowls in their garden. That's why they put up scarecrows. Bless his heart, Jesus was saying the kingdom of God is "for the birds"; the undesirables find a home in this little bush.

On Citizenship in Heaven and Being Born Again

You can look at Jesus' proclamation of the kingdom of God as another way of promoting "citizenship in heaven." Many of us grew up with this idea, singing songs like "I'll Fly Away" and "Swing Low, Sweet Chariot," which left us with the impression that our faith has very little to say about this world. But in a world that is falling apart, we ask if Jesus offers life *before* death. It seems some mean that heaven is sometime in the future and someplace out there, as if to say, "My citizenship *will be* in heaven." They may have a point. *Heaven* is certainly not the word to describe what life is like for many in the world today. And the Bible is not utopian, assuming that human hands and hearts can, with enough sweat and time, build heaven on earth. Without a doubt, evil is prevalent in and around us, and many efforts to rid the world of evil truly seem only to bring more in. The cure is worse than the disease.

And so the Christians speak of the "eschaton," the end times, when evil will be dissolved and every tear will be wiped away. But we must be careful not to speak of heaven, the end times, or heavenly citizenship before we fully understand what these concepts meant to the early followers of the Way.

In regard to Christian politics, some might say, "Sure my citizenship is *ultimately* in heaven, but I have to live in the 'real' world now." In other words, acting heavenly on earth is too risky; or, Jesus was the Son of God, but he was not realistic; or, following the Sermon on the Mount will not work on earth, so it will have to suffice in heaven. This interpretation basically comes to mean that my citizenship in heaven means nothing in the real world. Believers are then left with participating in the normal patterns of citizenship, with exploitative economy and violent militarism among its many sins.

But the problem is that Jesus' kingdom (and Paul's "citizenship in heaven") was about the real world, here and now. It was about allegiance.[45] Jesus and Paul were telling the people that they must live here with their identities as aliens. They must live by the rules of heaven amid the violent earthly powers. And to claim that one's citizenship is in heaven is to say that you pledge allegiance not to any of the kingdoms of the world but to Jesus and the body of those who take on his suffering, enemy-loving posture toward the world. This is what Peter meant when he called the church "a holy nation, a people set apart," a people who are supposed to live as "aliens and strangers in this land."

Jesus' spoke the same message when he said, "No one can see the kingdom of God without being born again" (John 3:3). The man to whom Jesus said this, Nicodemus, was a member of the Jewish ruling council and a Pharisee. He had a vested interest in maintaining the identity and pride of Israel. Nicodemus attempted to win Jesus' affection by praising him. But Jesus did not care about his praise and cut to the chase, insulting Nicodemus's Jewish piety and nationalism. "No one can see the kingdom of God without being born again."

Jesus insisted that the kingdom of God is not about your ethnicity and nationality. For he stated that being born of flesh (family, nation, ethnicity) is insignificant to being born of the Spirit.[46] Birth endows citizenship. (Think

45 Cf. Wright, *Resurrection of the Son*, 230.
46 Paul echoes this in Romans: "Not all who are descended from Israel are Israel. Nor because they are his descendants are they all Abraham's children" (Rom. 9:6–7). See also 1 Peter 1:23–25, where being born of "perishable seed" is equated with withering meaninglessness. This is more extensively illustrated in Lohfink, *Does God Need the Church?* 60–66.

of your birth certificate.) When you are born, you receive your identity and the boundaries that are worth defending and dying for.

But being born Israelite in the flesh, Jesus insists, is not of concern. God's people do not grow by having sex and making babies.[47] They grow by the Spirit of God weaving into and renewing identities and hearts, making them beat with love. As with Abraham and Sarah's children, it is the child who is born of miraculous means and God's initiative who carries the blessing. And that child, Isaac, must pass down blessing through the spirit of faith, not through the worldly inheritance of flesh and family. Through this lens, we can see how Jesus could honor and love his genetic family while also questioning, "Who are my mother and brother?"

So being born again redefines family; it grants a new way to see the world, a way to see right past the artificial borders we create and proclaim a deeper allegiance and affection. For those who pledge allegiance to the kingdoms of this world, Jesus preached good news: repent and become born again, "see the kingdom," and find a new identity. This is not a set of political suggestions for the world; this is about invoking and embodying the alternative. (More on that later.) All of this is an invitation to join a peculiar people—those with no king but God, who practice jubilee economics and make the world new. This is not the old-time religion of going to heaven; this is about bringing heaven to the world.

---

47 That the people of God are created through a multiethnic gathering, as opposed to mono-ethnic progeny, is evident throughout the Hebrew Scriptures and is not just a New Testament theme. (See Lohfink, *Does God Need the Church?* 58). The exodus was more than just the Hebrews but was enjoined by "a mixed crowd." The confederacy of tribes under Moses is described as a "gathering" from many different people groups. They, however, shared a common faith in one God (contrasted with the polytheistic Canaanite societies they withdrew from) and "an aversion to monarchy" (56–59).

Down-to-Earth Politics

Some might read the popular phrase, "My kingdom is not of this world," and mistakenly think that Jesus meant, "My kingdom is not *in* this world." But Jesus was speaking more about essence than location. In other words, he was talking about the "real world."

Jesus said this while on trial for insurrection. His kingdom had finally collided with the kingdoms of Herod and Pilate, and they wanted answers. Since Jesus' birth, he had been at odds with the establishment. They wanted him dead ever since the rumors about the other King of the Jews. Because of this Jesus had, for the most part, stayed on the fringes of public life, insisting that the kingdom he preached and represented be undetectable to the powers. But now he had paraded into the center of power, flipped over its tables, and hosted a public and critical teach-in, creating the conditions for his arrest. Now under government control, he is questioned:

"Are you the king of the Jews?"

"Is that your own idea," Jesus asked, "or did others talk to you about me?"

"Am I a Jew?" Pilate replied. "Your own people and chief priests handed you over to me. What is it you have done?"

Jesus said, "My kingdom is not of this world. If it were, my servants would fight to prevent my arrest by the Jewish leaders. But now my kingdom is from another place."

"You are a king, then!" said Pilate.

Jesus answered, "You say that I am a king. In fact, the reason I was born and came into the world is to testify to the truth. Everyone on the side of truth listens to me."

"What is truth?" retorted Pilate. ...

From then on, Pilate tried to set Jesus free, but the Jews kept shouting, "If you let this man go, you are no friend of Caesar. *Anyone who claims to be a king opposes Caesar.*"

When Pilate heard this, he brought Jesus out ... [48] "Here is your king," Pilate said to the Jews. ...

"*We have no king but Caesar,*" the chief priests answered.

[48] John 18:33–38; 19:12–15 (emphasis added).

Jesus didn't mean that his kingdom has no interaction with or claims to make about the world. Jesus even insisted that his whole life was a thrusting of truth into the world, affronting it. Nor did Jesus mean that his goal was to get people ready to die and go to heaven—as if the earth were just a waiting room for the afterlife. The people who were working for Jesus' execution understood that his identity wasn't just an abstract theological heresy or a threat to orthodox Judaism. His claims had political import, and the Jews agreed: the titles of King, Messiah, and Son of God (all used in the Gospels' accounts of Jesus' trials) were claims competing against the emperor in Rome. This scared the Jews to the point that they feverishly blurted, "We have no king but Caesar." But Jesus would rather invoke the great kingless history of Israel. What is Israel if it is not peculiar in the world? If it plays power politics and vies for thrones, it's just like every other empire destroying the world. Then it's like unsalty salt—worthless and not even good for a pile of manure.[49]

When Jesus said, "My kingdom is not of this world," he wasn't saying that his kingdom is apolitical; rather he was saying *how* his kingdom is political. He clarified his statement right after he made it: the essential difference is that in my kingdom, we do not fight to maintain the kingdom. Refusing to have a department of defense renders Jesus' kingdom neither meaningless nor irrelevant, just different. Just like the kingless confederacy of Israel in the Torah, the kingdom Jesus spoke of is a real political kingdom that is unique, confusing, and unheard of. His kingdom is not of this world because it refuses power, pledges a different allegiance, and lives love. In a world where truth has become smothered and rulers don't even know what it is anymore, Jesus embodies a truth that will set us free—even Pilate. If only we have eyes to see. Unfortunately, the crowd that day didn't. As we look back on it, it seems Jesus' politics are much more down to earth, and that Pilate's lofty thrones are "out there."

"We have no king but Caesar," the chief priests answered.

49 For more on the manure teaching, see Luke 14:35.

Take My Yoke, Not Rome's

A few years ago, some of the kids in our collaborative arts program created a play about a king whose crown was so *huge* (it took up the whole stage) that it was crushing him and his people.[50] There was a great song in the play called "Down with the Crown," in which the townspeople (albeit tiny townspeople, since most of them were under eleven) called on the king to lay down his crown before everyone died from the weight of its power. And, of course, another decent play called *Henry IV* has the old line, "Uneasy lies the head that wears a crown." One of Jesus' comforts for the burdened who were suffocating from Rome's crown was the image of the yoke. "Come to me, all you who are weary and burdened, and I will give you rest. Take my yoke upon you and learn from me. ... For my yoke is easy [more accurately, "good"] and my burden is light" (Matt. 11:28–29). The peasants to whom Jesus spoke knew the word *yoke* well. It had a lot of different meanings. It was the tool used for harnessing animals for farming. It was the word used for taking on a rabbi's teaching. Paul later used it in Galatians to describe the heavy burden of sin. But yoke was also the word used for the brutal weight of slavery and oppression that the prophets call us to break (see Isa. 58:6, 9, among other passages). The weary of whom Jesus speaks are a tired people who have labored under the yoke of empire. We can hear this same weariness echoed in African-American spirituals.

"WE ARE GOING"
✓ carrol Adair ✓

We are going through the valley
we are going on the road

We are wandering & weary
we are searching for our home

50 Yes! And ... is a community of artist-educators who work to reawaken imagination through collaborative arts (www.yesandcamp.org).

Don't miss that the words *labor* and *weary* are used over and over in Scripture for folks enslaved by power. And *weary* is the word Jesus used in contrast to the lilies, which do not labor or toil. They are free. The word *burdened* may also conjure up the time when Jesus scolded the religious folks for binding on people "heavy burdens" they could not bear. Burdens are the specialty of religious elites and power mongers.

Other ancient writers use the image of yoke as a metaphor for slavery to empires. According to 1 Enoch 103:10–15, "Sinners and oppressors have made their yoke heavy upon us," and according to Sibylline Oracles, "No longer will Syrian, Greek or foreigner or any other nation place their neck under your yoke of slavery." Even Josephus describes Roman imperial power as "the yoke of Rome."[51] The word *yoke* is used over and over (sixty-three times in the Hebrew text) and usually has to do with having control over someone, particularly political control or the imposition of harsh imperial power (Genesis 27; Leviticus 26; Isaiah 9, 47; Jeremiah 27; Lamentations 3). God continually "breaks the yokes" of the nations and kings oppressing Israel. Jesus did not move to break the Roman yoke but invited his followers to carry a new yoke altogether. And it is a *good* one. The adjective *good* (often mistranslated here as "easy") appears nearly thirty times in the Septuagint,[52] but never with the meaning "easy." It often is appropriately translated as "good" or "kind."[53] In the same way that the peace of God is not like Rome's peace, the yoke of God is not like Rome's yoke of slavery. It is good and kind. And to the weary imperial refugees, Jesus offers "rest." The word *rest* is used in the Hebrew Scriptures for the peace that comes after war and tremendous struggle (Deut. 12:9–10; 25:19; Joshua 1, 15, 11, 21, and others). Here Jesus gives the invitation

52 The Greek translation of the Hebrew Scriptures.

53 Warren Carter, *Matthew and Empire* (Harrisburg, PA: Trinity, 2001), 125–26. We are grateful for the scholarship of Warren Carter, whose work helped create this section and has helped us read Matthew with new eyes.

to rest—like the land on the Sabbath, like a people in a war zone after the bombs stop falling.

Jesus is ready to set us free from the heavy yoke of an oppressive way of life. Plenty of wealthy Christians are suffocating from the weight of the American dream, heavily burdened by the lifeless toil and consumption we embrace. This is the yoke from which we are being set free. And as we are liberated from the yoke of global capitalism, our sisters and brothers in Guatemala, Liberia, Iraq, and Sri Lanka will also be liberated. Our family overseas, who are making our clothes, growing our food, pumping our oil, and assembling our electronics—they too need to be liberated from the empire's yoke of slavery. Their liberation is tangled up with our own. The new yoke isn't easy. (It's a cross, for heaven's sake.) But we carry it together, and it is good and leads us to rest, especially for the weariest traveler.

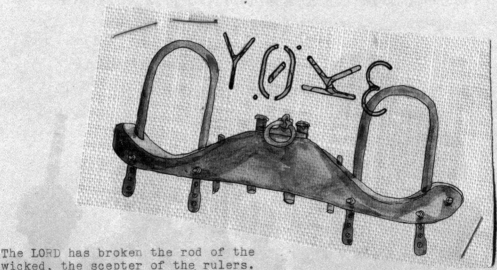

The LORD has broken the rod of the
wicked, the scepter of the rulers.
... All the lands are at rest and at
peace; they break into singing ...

> I WILL CRUSH THE ASSYRIAN IN MY LAND;
> ON MY MOUNTAINS I WILL TRAMPLE HIM DOWN.
> HIS YOKE WILL BE TAKEN FROM MY PEOPLE, AND
> HIS BURDEN REMOVED FROM THEIR SHOULDERS.

Isa. 14:5,7,25

Occupied by a Legion

Jesus wasn't just another politician with a lot to say and nothing to show. His politics came to life through healings, miracles, and exorcisms. And these weren't just "spiritual" acts. They were spiritual, political, and physical acts loaded with meaning. Since we can all think of some places that could use a little exorcising of the demons, consider this story from Jesus' campaign trail.

The "country of the Gerasenes" consisted of the ten federated cities of the Decapolis, east of the Sea of Galilee, under Roman occupation. It was a hub for much of the Roman military, and Gerasenes was known as a place where many Roman veterans with benefits were given land to dwell in, a veteran's settlement of sorts. As Jesus passed through the militarized zone, he met a man who could not be subdued because he was occupied (a word loaded with meaning, especially to a Galilean whose land was occupied by the Roman military, also a force that folks said no one could subdue) by an evil spirit (Mark 5:1–20). The evil spirit had made the man unclean by forcing him to live among the graves of the casualties of wars and riots, which violated the Hebrews' strict holiness

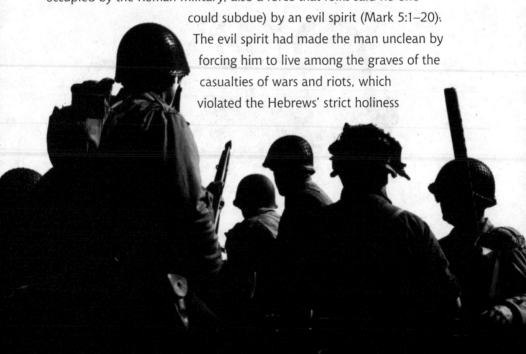

code.[54] He could not get the spirit out of his mind or body. The demon occupation led him to hurt himself, beating himself with hands possessed by violence.

Jesus asked the man his name, and he replied, "Legion," the same word for a division of Roman soldiers. Scholars note that a legion consisted of around two thousand troops, and there would have been several legions around the Decapolis. It's interesting that in the story, the demons beg to stay in the area. Nearby was a "band" of pigs, *band* being the same word used for a group of military cadets (and no, we aren't suggesting it's okay to call police officers "pigs").[55] The demons asked to be sent among the pigs, another symbol of uncleanliness. (Jews did not touch pigs.) Jesus invited the Legion to enter the pigs. And the pigs, specifically numbered at two thousand, "charged" into the sea to their deaths. And none of the listeners could have missed the subversive poetry, remembering the legion of Pharaoh's army that charged into the sea, where they were swallowed up and drowned (Exodus 14). Jesus healed people who had been made sick by the imperial system. They got the message. Imperial power is bad for your health.

Army Combat Suicides (per 100k)

2003 - 60 (12.8%)
2004 - 67 (10.4%)
2005 - 83 (19.9%)
2006 - 99 (20.4%)

RAW DATA FROM DOD
MORE INFO @ THERAWTRUTH.NET

1 out of every 4 ~~XXXX~~ non-combat deaths is 'self-inflicted'

No wonder the townspeople "begged" Jesus to leave their region.

54 Consider Isa. 65:4.

55 The pig was also the mascot of Rome's Tenth Fretensis Legion stationed in Antioch (Carter, *Matthew and Empire*, 71). It's interesting to note the places where Jesus drove demons out of people: often in the temple and in the militarized zones. The words "come out" that usually accompany an exorcism are the same words with which Jesus exorcized the temple, calling the money changers to "come out" because they had made a market of God's temple and marginalized visiting Gentiles. It's very much the same imagery as exodus and *coitus interruptus*. We're thankful for John Dominic Crossan, Ched Meyers, and the numerous scholars whose work on this text has given us new eyes to see.

Jesus and Taxes

As Jesus' influence and the controversy over his exorcisms increased, folks not only began to run him out of town, but people were always trying to trap him in the big questions of the day. For example, did he pay taxes? Keep in mind that Caesar's coins were floating all over the empire, stamped with Caesar's image and inscribed with the words "Long live the Son of God." The coins were a visual sign that the entire economy belonged to Caesar and that without him everything would fall apart. Historians point out that the Jews even started minting their own coins, branded with the palm leaf (their revolutionary flag). Josephus says that there was a group of Jews (which he calls the Fourth Philosophy) that refused to pay taxes. This group "refused to call any man master," believing they owed exclusive loyalty to God and could not render tribute to Caesar, who claimed to be Lord.[56] Peasants like Jesus' family in Galilee were usually so enslaved to debt and taxation that over 50 percent of their income went to Caesar. So it's not surprising that one of the traps that authorities tried to set for Jesus involved his taxes. (Remember, one of the things Jesus was accused of at his execution was trying to stop people from paying their taxes.)[57]

On one occasion, two unlikely groups conspired to trap him—one at odds with the Roman occupation (Pharisees) and one that represented it (Herodians). It was quite a broad net to cast over Jesus. But he shot back a beautiful riddle. First, when they asked him whether it was right to pay the

56 Josephus, *Jewish Antiquities* 18.5, 23.

57 "Then the whole assembly rose and led him off to Pilate. And they began to accuse him, saying, 'We have found this man subverting our nation. He opposes payment of taxes to Caesar and claims to be Messiah, a king'" (Luke 23:1–2).

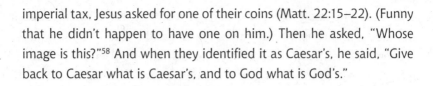

imperial tax, Jesus asked for one of their coins (Matt. 22:15–22). (Funny that he didn't happen to have one on him.) Then he asked, "Whose image is this?"[58] And when they identified it as Caesar's, he said, "Give back to Caesar what is Caesar's, and to God what is God's."

Some folks use this verse to say Jesus bowed to Caesar. But we think it was just the opposite. First, it was quite radical to speak of God and Caesar as two separate entities. Jesus then left it to the hearers to decide what was God's and what was Caesar's, though Jesus seemed to subtly point it out. Caesar could brand with his image coins, crowns, and robes, which moths would eat and rust would destroy. But life and creation have God's stamp on them. Caesar could have his coins, but life is God's. Caesar had no right to take what is God's. We are also reminded that just as Caesar stamped his image on coins, God's image is stamped on human beings. Even Caesar had God's stamp. God made Caesar, and Caesar was not God. But the hearer was left to ponder the riddle of what was God's and what was Caesar's.[59] No wonder Jesus often had to say, "Do you have ears to hear?"

Another time, the tax authorities asked Peter if Jesus paid the temple tax, and Peter said yes (Matt. 17:24–27). But later, when Peter saw Jesus, Jesus (after clarifying to Peter why he is exempt from paying taxes) did something bizarre. He told Peter to go catch a fish; inside its mouth would be the money to pay both his and Peter's tax. Again, Jesus is depicted in the scene as *not having money*. (If there is any lesson here, might it be that Jesus had no taxable income?) Peter went out and caught a fish, and it had the amount of their taxes in its mouth. Fish don't usually have money in their mouths. The whole

58 Since coins were a way for Caesar to communicate his message across the empire, Jesus' question might be equivalent to asking, "Who controls the media?" It's probably a good idea to have as few of Caesar's coins and TVs as possible.

59 No doubt conflict between the Pharisees and the Herodians reignited after this encounter with Jesus. The Pharisees would have celebrated Jesus' answer, emphasizing the idea of giving to God but not so much to Caesar, and the Herodians would have emphasized the opposite.

scene blew up into this big lampoon, a street theater.[60] Who cares about the taxes; a stinking fish had money in its mouth! That's cool. Jesus was saying, "You can have your money. I made that fish!" God created Caesar, and God created the heavens and the earth. Caesar cannot do that. Give to Caesar what is Caesar's. Once we've given to God what's God's, there's not much left for Caesar. And after Caesar returns to the dust, God will continue to live and to bring dust to life.

60 An old peasant proverb captures the humor and irony of what Jesus was up to: when the emperor passes, the peasant bows ... and farts. With revolutionary subordination, we give the empire what it asks, but not on its own terms. Caesar may have his coins, which rust will destroy, but life and nature are God's. And if Caesar takes our lives from us, we will rise from the dead.

Go Tell That Fox

The authorities continued to devise ways to trap Jesus. After Antipas had killed John the Baptist, it must have been maddening for him to see these undesirable troublemakers, these roaches, proclaiming another kingdom as quickly as he could stomp on them. As folks listened to Jesus, they wondered if the rowdy Baptizer had been raised from the dead for round two. Not only was Jesus preaching another kingdom, but he was sending his disciples out as ambassadors of that kingdom and inviting them to proclaim the same message throughout Herod's entire territory. The text in Luke says that they were going from village to village calling people to live under a different kind of king, and Herod the tetrarch was perplexed, saying, "I beheaded John. Who, then, is this I hear such things about?" (Luke 9:9). And then the text says Herod "tried to see him [Jesus]." Hmm … How does a king "try to see"? No doubt he sent some folks to check things out, maybe royal infiltrators to tap some phone lines and read some emails. Scholars point out that this is one reason why Jesus was always on the move, traveling constantly, with no real headquarters for the movement. And if you look carefully at his travels, you will notice that he always stayed one step ahead and never went into the two imperial cities ruled by Herod Antipas in Galilee—Sepphoris[61] and Tiberius.[62] He was as wise as a serpent (and as innocent as a dove).

61 Sepphoris was the capital for Herod Antipas. He ran the kingdom from this fancy city, which had water holes, courts, statues, a theater, and a gymnasium designed for royalty. With thousands of residents, Sepphoris was located up on a hill where all could see its glimmer of wealth. It was known as the city on a hill which cannot be hidden. You can imagine what it would feel like to look up at the spectacle from the poor little village below it, from the little town of Nazareth. Only a few hundred people lived in Nazareth, which had virtually no civic structures. Sepphoris was built on the backs of peasants like those in Nazareth. What must that have felt like?

62 Herod eventually built another town called Tiberius (named after a Caesar and built on a cemetery, again not scoring points with the Jews, who would have found it utterly offensive that it was built on death). And while Jesus stayed clear of Herod's headquarters, when his cousin John was arrested, the Gospels say Jesus left Nazareth and headed to Capernaum—a no-name town right next to Tiberius. Interesting. The Gospels make it a point to clarify exactly where Jesus was—"by the lake in the area of Zebulun and Naphtali." These towns were tribal allocations given by God to Abraham, not to Herod (Deuteronomy 34; Joshua 18; Isaiah 7). By using these names (repeatedly), the Gospel underlines the fact that this is God's land, not Caesar's. Jesus started preaching under Herod's reign, just down the shore from the palace and the jail, maybe as if John could hear him through the prison walls. And he reminded people why they had come to the desert to hear the good news. It was not to see "a man dressed in fine clothes." Those folks were in Tiberius and Sepphoris. It was to hear wild prophets in camel skin and rags who proclaimed a kingdom and a future other than Rome's.

WHAT DID YOU GO OUT INTO THE WILDERNESS
TO SEE? ... A MAN DRESSED IN FINE CLOTHES?
NO. ... A PROPHET? YES, I TELL YOU,
AND MORE THAN A PROPHET.
(LUKE 𝗫𝗫𝗫𝗫
7:24-26)

At one point in the Gospels, there is a fabulous encounter with some sympathetic Pharisees. They came to warn Jesus that Herod was looking for him, ready to kill him. And Jesus responded, "Go tell that fox, 'I will keep on driving out demons and healing people today and tomorrow, and on the third day I will reach my goal'" (Luke 13:32). This may seem like an obscure irreverent saying. But to his hearers, it was full of political satire.

Fox? Just as eagles and pigs and donkeys and elephants all have political meanings today, *fox* was richly symbolic. Calling Herod a fox instead of a lion was like saying the U.S. national bird is a vulture instead of an eagle. The rabbis spoke with images, one of which was the lion, an animal of power and prestige, often called the king of the wild. The fox was the opposite of the lion. The fox was often mistaken for a lion but wasn't king of anything. The fox was always lurking, scurrying off in cowardly reaction to every noise and movement. The fox was an impostor, a poser, a wannabe lion.

For I will be like a ... great lion to Judah.

Hosea 5:14

How do you call someone a fox or brood of vipers in love? I'm not sure I'd recommend trying it (could get you killed), but it's fascinating that such harsh language was reserved for kings and religious rulers who posed as God's gatekeepers but proclaimed another gospel and another master. They were dangerous impostors who caused the people to stumble away from God. You can see why people were so scared when they heard the things Jesus said. No doubt they were whispering to one another, "Did you hear that? Holy cow, he just called Herod a fox! He's going to get himself killed." Jesus took on the establishment, the most powerful rulers in the land, and rulers don't take that lightly. The way they deal with such treason is to cut off heads and hang people on crosses.

121

The Anti-Triumphal Entrance into Jerusalem

Jesus rode a donkey into Passover. Remember that Passover was the anti-imperial Jewish festival during which the Jews celebrated their ancestors' coming out of Egyptian slavery. With Roman soldiers lining the street, Jews gathered and waved palm branches, symbols of resistance to the empire.[63] Passover was a volatile time, often marked by riots and bloodshed. (Recall that Antipas killed thousands of Jews in the streets at the festival.) When Jesus rode a donkey into this festival, it was a lampoon, like street theater at a protest. Scholars call it the anti-triumphal entry into Jerusalem. Imagine the president riding a unicycle in the Fourth of July parade. Kings did not ride donkeys. They rode mighty war horses accompanied by an entourage of soldiers. So here is Jesus making a spectacle of violence and power, riding in on the back of an ass. (And a borrowed one at that!)

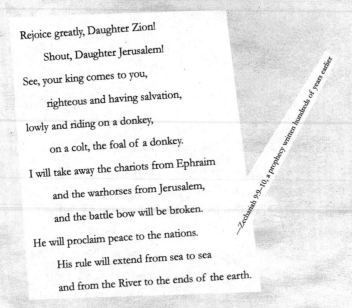

Rejoice greatly, Daughter Zion!
Shout, Daughter Jerusalem!
See, your king comes to you,
righteous and having salvation,
lowly and riding on a donkey,
on a colt, the foal of a donkey.
I will take away the chariots from Ephraim
and the warhorses from Jerusalem,
and the battle bow will be broken.
He will proclaim peace to the nations.
His rule will extend from sea to sea
and from the River to the ends of the earth.

—Zechariah 9:9-10, a prophecy written hundreds of years earlier

63 During the Maccabean revolt, generations before Jesus, the Jews cleansed the temple, which had been desecrated by the occupying powers, and "entered it with praise and palm branches, and with harps and cymbals and stringed instruments, and with hymns and songs, because a great enemy had been crushed and removed from Israel" (1 Macc. 13:51).

Ruling with a Towel

The disciples had a hard time trying to run after Jesus' vision of becoming the least to be the greatest. Over and over they argued about who was the greatest and who got to sit next to Jesus. At one point, the ambitious mother of James and John approached Jesus to intercede on their behalf. (Surely a little embarrassing for the boys.) She asked him, "Can my boys sit next to you on the throne?" How did Jesus respond? He gathered the whole group of disciples together and told them that if they wanted to be the greatest, they should become servants, not kings. If they wanted to rule in his kingdom, they'd better get ready to wash feet and clean toilets. This king rules with a towel, not a sword. In the kingdom of God, we descend into greatness.

"A dispute also arose among them as to which of them was considered to be greatest. Jesus said to them: 'The kings of the Gentiles lord it over them; and those who exercise authority over them call themselves Benefactors. But you are not to be like that. Instead, the greatest among you should be like the youngest, and the one who rules like the one who serves. For who is greater, the one who is at the table or the one who serves? Is it not the one who is at the table? But I am among you as one who serves'" (Luke 22:24–27).

The Last Prayer

Just before he was killed, Jesus prayed his longest recorded prayer (John 17). He was careful as he prayed to make it clear whom he was praying for:

"I am NOT praying for the world,

but for those you have given me."
(v.9, EMPHASIS ADDED)

He wasn't simply praying for the world to change or for Rome to be reformed. He prayed for the peculiar group of people to be set apart, for therein lies the hope of the world. He reminded his followers that...

"the world has hated them, for they are not of
the world
anymore than I am of the world" (v.14)

and he prayed that they would continue to be set apart and faithful to his way. As he had told them before, they should not be surprised when they collide with the world. As they live good, they will get beat up real bad. After all, look what the world had done to him, and he is the perfection of love.

Jesus' Inauguration Ceremony

Politics are very religious. When a president rises to power in the United States, an elaborate and religious ceremony inaugurates his presidency with sacred rituals like the twenty-one-gun salute. The inauguration has to be meaningful, holy, ceremonious, and big. The office of the President of the United States (and nearly all thrones of world governments) carries a spiritual and religious weight in our hearts, more than most of us would admit. Many people speak of the president as the most significant person who can "change the world" or "move world history." If you want anything done, the president can do it. The attention and reverence given to an inauguration confirms how seriously invested people's hopes are in the office of the (almost always) man in charge. And the attention and reverence (or even legitimating protests and riots) paid to presidents and rulers bestow on them a status something like "the Son of God." After all, being considered an omnipotent mover of history is a requirement for deity.

It wasn't all that different in Jesus' time. We all know of the Caesars and their insane, violent, and power-hungry egos. As we've mentioned, the Caesars and Roman emperors were worshiped as gods on earth. So the emperor gained the title Son of God. Inaugurations of Caesars were ornate, public, and meant to impress. The ceremony originated with the Greeks and was called a *thriambas*. Then the Romans adopted this ceremony (Latin: *triumpe*). At the center of these ceremonies was the triumphant person to be deified—the triumphator. Both the Greek and Roman ceremonies were affiliated with gods that died and rose again: Dionysus and Jupiter.

The Christians in the Roman Empire recognized the power and devotion of the imperial cult. They also recognized that you could not serve the god of the empire and the God of Jesus. This is why they did not choose small language to communicate about Jesus, language such as, "It's just a personal spiritual conviction, not political." No, they chose language and imagery with the weight of the empire behind their words. But probably the most poignant language in the Gospels that contrasts Jesus with the powers of his day is that of his crucifixion story in Mark. Ray Vander Laan[64] notes the following eight steps in the inauguration of a Caesar. Read these steps, and then note the powerful and satirical method Mark uses to paint what he sees as the true inauguration of Jesus, the suffering and loving triumphator—or the anti-triumphator.

64 Thomas Schmidt, "Jesus' Triumphal March to Crucifixion: The Sacred Way as Roman Procession," *New Testament Studies* (January 1995): 41:1 and *Bible Review* (February 1997): 30. Also, N. T. Wright, "Upstaging the Emperor," *Bible Review* (February 1988): 14:01. See also Ray Vander Laan, *Lord of Lords*, www.followtherabbi.com/Brix?pageID=2751.

Caesar's Coronation and Procession

1. The Praetorian Guard (six thousand soldiers) gathered in the Praetorium. The would-be Caesar was brought into the middle of the gathering.

2. Guards went to the temple of Jupiter Capitolinus, got a purple robe, and placed it on the candidate. The candidate was also given an olive-leaf wreath made of gold and a scepter for the authority of Rome.

3. Caesar was loudly acclaimed as triumphant by the Praetorian Guard.

4. A procession began through the streets of Rome, led by soldiers. In the middle was Caesar. Walking behind him was a sacrificial bull, whose death and blood would mark Caesar's entrance into the divine pantheon. Walking next to the bull was a slave, who carried an axe to kill the bull. Some accounts note that some people would spread sweet-smelling incense around the procession.

5. The procession moved to the highest hill in Rome, the Capitolene hill ("head hill"). On this hill is the Capitoleum temple.

6. The candidate stood before the temple altar and was offered, by the slave, a bowl of wine mixed with myrrh. He took it as if to accept, and then gave it back. The slave also refused, and then the wine was poured out either onto the altar or onto the bull. Right after the wine was poured, the bull was killed.[65]

7. The Caesar-to-be gathered his second in command on his right hand and his third in command on his left. Then they ascended to the throne of the Capitoleum.

8. The crowd acclaimed the inaugurated emperor. And for the divine seal of approval, the gods would send signs, such as a flock of doves or a solar eclipse.

---

65 Schmidt writes that within this procession is the theme of resurrection, "which is also confirmed by the similar dress worn by both the triumphator and the bull. In other words, the bull is the god who dies and appears as the victor in the person of the triumphator" ("Jesus' Triumphal March," 41:1).

Jesus' Coronation and Procession

1. Jesus was brought to the Praetorium in Jerusalem. And the whole company of soldiers (at least two hundred) gathered there.

2. Soldiers brought Jesus a wreath (of thorns), a scepter (an old stick), and a purple robe.

3. Sarcastically, the soldiers acclaimed, mocked, and paid homage to Jesus.

4. The procession began. But instead of a bull, the would-be king and god became the sacrifice, the bull. But he could not carry the instrument of death *and* be the sacrifice. So they stopped Simon (father of Alexander and Rufus, who were later young believers at the church in Rome) and gave him the cross.

5. Jesus was led up to Golgotha. (In Aramaic, Golgotha is not precisely "skull hill"—that's Calvary. To split hairs, Golgotha means "head hill," like the Roman Capitolene.)

6. Jesus was offered wine, and he refused. Right after, it is written, "And they crucified him."

7. Next came the account of those being crucified on his right and left. (The word for them—*lestes*—means "terrorist" or "insurrectionist.")

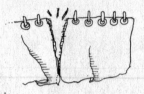

8. Jesus was again acclaimed (mocked) and a divine sign confirmed God's presence (the temple curtain ripped in two). (In other accounts, the whole sky became darkened, tombs burst open, and the dead walked about.) Finally, the Roman guard, who undoubtedly pledged allegiance to Caesar, the other "Son of God," was converted and acclaimed *this* man as the Son of God.

As Jesus was being "crowned king" and led to his inaugural execution, the symbolism was unmistakable to first-century eyes (but clouded to us by centuries of passion plays and bad movies). The crown of thorns, the purple robe, the royal staff—Mark's point is simple: at the very apex of the crucifixion, we read, "Surely this man was the Son of God!" (Mark 15:39). The first evangelist is a Roman centurion. Mark wants his readers to believe the same. But, knowing the context of this proclamation, we can know more of what the centurion meant by this. His belief in Jesus brings the text deeper into our politics and allegiance. For we know that the Son of God is not simply a title for a religious figure, a ghost of God beamed down to earth. No, with this name Jesus is placed here at the center of the universe—political, social, religious, economic, everything—because of how he died. Would you call a man who died like this the Son of God?

The suffering way of the cross is the ironic and astounding way to bring life to the world. Unless a seed dies, it cannot bring life. It's not that the cross is just some necessary step to accomplishing some religious plan of salvation—an abstract scheme that leaves Jesus politically meaningless. *The cross is the way.* It is a completely different way to view the world, success, and the meaning of history. "Here at the cross is the man who loves his enemies, the man whose righteousness is greater than that of the Pharisees, who being rich became poor, who gives his robe to those who took his cloak, who prays for those who spitefully use him.

The cross is not a detour or a hurdle on the way to the kingdom, nor is it even the way to the kingdom; it is the kingdom come.[66]

The cross is the culmination of all that the empire had to offer, where all the wrath of the world was poured out on God. And it is on the cross that we can see the ultimate power standoff. On the cross we see what love looks like when it stares evil in the face. We can hear what the Lover from Nazareth has to say to evildoers and torturers. "Father, forgive them, for they do not know what they are doing" (Luke 23:34).

131

66 Yoder, *Politics of Jesus*, 51 (or just read the whole book).

The Human Temple

When Jesus died on Friday, the world shook. The sun stopped. Creation stood still. Everyone Jesus loved waited in anxious bewilderment—only failed Messiahs hung on crosses. Even Jesus wondered if God had given up. Love died on that imperial cross. But then something beautiful happened that we shouldn't overlook: the veil of the temple was ripped in half (Luke 23:45). Scholars say that this curtain was enormous, bigger than a basketball court and as thick as your hand. It took more than three hundred priests to move it. And when Christ died, this curtain ripped open. We are left with the unmistakable image that God tore open the temple to set all the sacred things free. And this was something Jesus did his whole life. He offered healing and forgiveness for free, and outside the curtain. The Holy of Holies could not contain God. "The wildest being in existence"[67] would not be domesticated. The cross busted God out of the temple and religion, and brings God out into the streets and outside the city into the wild, where Jesus was executed.

As we've mentioned, the temple wasn't something God was happy about. The temple was a system that regulated access to God and was a centralized power symbol that made Israel "like the other nations." It is interpreted in 2 Samuel 7 as a compromise to God's tribal identity. Even more, the temple in Jesus' day was a project that had been sponsored by imperial Persia. (Years before, the Persian emperor Cyrus had released the Jews from Babylonian captivity and sent them home to Palestine. To keep the Jews indebted and connected to their liberators, Cyrus

67 A phrase coined by Wendell Berry in his book *Sex, Economy, Freedom, and Community* (New York: Pantheon Books, 1992), 101.

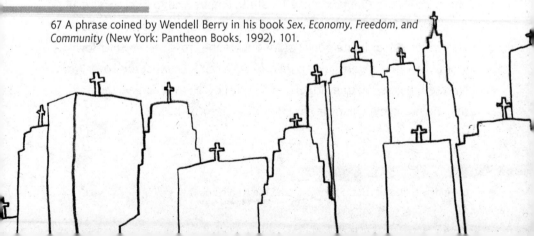

offered to rebuild their destroyed temple.) Instead of being a sign of the undomesticated God in the desert, this temple had sponsors and big-time financing. It could be seen as a way to control and contain the God who insists, "I am who I am, and I will be who I will be." Just as Jesus had proclaimed, there would be a day when we no longer worship in temples made by hands but worship in spirit and truth. We would not need buildings. And there would be no mediation.

Maybe Jesus saw what was coming—that only a few years later, the temple would be destroyed. At that point, the people of God would need to find their true center, an identity that ran deeper than a building. The tearing of the temple's veil was a sign of where things were going with Jesus: the new temple would be the people who lived in faith, hope, and love. It's a fulfillment of when Solomon built the temple but God turned the tables, in effect saying, "I'll make you into a living temple."

They ridiculed and mocked Jesus with an imperial inauguration and beat him to a pulp. Over this Pilate and Herod could agree; amazing how a common enemy can unite former adversaries. "That day Herod and Pilate became friends—before this they had been enemies" (Luke 23:12). So they united as friends to kill the one who supposedly was inciting the people to rebellion, the ultimate enemy of the state, the one who was being lauded as the King of Kings. But Jesus didn't flinch before the empire's sword. Death would soon die.

"He was oppressed and afflicted, yet he did not open his mouth; he was led like a lamb to the slaughter, and as a sheep before its shearers is silent, so he did not open his mouth" (Isa. 53:7).

It is as if he was saying, "What are you going to do, kill me? I am bigger than death."

Saturday,

The disciples had jumped ship and abandoned him. Some of them headed back to their old jobs and started fishing again, fishing for new dreams. Others denied that they had ever bought into the dream or knew the Dreamer. The women remained, crying, hoping, steadfast.

But the story doesn't end here.

On Sunday, the most incredible event in all of history happened. The tomb was empty. The slaughtered Lamb had risen from the grave. He had conquered death. He had triumphed over the Devil and all the powers of this world. And he had made a spectacle of them. Death, thou art dead. No king has ever gone this far to remind the world that it is loved. Long live the slaughtered Lamb. Long live the king who died at the hands of his enemies that they might know what love looks like. The inauguration ceremony that normally bolstered the pomp and arrogance of those who aspired for world power as "Sons of God" was turned upside down by Jesus as he ascended to the throne of the Son of Man. Crucified in humility[68] and full of enemy love, considered a good-for-nothing slave and an insurgent, Jesus shows us what true greatness looks like.

Then came the invitation. Jesus appeared to his disciples and gave them a great mission: Follow him. Drink of his cup. Become the body of Christ to teach the world how to love.

And they were to make disciples. Jesus' last commission was to "make disciples of all nations" (Matt. 28:19). They were to teach the nations a new way of living. One by one, these disciples would infect the nations with grace. It wasn't a call to take the sword or the throne and force the world to bow. Rather, they were to live the contagious love of God,

68 *Man* is a word for humanity or human being, which is rich with word connections: humiliation, humility—which means close to the ground (*humus*). Likewise, as we mentioned earlier, Adam is made from the *adama* (soil). Jesus is bringing the heavenly kingdom down to earth.

to woo the nations into a new future. "Nations" didn't mean states or governments; it meant all the world's peoples regardless of region, tribe, or clan. The covenant of God was open not just to Jews but to all the Gentile world. And making disciples didn't mean using cutting-edge small group curriculum; it meant disciplining themselves, training themselves to become the peculiar people of God set apart from Caesar's world.

Just like Abraham and Sarah starting a new family, these early disciples would soon become known as the new humanity, a people called out of the nations, of all different ethnicities, but with one thing in common: they were children of God, born again in a dysfunctional world where they were to become the change that they wanted to see. It was a call to become a new family, a people born not of flesh but of Spirit, a global sisterhood and brotherhood that ran deeper than nationality or biology. They were to be born again.

Making disciples meant that they were teaching the world to do the things Jesus did. To wash feet. To proclaim jubilee. To love enemies. To welcome strangers. And they would become known as the Way. Their community was more than just a group of people who shared religious beliefs. They were a group of people that embodied a new way of living, the way out of the empire, where slavery, poverty, war, and oppression were normal. They were to become the salt and the light of the world. The credibility of their gospel would rest on the integrity of their lives. For they were now to be the body of Christ. Jesus would live in them.

But it wouldn't be easy to make disciples of the nations. After all, the nations were also trying to make disciples of them.

SECTION THREE

When the Empire

Got Baptized

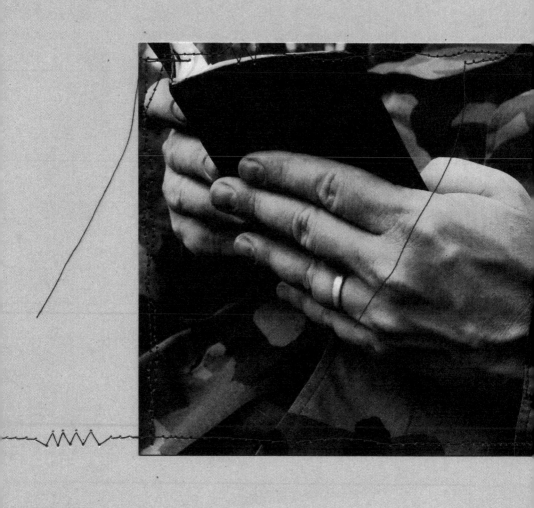

Jesus had warned his followers that they were to live the kingdom of God in this world and that the world would hate them for it. The powers would drag them before governors and courts, beat them and insult them, feed them to beasts, and hang them on crosses. Look what happened to Jesus. And hate his followers is what the world did—at least for the first couple of hundred years. The young church lived within the messy collision of kingdoms. The more the early Christians reflected on the life and message of their rabbi-messiah, and the more they tried to live the way of the gospel, the harder they collided with the state and its hopes and dreams, militaries and markets. In fact, Christians in those first few hundred years were called atheists[1] because they no longer believed in the Roman gospel; they no longer had any faith in the state as savior of the world. They were called

1 Robert L. Wilken, *The Christians as the Romans Saw Them* (New Haven, CT: Yale Univ. Press, 1984), 27.

all kinds of names—"renegade Jews," "rebel citizens," even "enemies of the human race." They were accused of incest because they called each other sister and brother even when they had no biological relationship. And they were accused of being cannibals because they had a strange ritual of eating something they called the body and blood of their Lord. They were enemies of the state.

Consider their own words and those of their contemporaries as they interacted with the empire:[2]

2 We are here indebted to the work of Eberhard Arnold's *The Early Christians: In Their Own Words* (Rifton, NY: Plough, 1970).

> The Christians form among themselves secret societies that exist outside the system of laws ... an obscure and mysterious community founded on revolt and the advantage that accrues from it.
>
> —Letter to Origen

> We are charged with being irreligious people and, what is more, irreligious in respect to the emperors since we refuse to pay religious homage to their imperial majesties and to their genius and refuse to swear by them. High treason is a crime of offense against the Roman religion. It is a crime of open irreligion, a raising of the hand to injure the deity ... Christians are considered to be enemies of the State ... we do not celebrate the festivals of the Caesars. Guards and informers bring up accusations against the Christians ... blasphemers and traitors ... we are charged with sacrilege and high treason ... we give testimony to the truth.
>
> —Tertullian

He called Abraham and commanded him to go out from the country where he was living. With this call [God] has roused us all, and now we have left the state. We have renounced all the things the world offers.

—Justin

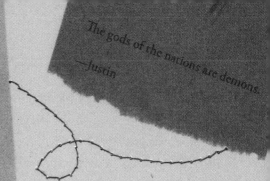

The gods of the nations are demons.

—Justin

[Origen, quoting Celsus:] "If everyone were to act the same as you Christians, the national government would soon be left utterly deserted and without any help, and affairs on earth would soon pass into the hands of the most savage and wretched barbarians." [Origen:] Celsus exhorts us to help the Emperor and be his fellow soldiers. To this we reply, "You cannot demand military service of Christians any more than you can of priests." We do not go forth as soldiers with the Emperor even if he demands this. [Origen goes on to say that if the Romans followed the teachings of Jesus, there would be no barbarians.]

—Origen

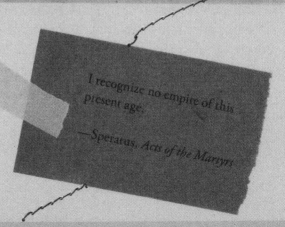

I recognize no empire of this present age.

—Speratus, Acts of the Martyrs

They charge us on two points: that we do not sacrifice and that we do not believe in the same gods as the State.

—Athenagoras

Washing the Dirty System Off of Us

For these early Christians, baptism was one of the rites of passage into the new life of the kingdom. Remember that one of the ways Jesus kicked off his public life was by having his cousin John baptize him in the Jordan River. Baptism was a sign of the new exodus from the contemporary Egypts; the old life was washed away and a new humanity emerged from the waters. As new believers confessed their faith and entered the community through baptism, they reconsidered and redefined everything about themselves. In the most constructive sense of the word, they repented, rethought their entire lives, and turned around to find a new way of living. Some people left their jobs when their old lives collided with their new ones, when their allegiance to Rome collided with their new allegiance to God's kingdom. For some early Christians, a true conversion meant that they became a new kind of tax collector or business person, and for others it meant that they would get fired. In the young Jesus movement, if you worked in the brothels and decided to give your life to Christ and his kingdom, then you needed to rethink your career. But it wasn't only people in the brothels who needed to do this reevaluation; so did folks who worked in the imperial games, made idols, served in the military,[3] or worked in the imperial courts, jails, and markets. And it was the responsibility of the Christian community to support these young converts as they rethought their lives outside the empire. To enter the church, many converts even went through a process of "exorcisms" to cast out the empires within.

3 "Celsus [a Roman intellectual], however, knew that most Christians refused military service and hence were unwilling to do their part in protecting the empire. Origen, writing seventy years later, confirms this. ... Christians not only refused military service but they would not accept public office nor assume any responsibility for the governing of the cities. ... By elevating the status of their society to divine status, they set up a rival to the one high God who watched over the empire" (Wilkins, *Christians as the Romans Saw Them*, 117–25).

Folks left their possessions for an economy of interdependence and abundance. Others left their biological families for a family of rebirth, with sisters and brothers living all over the empire as God's family. Consider how radically these early Christ-followers reimagined their lives.

The professions and trades of those who are going to be accepted into the community must be examined. The nature and type of each must be established ... brothel, sculptors of idols, charioteer, athlete, gladiator ... give it up or be rejected. A military constable must be forbidden to kill, neither may he swear; if he is not willing to follow these instructions, he must be rejected. A proconsul or magistrate who wears the purple and governs by the sword shall give it up or be rejected. Anyone taking or already baptized who wants to become a soldier shall be sent away, for he has despised God.

—Hippolytus, 218 AD

I do not wish to be a ruler. I do not strive for wealth. I refuse offices connected with military command. I despise death.

—Tatian

We ourselves were well conversant with war, murder and everything evil, but all of us throughout the whole wide earth have traded in our weapons of war. We have exchanged our swords for plowshares, our spears for farm tools ... now we cultivate the fear of God, justice, kindness, faith, and the expectation of the future given us through the crucified one ... the more we are persecuted and martyred, the more do others in ever increasing numbers become believers.

—Justin, martyred in 165 AD

You who are God's servants are living in a foreign country, for your own city-state is far away from this city-state. Knowing which is yours, why do you acquire fields, costly furnishings, buildings, and frail dwellings here? Anyone who acquires things for himself in this city cannot expect to find the way home to his own City. Do you not realize that all these things here do not belong to you, that they are under a power alien to your nature? The ruler will say you do not obey my laws, either observe my laws or get out of my country. Take care lest it prove fatal to you to repudiate your own laws. Acquire no more here than what is absolutely necessary. Instead of fields, buy for yourselves people in distress in accordance with your means.

—Hermas, 140 AD

On numerous occasions, soldiers who were chosen to execute their comrades suddenly decided on conversion and threw down their swords (for example, Lactantius and Tertullian). There is even documentation of "soldier saints" who left their swords and offices and, charged with treason, endured persecution and death. A church council in Elvira in 313 decided that Christians who held offices that participated in the violence of the state had to leave their jobs. Only a year later, this decision was reversed in the Synod of Arles, which was summoned by the emperor himself. The emperor made military service mandatory and excommunicated soldiers who disobeyed orders, as well as Christians who refused to serve as state officials even with the understanding that they wouldn't have to participate in emperor worship. (By that time, as in ours, the definition of "emperor worship" was a bit ambiguous.)

One of our favorite conversion stories is that of Minucius Felix, a lawyer in Rome who was well acquainted with imperial "justice"; he knew Rome's sword and Rome's distaste for Christians. Before his conversion, he wrote

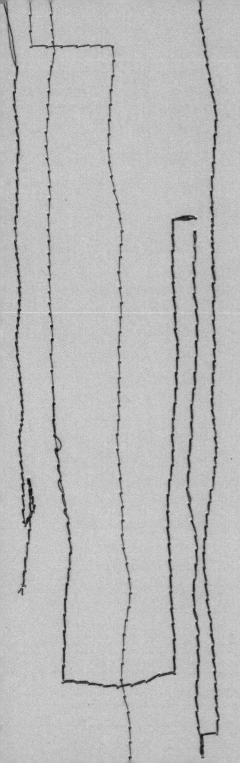

of Christians that "they form a rabble of profane conspiracy ... They despise temples as if they were tombs ... They despise titles of honor and the purple robe of high government office, though hardly able themselves to cover their nakedness. Just like a rank growth of weeds, the abominable haunts where this impious confederacy meet are multiplying all over the world. Root and branch, it should at all costs be exterminated and accursed. They love one another before being acquainted. They practice a cult of lust, calling one another brother and sister indiscriminately; under the cover of these hallowed names, fornication becomes incest."

After his conversion, Rome's clatter of death sounded very different to him. He wrote, "What a beautiful sight it is for God when a Christian ... mocks at the clatter of the tools of death and the horror of the executioner; when he defends and upholds his liberty in the face of kings and princes, obeying God alone, to whom he belongs ... Among us, boys and frail women laugh to scorn torture and the gallows cross and all the other horrors of execution."[4]

4 Arnold, *The Early Christians*, 89, 122–23.

The Empire Has No Clothes

Before there was Christianity or Christendom or even really a church, the movement of people following after Jesus became known as the Way, because their way of living stood in stark contrast to the ways of empire. They believed that new life through Jesus had begun—right now. Jesus' constant reiteration of his vision of the kingdom of God *coming on earth* still rang in their ears. They believed the kingdom's coming was so immanent, they could not help but start living it now. In a way, it was as if they had already died and gone to heaven and were now living heaven on earth. "Give 'em heaven," as we say, and they were givin' the empire heaven. The problem was that the world hadn't caught up. The globalizing economy in the first-century Roman Empire was exploitative and unsustainable. Some of the best anti-imperial and pro-kingdom images we have from the early church are from John's book of Revelation. The book's purpose is to reveal[5] the truth about the empire, and reveal he did, to the point that he was exiled to the island of Patmos. The careful scrutiny of those in power while he was in exile forced him to write using poetry, symbols, and images so the authorities wouldn't figure out what he was saying and do more than just exile him. Much of John's writing in Revelation is filled with bizarre beasts like those we read about in Daniel. But John offers another image of the global market and the kingdom of Caesar ... "the great whore."[6]

> We who formerly treasured money and possessions more than anything else now hand over everything we have to a treasury for all and share it with everyone who needs it. We who formerly hated and murdered one another now live together and share the same table. We pray for our enemies and try to win those who hate us.
>
> —Justin Martyr

5 The title *Revelation* can also mean "unveiling," much like the scene in the Wizard of Oz when the curtain is pulled away to reveal the wizard's fraud, or like the fable in which a kid points out that the emperor has no clothes.

6 We prefer the phrase "the great whore" to the term *prostitute*, because *prostitute* implies a context of poverty and male-domineering sexual exploitation, whereas *whore* implies seduction and adulterous licentiousness.

"Fallen! Fallen is Babylon the Great! ...
    For all the nations have drunk
                the maddening wine of her adulteries.

The kings of the earth committed adultery with her,
        and the merchants of the earth
                grew rich from her excessive luxuries.

        ...

  Come out of her, my people,
        so that you will not share in her sins
        so that you will not receive any of her plagues; .

    for her sins are piled up to heaven,
        and God has remembered her crimes. ..."

"The merchants of the earth will weep and mourn over her because
    no one buys their cargoes anymore--cargoes of gold, silver,
    precious stones and pearls; fine linen, purple, silk and scarlet
    cloth; every sort of citron wood, and articles of every kind
    made of ivory, costly wood, bronze, iron, and marble;
cargoes of cinnamon and spiceXXX
                        of incense, myrrh and frankincense,
of wine and olive oil, of fine flour and wheat; cattle and sheep;
  horses and carriages; and human beings being sold as slaves."

                                        (Rev. 18:2–5, 11–14)[7]

7 John was not the only one who criticized Rome's wealth. Here is a long poem from
the Sibylline Oracles: "Desire for treacherous gold and silver shall rule, for nothing
is greater than these in mortal eyes. Not the light of the sun, nor heaven nor sea
nor broad-backed earth. ... O source of godlessness, forerunner of disorder, Lord of
and means to all wars, hateful plague of peace, setting parents against children, and
children against parents! ... They will exploit the poor as if they wanted forever and
ever to keep the earth that feeds the masses of people, procuring land for themselves
and yet more land, boasting and putting down the poor. And if the vast earth did
not have its place far from the starry heavens, men would not share the light; it could
be bought for gold and would belong to the rich. For poor folk God would have to
prepare another existence. To thee, O stiff-necked Rome, shall come one day from
above the fitting blow from heaven! Then shall first thy neck bow down! Thou shalt
be razed to the ground and wholly consumed by fire, laid low and stretched out on
the ground. The whole of thy riches shall perish. Then thy ruins shall be the abode of
wolves and of foxes, and thou shalt be deserted as if thou hadst never been" (Arnold,
The Early Christians).

A few things about this quote should strike us. The *merchants* wept over Babylon. Merchants: the central cogs in the machine of the Roman dream. And all of the kings of the earth were involved in the sloppy affair. All of them. All the nations had grown drunk on her wine. Though the commodities she was buying and selling weren't intrinsically bad, the system of tumultuous greed itself was. The passage ends by saying she sold the bodies and souls of humanity. Sound familiar?

And she's drunk. John says that she is drunk with the blood of the saints. Her wineglass is filled with the blood she has shed throughout the earth— of "saints, prophets, and all who have been killed on the earth"—hers is the cup of empire, slaughter, genocide, and sweatshops. Everyone has grown drunk from the blood, and they stand back and marvel, "Who is like Babylon?" Babylon the beautiful. But there are those who do not drink from her cup, who do not grow drunk on the cocktails of culture.[8] Their cup is filled with the blood of the Lamb. It is the cup of the new covenant. The question becomes, From which cup will we toast?

8 Just as Daniel refused to eat the meat at the king's table when he was held captive in the imperial courts (Dan. 1:8).

Babylon was considered to be great. John's point was to reveal as a fraud what was every day considered normal, insisting that normal is not the same as good. Rather, "What people value highly is detestable in God's sight" (Luke 16:15). The world around John is detestable not according to Rome's standards (Rome was certainly "respectable") but according to the standards of his great prophetic tradition, flowing backward from Jesus, to Daniel, to Elijah, and to Moses. The economy of Rome is not worthy of God's creation, according to this tradition. Rather, we should look to Moses' anti-imperial politics of debt forgiveness, land redistribution, welcoming immigrants, gleaning fields for the poor, taking care of the elderly, keeping honest scales in the market, not charging interest or defrauding your neighbor, and helping even one's enemies—all of it worlds apart from the Roman Empire. And for the early Christians, this was a major point of debate: Can they eat the meat and wine of Rome? Can they eat the food that is polluted by the imperial cult?

John's language couldn't be clearer: we are to "come out" of her, literally to pull ourselves out. Let's be honest here: this is rated R. Kids, go ahead and flip the page and look at the pictures. Scholars point out that this is erotic language and that the words John uses are the same ones used for *coitus interruptus*—to interrupt sexual intercourse before climax. As John is speaking of this steamy love affair with the empire, he calls the church to "pull out of her"—to leave the romance with the world and be wooed by God, to remember our first love, to say no to all other lovers. Certainly he made his readers blush. And it's not easy to pull out of a relationship of dependency and romance, of lavish gifts and captivating beauty, especially with a bride as beautiful as Rome or America.

We may live in the best Babylon in the world ...
but it is still Babylon, and we are called to come out of her.

--Tony Campolo

But how do you go to the grocery store when you know it is part of a system of greed, exploitation, and unsustainability? What can you eat when it seems like every food has been defiled? This was a question asked by people in John's time. The supermarket of their day was called the *agora*. Just as Home Depot and Wal-Mart have an American flag waving above their entrances, so too the agora existed under the mythology of the powers. And just as our money says, "In God We Trust," so did Rome's, because the things they were selling promised to feed not just the mouth but the soul. To enter the agora, in order to buy and sell, one needed to pledge allegiance, so to speak, to the economy patronized by Caesar. And no one thought about it; after all, few could tell the difference between Caesar and God. This pledging of allegiance was often done by dropping a pinch of incense before an image of Caesar or by giving some other sign of recognition before entering the market. After all, monetary economies are based on the belief in central authority (like Caesar), or else currency is just paper or scraps of metal. After affirming the center of the imperial economy, the person visiting the market would receive a mark on their right hand, allowing them to enter and to buy or sell. John the Revelator illustrates the tension: "[The Beast] forced all people, great and small, rich and poor, free and slave, to receive a mark [*charagma*] on their right hands or on their foreheads, so that they could not buy or sell unless they had the mark, which is the name of the beast or the number of its name" (Rev. 13:16–17).

Scholars Wes Howard-Brook and Anthony Gwyther help clarify what's happening in this text: "The mark [*charagma*] of ancient Rome was not some esoteric symbol but a stamp used to certify deeds of sale, and the impress of the emperor's head on the coinage. ... John knew that while the right hand was holding the Roman coin, empire would transfix the mind of the bearer."[9] It's a way the empire branded you.

The greatest sin of political imagination is thinking there is no other way except the filthy rotten system we have today.

Christians in the empire faced the question of whether (and if so, how) they would participate in the market. The market was part of the empire's abuse of the earth and its idolatrous dominance. If Christ was truly risen and God's kingdom was real, believers wanted all things in their lives to embody those realities. But it wasn't easy to resist the temptations of empire, just like the Israelites longed for the stew they ate back in Egypt. "We have to eat," they might have said. "Just cross your fingers and acknowledge Caesar." And so John had to write compelling arguments against the market that saw everything in "the big picture." He did not simply argue that various aspects of the market exploit this or that; rather he placed his concerns in light of a cosmological struggle between right and wrong. This, indeed, is a challenging call from the prophet John. Is he saying we should not take the mark at the entrance to the supermarket? If we don't take the mark, we can't get in; how do we live and eat? We cannot live without the empire's supermarket! But it seems that John has brought his readers to see the greatest sin of political imagination: thinking there is no other way except the filthy rotten system we have today. Is it possible we can't see the destructiveness of our economy not because we don't know it's terrible but because deep down, we feel that it's necessary and that therefore it's hopeless to criticize it?

9 Wes Howard-Brook and Anthony Gwyther, *Unveiling Empire: Reading Revelation Then and Now* (Maryknoll, NY: Orbis, 1999), 175. See also Adolf Deismann's *Light from the Ancient East* (London: Hodder and Stoughton, 1910), 341, and G. B. Caird's "On Deciphering the Book of Revelation: Heaven and Earth," *Expository Times*, 74:13–15 (1962): 173.

While John's letter to the churches is aggressive and wild in its language, many of the details (such as emperors, cities, and names) are veiled. Maybe John wanted his readers to come to conclusions themselves, like Jesus often wanted when he told his obtuse parables. Or maybe he just didn't want to get killed, since his letter was to be screened by prison guards. In any case, John writes, "This calls for wisdom. For those who have insight, calculate the number of the beast, for it is the number of a man." Hundreds of years earlier, the prophet Daniel had seared into Israel's consciousness the sense of empires as "beasts" (as we mentioned in section 1). John alludes to this, naming the beast 666, the number of the beast who began the long drama of killing the people of Jesus. Sorry to burst the apocalyptic bubble and ruin all the wild movies, but the Antichrist isn't who any of us grew up thinking it is. Just as the letter X in Roman numerology stands for ten and V stands for five, so too do Hebrew letters hold numerical value, and the letters of Nero Caesar add up: *nrwn qsr* = 666.[10] Of course, this took a bit of calculation to figure out, as John warned, but it would not have been too hard to see what he was alluding to. His other contemporary allusions, like to Emperor Vespasian's recovery from a war wound (13:12), underscore his awareness of and aversion to power and empire. Today, someone writing in John's style might use a phrase such as "mission accomplished" or describe the image of a flaming oil field under a sky of black smoke. Someone writing like this isn't naming names but draws on enough political memory to help readers weave their own poetic re-readings of history. We might even say that, in some sense, John was rewriting history from the perspective of the Lamb of God— Rome is no longer the prestigious guarantor of freedom at the height of its prosperity (as historians might read the times of John's writing) but is the power that conspires to slaughter God's love in the world. In other words, John's political imagination pierces the popular, but false, appearances: he proclaims, "Rome is fallen!"

10 "50 + 200 + 6 + 50 + 100 + 60 + 200 ... The Beast is the Roman Empire— more precisely, all the cruelties of the Roman political domination—personified by Nero Caesar" (Thomas Cahill, *Desire of the Everlasting Hills* [New York: Doubleday, 1999], 163).

So among the book of Revelation's many messages is a clear message to believers: come out of that maddening whore of an economy that is pillaging the world. As we shared earlier, "coming out" for the early Christians meant sharing all things in common, selling possessions, and giving to anyone in need (Acts 2; 4). Just as ancient Israel was an alternative to the exploitive economies in Egypt and Canaan, so too these early Christians understood themselves as set apart in all areas of their lives, including economic. Christians didn't need Caesar's power to create an alternative society. They lived life in the spirit of jubilee. They practiced radical economic sharing, so much so that it could even be said they ended poverty in the small pockets they lived in. One of the results of the birth of the church at Pentecost was that the church ended poverty: "and there were no needy persons among them." The community itself became good news to the poor. They lived near one another, sharing a common rule of life, daily sharing worship and friendship. They, as their hearts became softened to the love of God, enacted "release to the captives" and "freedom for the prisoner," slowly dissolving the structures of oppression within their households. To a world gone blind from "an eye for an eye," they gave sight, living out Jesus' teachings on enemy-love.

Indeed, the early movement of Christ-followers enacted God's hopes for Abraham and Sarah: they had been blessed to be a blessing to the world. They were a stateless society that would infect the world like a mustard seed. This community would be the yeast of God kneaded into the dough of the world. But this was more than just a renewed Israel. The definition of the "people of God" took on a different and expanded shape when it became apparent that many of the Hebrews would not pledge allegiance to Jesus. The enlarged scope of God's people would be called "the church," a sort of hybrid people of Jews *and* Gentiles grown from the Israelite story. This is the people who have fallen in love with Jesus and are grafted into his story of a peculiar people. The image John the Revelator leaves us with is of the City of God that has come to earth, the New Jerusalem, where mourning is turned to dancing, death is no more, the gates are left open for everyone, and the gardens take over the ghetto.

On the Political Fringes of Empire

It's easy to see why Rome acted to silence the voices of dissent, or at least exile them to an island where no one could hear them. *Martyr* means "witness." Just as Christians wanted to live like Christ, they also wanted to die like Christ. This meant loving their enemies, even as their enemies fed them to beasts. There was no greater honor than to show the world what love looks like in the face of tremendous evil.

No wonder word spread so quickly about "these men who have caused trouble all over the world" (Acts 17:6). In the early days, the movement was filled with those who had been left in the wake of imperial progress—day laborers, working children, old folks, feisty revolutionaries, single working mothers, those with disabilities, immigrants, and others who just had nothing to lose (except Rome's heavy yoke). Especially during the persecutions, martyrs came from the lower classes on the fringes of wealth and power (certainly many from the

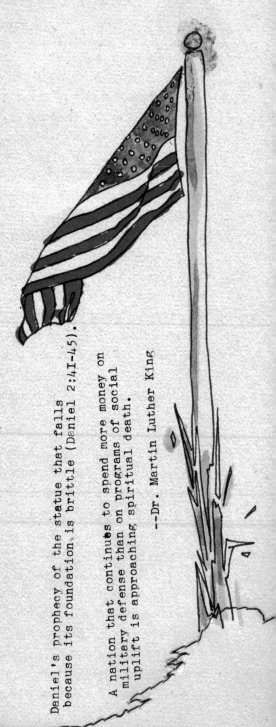

Daniel's prophecy of the statue that falls because its foundation is brittle (Daniel 2:41–45).

A nation that continues to spend more money on military defense than on programs of social uplift is approaching spiritual death.

--Dr. Martin Luther King

ranks of Rome's disenchanted youth). But Christianity spread like wildfire. Grace and community are magnetic, and even in the Gospels we see centurions and soldiers, rich rulers and CEOs, tax collectors and politicians catching the fire of God's love.

It just became harder and harder to pinch off a little incense. There were Christians who insisted that they could not bow to Caesar in any form. Others, especially those from positions of relative comfort, held a more moderate position that, while Christians could not offer sacrificial tribute to Caesar, they could falsify the census documentation saying that they did (to avoid getting killed). After all, what's a pinch of incense, right? Christians, often divided into camps of "rigorists" and "laxists," debated these issues incessantly, even to the point of excommunicating bishops and shedding blood. (At one point, a bishop condoned the attack of Caesar's army on a parish of noncompromising Christians who refused homage.)

A common misconception about the early martyrs is that they just "believed in Jesus" too much. They had serious "religious convictions," and the Romans found this offensive. Sometimes the lingering caricature of the early Christians is that they held up their crosses with fundamentalist vigor in the face of pagan Rome and were then dragged away by atheistic brutes. But the fact is that the Roman Empire was very tolerant of other religions, thoroughly committed to lawful processing, and quite pious.

> Wish yourself a martyr's death. Blushing for shame you will be dragged before the public. That is good for you, for he who is not publicly exposed like this before people will be publicly exposed before God. Power streams forth when you are seen by men.
>
> —Maximilla

Alluring, Pious Rome

Rome was not just an "evil empire." It was dazzling, magical—the world stood in awe of her. Rome was known for her roads, progress, culture, art, architecture, and security. She was the best empire there ever was, some might say. Christians longing for the world to be God's began to think maybe Rome's hands would be the next best thing. There is no question that there was a great splendor in Rome. The question was, What is the cost of that splendor?

Rome caught the attention of the world, even the secret admiration of its adversaries. The Jewish historian Josephus (whom we love to read) was in command of Jewish rebels in Galilee. When defeated, he somehow became an admirer of Rome (can't beat 'em, join 'em). He went on to call Rome's military might "irresistible" and became a spokesman of Rome and a worshiper of the emperor. Josephus was so impressed by Rome's power, he could explain it only by pointing to God's favor and ended up saying Jewish rebels were "waging war not only against the Romans but also against God".

From the Cheneys[11]

"And if a sparrow cannot fall to the ground without His notice, is it probable that an empire can rise without His aid?"
- Benjamin Franklin

11 This was an actual message from the 2003 Cheney Christmas card. Check out http://www.nytimes.com/2007/07/01/weekinreview/01goodheart.html?_r=1&pagewanted=all&oref=slogin or http://www.commondreams.org/views04/0415-12.htm.

Every empire has its prophets. And every empire also has its poets and troubadours.

Cities now gleam in splendor and beauty and the whole earth is arrayed like a paradise (Wengst, 8).

The author of this "paradise" new world order was Rome.

An inscription in Halicarnassus, in Asia Minor, celebrates Augustus as "Savior of the whole human race." "Land and sea have peace, the cities flourish under a good legal system, in harmony and with an abundance of food, there is an abundance of all good things, people are filled with happy hopes for the future and with delight at the present." Jesus lived during the "golden age" of Rome.

"If anyone wants to see the beauty of the earth, he should travel the world or just come to Rome. For what grows and is produced among individual peoples is always here and here in abundance. ... Anything that you do not see here does not count among what exists or has existed."

—Aristides

Rome's subjugation of the world was frequently symbolized in the globe, which even began appearing on coins. On the heels of what Alexander the Great had started years earlier with military conquests galore, Rome was advancing globalization. The Divine Augustus subjected the world to the rule of the Roman people, "made the boundaries of the empire equal to the boundaries of the earth, and safeguarded the revenues of the Romans (Diododorus Siculus 40:4/22).

Revolutionary Subordination

A curious politics is emerging here: the early Christians weren't trying to overthrow or even reform the empire, but they also weren't going along with it. They were not reformists offering the world a better Rome. They offered the dissatisfied masses not a better government but another world altogether.[12] In a world gone respectably insane, Christians, as they lived God's kingdom, embodied revolutionary subordination toward the kingdoms of the world, exemplified in the suffering humiliation of the crucified Messiah, the slaughtered Lamb who exposed the greed and violence of the world as he died naked on the cross.

One way the church stated its relationship to the powers was, "We must obey God rather than human beings!" (Acts 5:29). Maybe this is what St. Augustine was getting at when he said, "An unjust law is no law at all." But the attitude of Jesus and the church ran deeper than the usual Christian politics—that you obey the authorities when they are doing good and disobey them when they are doing bad. Rather, the church was always revolutionary through its subordination (just like carrying the pack two miles).

Very few Scriptures can be construed to say that we are unquestioningly to follow whatever kings and presidents dictate, no matter how out of line they seem to be. But some writings, like Romans 13, often surface as justification for such servitude. Nazi Germany, however, caused Christians to rethink blind obedience to the authorities. The church could not help but wonder, "When the Bible says 'be subject,' either the Bible must not have thought that one through (and it is wrong), or we really are supposed to go along with the Nazis as God's will. Or ... maybe there is something deeper going on here."

12 You might say they were not trying to fit their "new wine" (or life) into the old wineskins of the world's structures (Matt. 9:17). Jesus' way would not work in (or would burst) the world's crusty old patterns.

When we are careful to situate Paul's writing in the context and culture in which he wrote (see appendix 2), we find that Paul offered a biting critique of power and a creative path of revolutionary love. We might remember Paul urging his friend Philemon to illegally welcome back home a fugitive slave, Onesimus, as a brother, instead of killing him for running away. This is a scandalous subversion of Roman hierarchy. Paul was just as radical as Jesus. Remember that the Paul who wrote "be subject to the authorities" is the same Paul who was stoned, exiled, jailed, and beaten for subverting the authorities.[13] This could explain why Paul used the same word for authorities when he said in Ephesians, "We wrestle not against flesh and blood but against the authorities [exousia] of this dark world."

Is it possible to submit and to subvert? Paul's life gives a clear yes, as does Jesus' crucifixion. Paul points out that the very act of submission is what "disarms the powers" by making a spectacle of their evil:

For it seems to me that God has put us apostles on display at the end of the procession, like those ▨▨▨▨▨▨▨ condemned to die in the arena. We have been made a spectacle to the whole universe, to angels as well as to human beings. We are fools for Christ, but you are so wise in Christ. We are weak, but you are strong! You are honored, we are dishonored! To this very hour we go hungry and thirsty, we are in rags, we are brutally treated, we are homeless. We work hard with our own hands. When we are cursed, we bless; when we are persecuted, we endure it; when we are slandered, we answer kindly.

> We have become the scum of the earth, the garbage of the world--right up to this moment.

I Cor. 4:9-13

Scum of the earth ... this is Paul's snapshot of the early Jesus movement. Do we have the courage to follow?

13 See Acts 17:6–8 for an example of how Paul's sermons were heard.

Constantine and the "Fall"[14]
of the Church

The Roman Empire had its struggles. At one point, power was divided between many rulers because running everything under just one Caesar had gotten crazy. Other groups had invaded all sorts of regions, the economy began to crumble, and civil wars abounded. Then entered the man Gaius Flavius Valerius Aurelius Constantinus—or just Constantine. He emerged from the imperial tumult through several military conquests, the most popular of which was the Battle of the Milvian Bridge in the year 312. Before he entered into battle, so the legend goes, he saw a sign of the cross and heard a voice saying, "In this you will conquer." Hmm … ironic, considering that for Jesus the cross meant refusal of worldly ways of conquering. Nevertheless, Constantine's

> Better to die for the sake of Jesus Christ than to be king over the utmost ends of the earth.
>
> —Ignatius

> I do not wish to be a ruler. I do not strive for wealth. I refuse offices connected with military command. I despise death.
>
> —Tatian

> The desire to rule is the mother of heresies.
>
> —John Chrysostom

> Emperors could only believe in Christ if they were not emperors—as if Christians could ever be emperors.
>
> —Tertullian

14 The roots of this fall are earlier and deeper than in just one emperor and one edict. The compromise began years earlier in the church's inability to reconcile Jew and Gentile. After several decades, the difficulty of holding these two groups in one body became too great. The church that began largely as Jews, welcoming in the Gentile converts, turned into a mainly Gentile affair. But then the greater political story we have illuminated in this book was lost: the church is that minority group, the alien people, the exodus tribes, unlike "the other nations." After these roots withered, it was not difficult to uproot the tree and plant it squarely in the state. It is difficult to see how those wounds can be healed. The process might begin by acknowledging that the very essence and identity of church are bound up in these ancient, anti-imperial desert tribes. One might argue that the Reformation didn't make a radical enough critique; it didn't go far enough back. What needed treatment were not just the papacy, its hierarchical structures, and mutated rituals but also the very assumptions of power in the Constantinian shift and in its split with Judaism.

army won the battle, with crosses painted on their shields, securing Constantine's power as the Western Roman emperor. With his gained appreciation for Jesus helping him win the war, he later passed the Edict of Milan, which granted tolerance to all religions, especially Christianity.

And years later, as the love affair between church and empire grew more intimate, the emperor Theodosius proclaimed Christianity as the state religion of the empire, making it a crime not to be a Christian. That's when things got even messier. The first recorded instance of Christians killing pagans occurred shortly after, and before long, the militant church conquered lands and people throughout Europe, compelling them to be baptized or die. Under Theodosius' decrees, temples from other religions were ordered to be destroyed, if not just declared abandoned, to be renovated and reused later as Christian temples. And those who had formerly renounced the sword now filled the Roman army; every Roman soldier would be required to be a Christian.

Many years later, Charlemagne, drunk on this power, instructed his Christian soldiers in their conquest of the Saxons, "If there is anyone of the Saxon people lurking among them unbaptized, and if he scorns to come to baptism ... and stay a pagan, let him die."[15]

Moving from persecuted to persecutor, the church had become the church militant and triumphant. The kingdom of God that had been known through a king who rules with a towel, a donkey, and a cross had become the empire of Christendom. In the name of the one who taught us to love our enemies, the church burned its enemies alive.

15 H. R. Loyn and J. Percival, eds. and trans., *The Reign of Charlemagne: Documents on Carolingian Government and Administration* (New York: St. Martins, 1975), 52.

Dear world, this is not my Jesus.

Compassionate Imperialism

Was the shift to Christian emperors the best thing or the worst thing that happened to Christianity? Was it God's voice or the Devil's? This shift in the fourth century illuminates a strange tension evident throughout church history: Christianity is at its best when it is peculiar, marginalized, suffering, and it is at its worst when it is popular, credible, triumphal, and powerful.

Imperial Christianity grew quickly from five million to twenty-five million people. Constantine flung open the doors of the church to the rich and powerful, but it was at a great cost. Repentance, rebirth, and conversion were exchanged for cheap grace, and the integrity of what it means to be a disciple of Jesus faded. People joined the church in droves, but Christian disciples were hard to come by. Christianity had an identity crisis.

It's the same old story of the forbidden fruit—it's the beautiful things that get us. It's the things that seem good, but are not quite of God, that steer us off the course of holiness into destructiveness. The bishops and elders of the church had good things in mind. Weary after years of suffering cultural prejudice, prison terms, and state-sanctioned executions, the leaders of the Way saw these new propositions of the state as a possible way to end their marginalization and spread the good news of Jesus to as many people as possible. Influencing politicians, or even becoming people of political influence themselves, they could make their way of life standard for the whole empire. Not only would their persecutions end, but they could finally see their way of life adopted by everyone. Now the church could be relevant. In their pursuit of "making disciples of every nation" and baptizing all those within the empire, they stumbled into baptizing the empire itself, thus turning sacrament into sacrilege, producing what so many liberal and conservative Christians want today—an empire run on the blood of Jesus Christ, a holy Christian state.

Through inheriting all the "kingdoms of the world," the church became the kind of beast that Jesus worked and taught against. The history of the church has been largely a history of "believers" refusing to believe in the way of the crucified Nazarene and instead giving in to the very temptations he resisted—power, relevancy, spectacle.

Today the logic goes something like this: "Calling a ruler 'Son of God' is out of style. No one really does that nowadays. We can support a president while also worshiping Jesus as the Son of God." But how is this possible? For one says that we must love our enemies, and the other says we must kill them; one promotes the economics of competition, while the other admonishes the forgiveness of debts. To which do we pledge allegiance? Surely, one of them must have the wrong idea of how to move history. Can a servant serve two masters? To say that we must kill our enemies and join the popular project to "rid the world of evil" is to call Jesus unrealistic. And that is possibly desirable for many; surely his ideas do not resonate with any common wisdom. But can you call Jesus the Son of God and also say, "He just doesn't understand the world today"?[16] How ironic is it to see a bumper sticker that says "Jesus is the answer" next to a bumper sticker supporting the war in Iraq, as if to say "Jesus is the answer—but not in the real world." Remember, Jesus' followers were burned alive, beheaded, or fed to lions. They knew evil and the "real world." They would meet it face to face. If there was anyone who tried to deal with evildoers and terrorists, it was certainly first-century Christians.

When the church takes affairs of the state more seriously than they do Jesus, *Pax Romana* becomes its gospel and the president becomes the Son of God. After all, what is the point in calling anything God if it does not also hold sway in every part of one's life—especially one's politics?

16 Dallas Willard puts it well: "'Jesus is Lord' can mean little in practice for anyone who has to hesitate before saying, 'Jesus is smart'" (*The Divine Conspiracy* [San Francisco: HarperSanFrancisco, 1998], 95).

For Jesus and his followers, the central question was, How do we live faithfully to God? But then the church inherited a kingdom. And it wasn't the kind of servant kingdom Jesus imagined and incarnated, not the kingdom of the slaughtered Lamb; it was the dominant and coercive force in charge of the world, even in its pursuit of establishing "justice for all." Instead of faithfulness, the question was, How do we run the world as Christians? This question would echo throughout the centuries in questions like, How do I run this profit-driven corporation as a Christian? How can we make culture more Christian? How would a responsible Christian run this war? But Jesus taught that his followers—or even the Son of God!—should not attempt to "run the world."

Another Exodus

Ever since the empire warmed up to Christianity, the church has made some effort to refrain from power. The Nicene Creed, written at the request of Constantine himself, still has nuggets of the revolutionary spirit embedded in it. At one point the creed states, "We believe in one Lord Jesus Christ, the only Son of God." Athanasias, who fought so hard to put this in the creed, faced serious opposition from state-sponsored Christians. The problem was that calling Jesus the Son of God wasn't just an extreme theological claim but also an exclusive theological and political claim. It was a serious problem because Constantine himself, like most emperors, had inherited the political title Son of God. Could they both hold the title? Could they pledge allegiance to both? That'd be like saying there are two presidents, two emperors. But maybe they could just demote the emperor a little bit—like a vice president. From this argument came a rare accomplishment: the underdog, Athanasius, won. At the end of the day, they would make the creed say that there is only one Son of God.

If only the church had retained this conviction. For in the coming centuries, the church would bend over backward to insist that there were two emperors—Jesus and Caesar. This has come at the cost of a widespread schizophrenia still alive today. It is hard to imagine a gospel that is more of an antithesis of Jesus' gospel and the Beatitudes than what we hear today in the church: "Blessed are the rich"; "Blessed are the troops"; "We will have no mercy on the evildoers."

During the reign of Constantine, another movement developed in Christianity—an underground of sorts. People left the centers of power and wealth and headed to the desert. Some of these monks described their society as a shipwreck, and folks swam into the desert to find God. They began to rethink what it means to be Christian, and their life on the margins called everything relevant into question. The desert became a place where clusters of people rethought their faith and culture. Some of them wrote that there was such an exodus of imperial misfits, the desert became a city filled with criminals and saints, none of whom saw the empire as a good place for the saints. They were not just fleeing society; they were going to the desert to save society, or at least themselves.

And about every five hundred years there has been another exodus. During the crisis of the Roman Empire's crumbling, there were the desert fathers and mothers and the Benedictines. And during the difficulties of the Crusades and the split between East and West in the church, orders like the Franciscans,[17] Poor Clares, and Dominicans were birthed. And during the church's identity crisis throughout the Enlightenment, the Reformation proclaimed its critiques not just through the reconsideration of doctrine but through community movements like the Moravians and Anabaptists. All of these waves of history are signs of people seeking an alternative to the god of power, instead praying low to the ground, seeking the faithfulness of God's people.

Maybe it's time once again to go to the desert, to the abandoned places of the empire in which we find ourselves.

17 In the thirteenth century, Francis found himself in a troubling culture in which the Christian identity was all but lost in Italian riches and the Crusades. In a brilliant act of faithfulness, he cast aside his warhorse and armor and walked unarmed to meet the Muslim sultan, with whom he became friends. He threw his belongings out the window to the beggars below his palace and danced naked out of the town of Assisi to live like the lilies and the sparrows. An entire countercultural youth movement followed; the best of Assisi's youth rejected the imperial dreams of conquest and expansion for the dreams of rebuilding the church among the poor. And they did it in an old abandoned cathedral called San Damiano. They called into question all that was relevant in their culture as they left for the margins.

The Collision of Identity

"I am astonished that you are so quickly deserting the one who called you by the grace of Christ and are turning to a different gospel—which is really no gospel at all. Evidently some people are throwing you into confusion and are trying to pervert the gospel of Christ" (Gal. 1:6–7).

Who needs a Creator when
we can sculpt mountains?

Who needs a Great Physician when we can heal ourselves?

Who needs Providence for food when we can
clone animals for food?

Who needs
a Savior when we have a four hundred
billion dollar defense shield?

Who needs a Deliverer when the empire has become
a democracy?

Who needs a God when we are worthy of worship ourselves?

"For although they knew God, they neither glorified him as God nor gave thanks to him, but their thinking became futile and their foolish hearts were darkened. Although they claimed to be wise, they became fools and exchanged the glory of the immortal God for images made to look like mortal human beings" (Rom. 1:21–23).

The Imperial Baptism Continues

Fast-forward from Constantine in the 300s to the Conquistadors invading (or settling, depending on your perspective) North America, circa 1600s. These folks were increasingly fed up with Europe's religious and political systems. But instead of working it out, along came the prospect of divorce. Conquistadors had years earlier found land abroad that they too could take. The Americas were soon violently swiped from the native inhabitants. This pillaging was powered largely by Christians, who often interpreted their "success" as a reenactment of the Israelite conquest of Canaan. Some pastors see George Washington as America's Joshua. Moving from Europe to the Americas might have been interpreted as their own exodus. (But many biblical scholars can read the Canaan conquest stories in Joshua and understand that they were not meant to convey for their audience a militant, colonialist attitude. Even Jesus knew these stories from his ancestry and still commanded enemy-love, insisting along the way that he was not contradicting but embodying the Law and the Prophets.)[18]

Nevertheless, religious pioneers like John Winthrop provided much of the theological fuel for this conquest. He wrote of the creation of a new church-state in the Americas as embodying a new Israel, a city on a hill. Later, Ronald Reagan, a fan of Winthrop, recycled this language in

---

18 Yoder puts it well in *The Original Revolution*: "When the Israelites want to have a king like the other kings and a standing army like other nations have, *the holy wars come to an end.* What the original experience of the holy wars meant in the life of Israel was that even at the very crucial point of the bare existence of Israel as a people, their survival could be entrusted to the care of Yahweh as their King, even if He told them to have no other kings. ... The point made by the prophets is rather, 'Jahweh has always taken care of us in the past; should we not be able to trust His providence for the immediate future?' Its impact in those later prophetic proclamations was to work *against* the development of a military caste, military alliances, and political designs based on the availability of military power" (99). See also Yoder's *The Politics of Jesus* (Grand Rapids: Eerdmans, 1994; esp. chap. 4, "God Will Fight for Us"), Norman Gottwald's *The Tribes of YHWH* (Maryknoll, NY: Orbis, 1981), and Gerhard Lohfink's *Does God Need the Church?* (Collegeville, MN: Liturgical Press, 1999, 55).

his defense of the US as a militant and unaccountable maverick in the world, a conviction known as "American exceptionalism." This sense that "America"[19] is a special, holy force in the world, immune to criticism, has its roots in the Constantinian shift hundreds of years earlier.

"There's power, wonder-working power, in the goodness and idealism and faith of the American people" (President Bush, 2003 State of the Union Address). Putting "America" in where the old gospel hymn places "the blood of the Lamb" is not only idolatry, it also just doesn't have the same ring to it; try singing it on Sunday morning.

"The ideal of America is the hope of all mankind. ... That hope still lights our way. And the light shines in the darkness, and the darkness has not overcome it" (George W. Bush, Ellis Island, 2002).

And the recent words of Barack Obama on *The Late Show with David Letterman* (April 9, 2007): "This country is still the last best hope on earth."

19 By America, many people seem to mean "the United States." To be more careful with language, we would do well not to implicate the rest of the American continent in the project of "the United States."

These religiously inspired settlers, instead of embodying Jesus' peculiar society, which is both revolutionary and subordinate, aimed to be solely revolutionary by creating a competing state that would exist on the world's terms of power and violence. They eschewed the upside-down politics of the mustard seed kingdom of God, while retaining the language of piety. They refused Jesus' call to be a humble people (to the surrounding natives, to say the least!)[20] and instead seized land to colonize. If we look hard, we might find some sincere Puritans with admirable qualities (as with any person or group), but essentially their identity was less in being the church and more in becoming a state with church words and practices sprinkled in.

Some congregations have identified this historical mistake and attempted to correct it. But in many cases, the treatment doesn't get to the root of power. Take the great project to "take back America for God" as an example. This project, of course, is rooted in the thought that the United States was initially founded "on God," a seriously contested claim.[21] But even more, this grand goal, while it sounds pious, attempts to grasp power the same way the world does. The American project may have been a result not so much of malicious people as of bad theology—or wanting the right thing but pursuing it by the wrong means.

20 A Puritan captain, John Mason, said of the Pequot tribe after they massacred them, "God laughed his Enemies and the Enemies of his People to Scorn, making them as a fiery Oven. ... Thus did the Lord judge among the Heathen, filling the Place with dead Bodies" (Charles M. Segal and David A. Stineback, *Puritans, Indians and Manifest Destiny* [New York: Putnam, 1977], 111–12, 134–35). For more details, see Howard Zinn's *A People's History of the United States of America* (New York: Harper Collins, 1980), esp. chap. 1.

21 Greg Boyd has done some of the best recent work on this in his book *Myth of a Christian Nation* (Grand Rapids: Zondervan, 2006).

Greg Boyd describes the "religion of American democracy" like this: "Like all religions, this religion has its own distinctive, theologized, revisionist history (for instance, the 'manifest destiny' doctrine whereby God destined Europeans to conquer the land). It has its own distinctive message of salvation (political freedom), its own 'set apart' people group (America and its allies), its own creed ('we hold these truths to be self-evident'), its own distinctive enemies (all who resist freedom and who are against America), its own distinctive symbol (the flag), and its own distinctive god (the national deity we are 'under,' who favors our causes and helps us win our battles)" (Boyd, *Myth of a Christian Nation*, 150).

So are we saying the United States of America is not a Christian nation?

The United States is Christian inasmuch as it looks like Christ. *Christian* came to refer to those disciples who saw themselves as "little Christs," people who were literally the body of Christ, the hands and feet of Jesus alive in the world. As our brother Rob Bell says, Christian is a bad adjective, but a good noun.

An Excerpt from Shane's Iraq journal from his time in Baghdad during the bombing:

I had a live interview on CBS this morning where they asked what I thought about America, and within the first minute they hung up on me. Hmm. They have been very interested in the dramatic fact that we could face up to twelve years in prison if we are convicted of treason ... so they have been asking if we are "traitors." I wrote this little ditty in response:

Traitor?

If this bloody, counterfeit liberation is American …
I am proud to be un-American.

If depleted uranium is American …
I am proud to be un-American.

If US sanctions are American …
I am proud to be un-American.

If the imposed "peace" of *Pax Americana* is American …
I am proud to be un-American.

But if grace, humility, and nonviolence are American …
I am proud to be American.

If sharing to create a safe, sustainable world is American …
I am proud to be American.

If loving our enemies is American …
I am proud to be American.

Regardless, I would die for the people of New York, but I will
not kill for them … my kingdom is not of this world.

I would die for the people of Baghdad, but I will not kill for them
… my kingdom is not of this world. I will stand in the way of
terror and war … my kingdom is not of this world.

I will pledge an allegiance deeper than nationalism, to my God
and to my family … my kingdom is not of this world. I will use
my life to shout, "Another world is possible" … for my kingdom is
from another place. "My kingdom is not of this world. If it were,
my servants would fight … but now my kingdom is from another
place" (Jesus; John 18:36).

How "Christian" was America? Listen to the words of a former slave, Frederick Douglass:

"Between the Christianity of this land, and the Christianity of Christ, I recognize the widest possible difference—so wide, that to receive the one as good, pure, and holy is of necessity to reject the other as bad, corrupt, and wicked. … I love the pure, peaceable, and impartial Christianity of Christ; I therefore hate the corrupt, slaveholding, women-whipping, cradle-plundering, partial and hypocritical Christianity of this land. Indeed, I can see no reason, but the most deceitful one, for calling the religion of this land Christianity."[22]

22 Frederick Douglass, *Narrative of the Life of Frederick Douglass, an American Slave, Written by Himself* (1845; New York: Signet, 1968), 120.

When we ponder the wisdom of Christianity gone militant and triumphant, we need only to look on the ruins of Christendom in the regions where Christians ruled by the sword. Look at Europe—England, Sweden, Denmark, perhaps post-Christian USA in a few years. To find Christianity at its best, and the church alive, we need only look to the areas where it is persecuted and peculiar. It's hard to walk away with any other conclusion but that the best way to defeat the kingdom of God is to empower the church to rule the world with the sword, for then it becomes the beast it wishes to destroy.

> "We have the ability to take [Hugo Chavez] out, and I think the time has come that we exercise that ability."
>
> —Pat Robertson, *The 700 Club* (August 22, 2005)

What good is it to gain the whole world but lose your soul?

Caesar seemed to be able to do anything in the world. But Caesar could not wash feet.

> "We should invade their countries, kill their leaders and convert them to Christianity. We weren't punctilious about locating and punishing only Hitler and his top officers. We carpet-bombed German cities; we killed civilians. That's war. And this is war."
>
> —Ann Coulter

> "You've got to kill the terrorists before the killing stops. And I'm for the President to chase them all over the world. If it takes ten years, blow them all away in the name of the Lord." —Jerry Falwell

"The ethic of conservation is the explicit abnegation of man's dominion over the Earth. The lower species are here for our use. God said so: Go forth, be fruitful, multiply, and rape the planet—it's yours. That's our job: drilling, mining, and stripping. Sweaters are the antibiblical view. Big gas-guzzling cars with phones and CD players and wet bars—that's the biblical view."
—Ann Coulter

"You can no more have a Christian worldly government than you can have a Christian petunia or aardvark."

—Greg Boyd, *Myth of a Christian Nation*, 54

"The government of the United States of America is not, in any sense, founded on the Christian religion."

—John Adams

Few of us step out of the matrix to observe the military industrial complex in which we live. And statistics are tricky, because they often seem lifeless, so we won't overwhelm you (besides, statisticians say 80% of statistics are wrong anyway, wink). But consider this…

The US arsenal is the largest stockpile of nuclear weaponry in the world, equivalent to over 150,000 Hiroshima bombs. (www.warresisters.org). The US military budget is over 450 billion per year, and it would take the combined budgets of the next 15 countries to equal that of the US (Russia is the next biggest spender at around 70 billion, China at 50 billion, and the entire "Axis of Evil" is less than 10 billion (truemajority.com).

Just to show one clear example of the absurdity… one Minuteman III bomb carries 170-300 Kilotons (a kiloton is 1000 tons of TNT, approximately equivalent to the Oklahoma City bombing), and the US has nearly 500 of these bombs (450 of them ready to deploy). The smallest of these (170 Kilotons) is equivalent to 170 Oklahoma City bombings, or 10 times the Hiroshima bomb… and there are 49 of them in Colorado alone. (from the film "Conviction" by Zero to Sixty Productions www.ztsp.org)

Dare we call this land called America an "empire"?

The Gospel of America and Beyond

> Not since Rome has one nation loomed so large above the others. Indeed the word "empire" has come out of the closet.
>
> —Harvard Joseph Nye, *Washington Post*

> What word but "empire" describes the awesome thing that America is becoming. ... [This nation] fills the hearts and minds of an entire planet with its dreams and desires.
>
> —*New York Times Magazine*, January 5, 2003 (22–23).

Throughout all of the world wars, border disputes, and cutthroat economic boom of the twentieth century, a conviction increasingly developed that the United States needed to solidify its control of the global scene. Among the myriad critics of this global-dominance project was Martin Luther King Jr., who initially aimed at race and class issues but later voiced criticism of the US as an imperialistic "policeman of the whole world."[23] He wasn't killed without reason. Even a glance at a high school history book shows that the United States' imperial objectives are all too clear. The Stars and Stripes fly over more than seven hundred military stations in more than one hundred countries all around the globe. The US has claimed lands far and wide as its own (Alaska, Puerto Rico, Hawaii, Guam, Guantanamo Bay [in a country it explicitly opposes through sanctions], the Virgin Islands, American Samoa, etc.). It participated in and escalated the most belligerent and out-of-control weapons race ever known to humanity:

23 How ironic that he was granted a national holiday by the nation he called "the greatest purveyor of violence in the world today." Reminds us of when Jesus pointed out that the Pharisees erected monuments to the prophets that their forefathers killed.

the stockpiling of tens of thousands of nuclear weapons.[24] More than one hundred fifty countries have had arms contracts with US corporations such as Lockheed Martin. The US is arming over 75 percent of the world, while it tells folks to disarm, which is like handing out guns to kids in our neighborhood and telling them not to shoot each other.[25] This history, along with the CIA's many covert operations to overthrow governments (some democratically elected), is not "hidden."[26]

One of the groups that has worked very hard to maintain US global dominance is the Project for the New American Century,[27] headed and supported by many self-professing Christians. There is dangerous theology behind the American enterprise. This think tank's claim to fame is a seventy-six-page document produced in 2000 titled "Rebuilding America's Defenses: Strategy, Forces and Resources for a New Century."

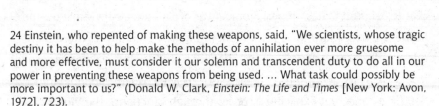

24 Einstein, who repented of making these weapons, said, "We scientists, whose tragic destiny it has been to help make the methods of annihilation ever more gruesome and more effective, must consider it our solemn and transcendent duty to do all in our power in preventing these weapons from being used. ... What task could possibly be more important to us?" (Donald W. Clark, *Einstein: The Life and Times* [New York: Avon, 1972], 723).

25 This is what the Iran-Contra scandal was about. The US armed both sides of a war and made some serious money at it.

26 Classic texts like Howard Zinn's *A People's History of the United States* or much of Noam Chomsky's research describe these hubristic exploits in great detail.

27 The PNAC originated in 1991 in a memo from Undersecretary of Defense Paul Wolfowitz to President Bush Sr. titled "Defense Policy Guidance 1992–1994." The memo called for a surge of funds to swell the size of the military and stated that the United States had the responsibility to use preemptive attacks to ensure that its interests around the world would not be threatened. Wolfowitz's ideas gained momentum in 1997 when *Weekly Standard* editor William Kristol organized a think tank based around many of the precepts found in Wolfowitz's memo.

Its opening lines should make us shiver:

> [T]he United States stands as the world's preeminent power. Having led the West to victory in the Cold War, America faces an opportunity and a challenge: Does the United States have the vision to build upon the achievements of past decades? Does the United States have the resolve to shape a new century favorable to American principles and interests?
>
> [What we require is] a military that is strong and ready to meet both present and future challenges; a foreign policy that boldly and purposely promotes American principles abroad; and national leadership that accepts the United States' global responsibilities. ... The history of the past century should have taught us to embrace the cause of American leadership.

Among the many connected with the PNAC are George W. Bush, Dick Cheney, Karl Rove, Donald Rumsfeld, Jeb Bush, Paul Wolfowitz, and Lewis Libby. We would pick on the Democrats too, but they just don't happen to have their theology together yet. (But be warned, they sure are working hard on it.) It's no surprise for many that the United States hopes to maintain global dominance. Just like the history of the US, this group is not secretive and is readily located; myriads of its documents are on the internet. It is more than eerie to find the Roman Empire's description of itself as the *Pax Romana* regurgitated by this group:

> The American peace has proven itself peaceful, stable, and durable. It has, over the past decade, provided the geopolitical framework for widespread economic growth and the spread of American principles of liberty and democracy. Yet no moment in international politics can be frozen in time; even a global *Pax Americana* will not preserve itself. (pp. 1, 11, 13)[28]

28 It's no coincidence that the federal *National Security Strategy for the United States of America* and PNAC's *Rebuilding* packet mirror each other, not only in their language and style but in their aspirations for a globally enforced *Pax Americana*.

But the PNAC is certainly not the only power player here. The web of domination the church has been lured into and gotten entangled in is much more vast and complicated. If only imperialism were so simple. In the old days, "the empire" often referred to a single powerful nation which invaded weaker nations and subjected them to serfdom. But things have changed. Pharaoh isn't as easy to name as he used to be.

In the introduction of his book *In Search of Paul: How Jesus' Apostle Opposed Rome's Empire with God's Kingdom*, biblical scholar John Dominic Crossan asks this haunting question: "Who now is Caesar and where now is Christ?" As we consider the theology being preached from the pulpits by both pastors and politicians (and these days, its hard to tell them apart), we need to contemplate this question. Fortunately, more and more Bible-literate Christians are deeply disturbed by the skewed theology of empire. It is becoming more and more clear that the *Pax Americana* is not helping the world get any closer to understanding the crucified Christ and his gospel of grace.[29]

Seneca says that peace, freedom and liberty are things that sound beautiful "but are hard to touch." He said they belong to all, but only as a slogan, because "no one really knows what they are anymore."

In the speech of Cerialis in Trier after the plundering of Germani: "*Freedom*, however, and other specious names are their pretexts: but no man has ever been ambitious to enslave another or to win dominion for himself without using those very same words."

—Wengst

29 The essence of our book is not dependent on whether the United States is truly a prideful empire. Christianity proclaims an alternate allegiance even to citizens of humble nations. And the point is certainly not that only the United States is one of the beastly powers. Among Russia, China, Rwanda, Belgium, and countless others, it would be quite a competition as to which dictatorship tops the list of most blood shed and worst publicly legitimated insanity. But to see the bad fruits of power is an important connection to make for those who have a white-knuckle grip on both the cross and the flag. When we take a good look at the history of the United States, we must face the reality that the US is not, as Barak Obama (and countless others) said, "the last great hope for humanity." This not only is false according to the standards of secular history but also is heretical for us in the church. This is the kind of stuff that made John of Patmos seethe (not to mention God). And in the scope of history, the United States is a young project that doubtlessly will fall—whether in a few or in many years.

Obviously, people didn't like war or bloodshed, and Aristides goes so far as to say that even though people would say they did not like war, nonetheless, "waging war is a tradition among you." For the Romans, war was omnipresent, normative, nihilistically acceptable.

Tacitus puts these words on the lips of the Briton Calgacus, in a speech delivered to his countrymen before a decisive battle against Agricola's troops: "If their enemy has wealth, they have greed; if he is poor, they are ambitious ... they behold with the same passion waste and want. To plunder, butcher, steal, these things they misname empire; they make a desolation and call it peace."

Tacitus said that people "feared the peace of Rome" (Wengst, 13), because streams of blood and tears of unimaginable proportions followed in the "peace." Pliny, a Roman gentleman and writer, said he writes "not so much to commend the Romans as to comfort those who have been conquered by them," those who came to suffer Rome's peace firsthand. This is why Jesus said he does not "give peace like the world gives peace."

They must see us as strange liberators.
— Dr. Martin Luther King Jr.

We are dying and killing for
abstract nouns like freedom
and democracy...but this
is not the gospel of Jesus Christ.

— Letter from a US soldier in Iraq

Idols and images

Exodus 20:4: "You shall not make for yourself an idol in the form of anything in heaven above or on the earth beneath or in the waters below."

Lev. 26:1: "Do not make idols or set up an image or a sacred stone for yourselves, and do not place a carved stone in your land to bow down before it. I am the LORD your God."

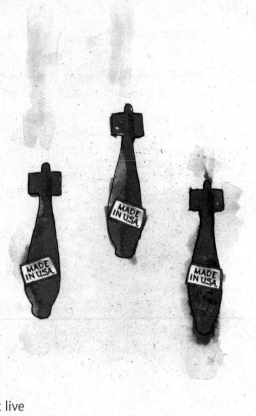

4 Ezra 4:11: "Therefore, you will surely disappear, you eagle ... so that the whole earth, will be freed from your violence." The Eagle will not live forever, blessed be the Lamb.

Dominic Crossan: Over 50 percent of the Roman budget went towards the Roman military.

Of each dollar paid in taxes, 36 cents goes toward the military of the United States.

Only God can make an image of God's self... and God did. Look in the mirror or look in the slums.

ONLY SOMETHING SACRED CAN BE DE*SACRATED.

If you cannot win them ...

you must buy them ...

or at least entertain them ...

quote from Hauerwas (quoting Bush after 9-II):

"We must keep shopping."

> Juvenal: "The people that once bestowed commands, consulships, legions and all else, now meddles no more and longs vaguely for just two things—bread and games."

Gladiators and athletes waved their flags in imperial games that catalyzed competition and climaxed in the glory of Rome, just like the Olympics. Tacitus writes of one rebel under Civilis who called on the rebels: "away with those pleasures which give the Romans more power over their subjects than their arms bestow."

Superbowl ? Imperial Games ?

It was once said, if you want to know your idols, consider what you are willing to kill for.

WHAT ARE OUR IDOLS?

KILL YOUR TV

Hey, Uncle Sam put your name at the top of his list,

And the Statue of Liberty started shaking her fist.

And the eagle will fly and it's gonna be hell,

When you hear Mother Freedom start ringing her bell.

("Courtesy of the Red, White, and Blue")

There is no doubt that America has its charm and beauty.

Just as Caesar had his image on everything, America has its stamp. The world is branded with America.

To some, being conquered by Rome was a humiliation, and to others, it was a privilege, for now they could join the ranks of Roman citizens. (We're reminded of an Iraqi civilian who, when asked what he thought of his country now that Saddam was gone, replied, "Oh, this is not my country. This is your country now.")

"Such vast quantities of the spoils of wars came home that in Syria a pound of gold was sold for half its former value." (Josephus)

Aelius Aristides: "Now the earth itself and its inhabitants have been granted universal security which is evident to all. Every war begins with fear."

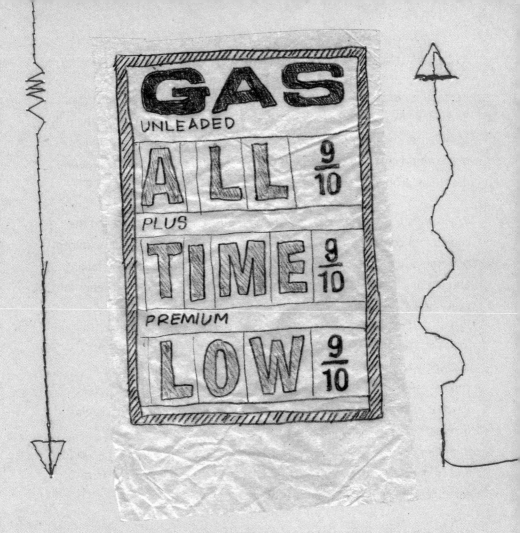

Horace was delighted to be able to say of Augustus, "Neither civil strife nor death by violence will I fear, while Caesar holds the earth."

According to Suetonius, Augustus "so beautified things that he found them in brick and left them in marble." NAFTA? CAFTA? Developing Countries?

What was so evil about Sodom? "Now this was the sin of your sister Sodom: She and her daughters were arrogant, overfed and unconcerned; they did not help the poor and needy" (Ezek. 16:49). That's not what we learned in Sunday school.

In the Market We Trust

Remember, Israel's desire for a king led them down a path of destruction. Becoming "like the other nations" would make Israel a chaotic society, full of violence, cheating, and harm (1 Samuel 8). Not only would the ways of the world corrupt their society, but they would murder God's creation itself. The prophets then cried out against the abuse of creation.[30]

When we are talking about a baptized empire, one that has dazzled the church into conformity, we are not just talking about the violent militarism of Rome or the United States or Iran or North Korea. We are also talking about a much more prevalent, subtle, and powerful empire that seeps into every home—our daily global lifestyle.[31]

In the last few hundred years, the average person's life has become dizzyingly complicated. Even the seemingly simple act of drinking a cup of coffee involves an intricate international system of bean pickers, international shipping (fueled by oil from who knows where), packaging (in what?), roasting (by energy from who knows where), domestic shipping, driving to get it (using car parts and gas from around the world), and so on.[32] It's like the cup of coffee has been dragged halfway across the earth, leaving trench-like trail marks along the way.

Another, possibly the greatest, unholy aspect of our economy is its exploitation of people. While our economy floats on cheap oil, it too is carried on the backs of cheap laborers. If we ask, Why do so many of our products come from China? we can certainly say this is aided by cheap oil for shipping, but it's essentially founded on easily exploited labor.

30 See Isa. 24:4–7; 32:15–20; Jer. 12:4; 23:10; Hos. 4:1–3; Joel 1:10, 18, 20; Nah. 3:16; Rev. 11:18.

31 Scholars tend to use the words "global [post] industrial capitalism."

32 These concerns are developed with greater economic precision by authors like Lester Brown, Wendell Berry, Rachel Carson, Jared Diamond, Paul Hawken, Bill McKibben, and countless others.

The hundreds of thousands of jobs that have been lost in the United States testify to "job creation" in foreign countries. Left in the wake are our neighborhoods, blighted with hundreds of abandoned factories and hundreds more abandoned homes. Christians have no problem helping the poor. But question whether our "blessings" are borne on the backs of the poor and things get messy. The call to "Make poverty history" needs a partner: "Make affluence history."[33]

Years ago, some folks from our communities attended a rally against overseas sweatshops. They had not invited the typical rally speakers—lawyers, activists, and academics. Instead, they brought the kids themselves from the sweatshops to speak. We listened as a child from Indonesia pointed to the giant scar on his face. "I got this scar when my master lashed me for not working hard enough. When it began to bleed, he did not want me to stop working or to ruin the cloth in front of me, so he took a lighter and burned it shut. I got this making stuff for you." We were suddenly consumed by the overwhelming reality of the suffering body of Christ. Jesus now bore not just the marks from the nails and scars from the thorns but a gash down his face, for when we have done it to the "least of these," we have done it to Christ himself. How could we possibly follow Jesus and buy anything from that master? The statistics had a face. Poverty became personal. And that messes with you.

Into the economics of the world, the letter of James speaks a word of rebuke: "The wages you failed to pay the workers who mowed your fields are crying out against you. The cries of the harvesters have reached the ears of the Lord Almighty" (5:4). This isn't simply about fairly paying the immigrants who mow our lawns; it's about the way our world's economy siphons wealth from the poor up to the rich. And we are all part of it.

33 Thanks to the editors of *Geez* magazine who coined this tongue-in-cheek slogan.

But the god of mammon calls out, "How could we buy cheap shirts without the sweatshops of Honduras? How could we get cheap fast food without the migrant tomato farmers in Florida?" God hears the workers' groaning.

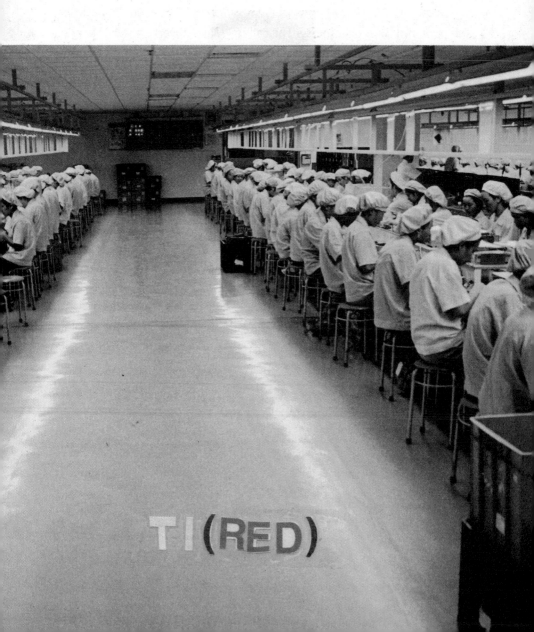

As God's kingdom collides with this disastrous empire (as it has with all empires), more than life and death are at stake. God's gift of the earth itself is at stake. Wendell Berry writes,

"The sense of the holiness of life" is not compatible with an exploitive economy. You cannot know that life is holy if you are content to live from economic practices that daily destroy life and diminish its possibility. And many if not most Christian organizations now appear to be perfectly at peace with the military-industrial economy and its "scientific" destruction of life. Surely, if we are to remain free, and if we are to remain true to our religious inheritances, we must maintain a separation between church and state. But if we are to maintain any sense or coherence or meaning in our lives, we cannot tolerate the present utter disconnection between religion and economy. By "economy" I do not mean "economics," which is the study of money-making, but rather the ways of human housekeeping, the ways by which the human household is situated and maintained within the household of Nature. To be uninterested in economy is to be uninterested in the practice of religion; it is to be uninterested in culture and in character.

Probably the most urgent question now faced by people who would adhere to the Bible is this: What sort of economy would be responsible to the holiness of life? What, for Christians, would be the economy, the practices and the restraints, of "right livelihood"? I do not believe that organized Christianity now has any idea. I think its idea of a Christian economy is no more or less than the industrial economy—which is an economy firmly founded upon the seven deadly sins and the breaking of all ten of the Ten Commandments. Obviously, if Christianity is going to survive as more than a respecter and comforter of profitable iniquities, then Christians, regardless of their organizations, are going to have to interest themselves in economy—which is to say, in nature and in work. They are going to have to give workable answers to those who say we cannot live without this economy that is destroying us and our world, who see the murder of Creation as the only way of life."[34]

34 Wendell Berry, *Sex, Economy, Freedom, and Community: Eight Essays* (New York: Pantheon, 1993), 99.

Co-opted and Confused

Two of our favorite Roman dropouts were Propertius and Tibullus. They called Rome's treasures of war "hateful gold," and they called the metals of imperial war "cruel steel." Tibullus declared, "But may my lot bring me a modest and tranquil life. There would be no war if the cup that one used at a meal were made simply of wood" by one's own hand.

These dropouts went to the margins to farm—as poets to find an imagination beyond the imperium, marked by a return to the land.

We must see what is going on today. Something different is happening. We have wasteful technologies used by billions of people growing exponentially, more expansive exploitation, more powerful bombs. And yet people's hearts are the same as they were thousands of years ago: a chaotic mix of love and hate, creativity and destructiveness. But this is the problem. Our tools have "advanced," but we haven't advanced spiritually or morally. And so we, normal people, with the tools of destruction and wastefulness available daily for purchase, cannot handle the power. With all of the destruction that has ravaged the earth since the Industrial Revolution, one wonders if we can even call it advancement. Those who are convinced that we are at "the end of history," at the apex of civilization's development, fail to notice that the twentieth century was the bloodiest and most toxic in world history. And to sanctify this chaos, as our friend and priest Michael Doyle has said, the church's precious words have been co-opted for profit: trust, fidelity, liberty, mutual equity. We can see them all around us in bank statements and on billboards.

Maybe, as a response, we in the church work for legislation that attempts to turn the tide, but these efforts often do not change the way we, as communities, live or think. Addressing our needs versus our wants and making sacrificial choices to buy less or differently is not something the state can do for us. We can see one reason why Jesus exorcised unclean spirits and opened eyes—the state wasn't doing it. It's the small things we do every day—the logs in our eyes[35]—that are of great significance. (Even worse, in the face of escalating tension in the world, after 9/11 the government called us not to be frugal and thoughtful but to go shopping.[36] One wonders if a nation that wholeheartedly buys into this scheme while launching two costly wars should have dangerous weapons anywhere near them.) We might hope to change the world through better, bigger programs to stop global warming, but global warming will not end unless people become less greedy and less wasteful, gaining a fresh vision of what it means to love our global neighbor.

And so, if we recognize that the empire of violence and nationalism has crept into the church, we must also recognize that the economic and ecological destruction of God's creation has come along with it.

Answers to this problem are manifold. In the fourth section of this book, we will address some practices for the church, but there is no easy solution. In fact, it seems the Bible's criticism of civilization is more serious than we might be ready to see or accept (see appendix 1), which has even more radical implications on how we live.[37] We share a sneaking suspicion that the economic future of the church may have more in common with the Amish than with the activist's organic, fair-trade latte.

35 Matt. 7:1–6.

36 In a September 2001 address, the president's charge was for "continued participation and confidence in the American economy," and five years later, after appraisal of the war on terror, he once again urged America, "I encourage you all to go shopping more" (Dec. 20th, 2006). http://www.whitehouse.gov/news/releases/2006/12/20061220–1.html.

37 We even wrestled with writing this book at all, because publishing it relies on the industrial world made possible by computers, fossil fuels, deforestation, international shipping, and so on. (See Wendell Berry's provocative essay "Why I Won't Buy a Computer" in What Are People For? [North Pointe Press, 1990].) For this reason, we have made a modest compromise by giving back to the earth 10 percent of our book earnings through "carbon fixing," planting trees, and sustaining nature.

Horace complained that in many cultures youth received the gifts of art, imagination, the magic flow of discourse, but Rome's youth were learning to divide the tiny copper coin into a hundred pieces.

The danger is that we can begin to read the Bible through the eyes of America rather than read America through the eyes of the Bible. We just want Jesus to be a good American.

> "Some emergent types [want] to recast Jesus as a limp-wrist hippie in a dress with a lot of product in His hair, who drank decaf and made pithy Zen statements about life while shopping for the perfect pair of shoes. In Revelation, Jesus is a prize fighter with a tattoo down His leg, a sword in His hand and the commitment to make someone bleed. That is a guy I can worship. *I cannot worship the hippie, diaper, halo Christ because I cannot worship a guy I can beat up.*"
>
> —Mark Driscoll, *Relevant* magazine (January–February 2007)

?

I PREACH CHRIST CRUCIFIED. - Paul.

Flags on Altars

On July 4, 2007 Robert Schuller, pastor of the renown Crystal Cathedral in California delivered a sermon written first person from the perspective of the American flag. Amid the usual triumphal viscera of the 10,000 windows, 90 foot doors, and 17 foot 18 karat gold cross, there was a military band in full uniform at the altar, flags blazing.

Adopting the persona of the flag, Schuller's delivery was a message directly from the flag to her people. He began it like this:

```
At a time like this, it is
good for us to listen to the
message of our American flag...
```

And continued like this.

```
I am the American Flag. I speak from the
wisdom of a long life. I first felt the vigor
of wind on my multicolored face when I unfurled
my thirteen stars over two-hundred years ago.
Since then, I have known forty-three presidents.
I have traveled across continents, oceans, and
deserts; I have soared through space, until I
stood proudly on the moon. I have lived long
and traveled far to bring peace and freedom to
oppressed people...
```

As a grand finale a flag was dropped from the ceiling to the floor of the monstrous cathedral. One person mentioned how troubling it was to see the entire altar and cross hidden by the flag.

The American flag has smothered the glory of the cross. Many people can't see the beauty of the cross because everything the American flag represents to them is in the way. We used to attend a congregation that considered itself "seeker friendly." To separate itself from the confusing world of religion and to appear more relevant to the image-driven modern world around them, this community chose not to display the cross in the church, since, because of misrepresentation through the years, the cross conjures unclear religious or moral associations. They felt that the cross should be understood as a historical and offensive reality of torture and execution. The cross is not about religion, per se, but about how Jesus died.

This is a fine start. But after the September 11th attacks, there began a great national fervor to display the American flag. Even antiwar activists waved flags and banners, trying to sell peace under the auspice of Americanism; "Peace Is Patriotic" banners and pins decorated their marches. What this all meant was not always clear. Was everybody just trying to remind each other that, lest we forget, we are in the United States? It often seemed to mean not just that the displayer mourned the deaths of those killed in the terrorist attacks (how a national flag might do this is still unclear) but that he or she stood behind the increasing patriotism. It was indeed confusing.

And the church at large jumped on the bandwagon. Shortly after, as the emphasis shifted from popular nationalism to the "war on terror," this particular congregation began displaying a US flag at its entryway. But then came the question: how is it that a congregation could refrain from displaying its essential symbol (a cross) because of public confusion, but could display an even more confusing symbol? It's a dangerous thing when the church has a flag but no cross. One of us called the leadership to ask. The answer was as expected: the leader had not really noticed it, but she knew that many attendees have relationships to the military, and the church wanted to make known its general support of the troops. What made this all so confusing was Jesus and his way: being born again radically dissolves affection for national borders. Maybe this would have all been less confusing if the church, out of concern for and in solidarity with all of God's family, displayed Afghan and Iraqi flags next to the US flag. Or maybe it would have been better if the church had taught the politics that *everybody* is made in God's image, no matter what lines are drawn in the sand.

Maybe it's time for Christians all over the world to lay down the flags of their nations and together raise the banner of God. The Christian icon is not the Stars and Stripes but a cross-flag, and its emblem is not a donkey, an elephant, or an eagle but a slaughtered lamb.

HAS CÆSAR COLONIZED YOUR IMAGINATION?

"The divine banner and the human banner do not go together, nor the standard of Christ and the standard of the Devil. Only without the sword can the Christian wage war: the Lord has abolished the sword."

—Tertullian

*Here's an interesting experiment. If your congregation has a US flag at the altar, erect the Iraqi or Afghan flag beside it to remember everyone suffering from the horrors of war and terror.

HE LEADS IN A WAY THAT THE GOOD LORD TELLS

HIM IS BEST FOR OUR COUNTRY.

- Marine General Peter Pace,
  Chairman of the Joint Chiefs of Staff

God Bless America

Our friend Ched Myers does great work with the idea of "God Bless America" in his article "Mixed Blessing: A Theological Inquiry into a Patriotic Cant," published in the November 2001 issue of *The Other Side* magazine (www.bcm-net.org). What he finds is startling. In the Hebrew Bible, the imperative "Bless!" occurs only thirty out of the several hundred times the verb *barak* ("to kneel," as before a king) appears. Of those thirty occurrences, the majority are liturgical exhortations to "bless the Lord," mostly in the Psalter (e.g., Ps. 66:8; 96:2; 104:1). In other words, the act of blessing is most often directed *toward* heaven, not solicited from it! Only four times in the entire Hebrew scriptural tradition do we find requests in the imperative for divine blessing. Even more interesting (or troubling, from the point of view of the "patriots") is the use of *blessing* in the New Testament. Of the forty-one appearances of the Greek verb *eulogeoo* ("speaking a good word"), only twice do we find it in the imperative mood. In neither case does it involve God. It does, however, involve us—*and our enemies*. In his famous Sermon on the Plain, Jesus invites his disciples to "bless those who curse you" (Luke 6:28). These instructions are later echoed by the apostle Paul: "Bless those who persecute you; bless and do not curse" (Rom. 12:14). The lesson is unmistakable: we would do much better to ask God's blessing on the world, and to bless God by loving our enemies.

Some folks may be really bummed to find that "God bless America" does not appear in the Bible. So often we do things that make sense to us and ask God to bless our actions and come alongside our plans, rather than looking at the things God promises to bless and acting alongside of them. For we know that God's blessing will inevitably follow if we are with the poor, the merciful, the hungry, the persecuted, the peacemakers. But sometimes we'd rather have a God who conforms to our logic than conform our logic to the God whose wisdom is a stumbling block to the world of smart bombs and military intelligence.

As President Harry Truman said, after dropping the atomic bomb on Nagasaki on August 9, 1945, "Having found the atomic bomb, we have used it. We shall continue to use it. ... It is an awful responsibility which has come to us. We thank God that it [the atomic bomb] has come to us instead of to our enemies and we pray that he may guide us to use it in his ways and for his purposes."

In times of war, our leaders always speak of their prayers. They wish us to know that they say prayers because they wish us to believe that they are deeply worried and that they take their responsibilities seriously. Perhaps they believe or hope that prayer will help. But within the circumstances of war, prayer becomes a word as befuddled in meaning as liberate or order or victory or peace. These prayers are usually understood to be Christian prayers. But Christian prayers are made to or in the name of Jesus, who loved, prayed for, and forgave his enemies and who instructed his followers to do likewise. A Christian supplicant, therefore, who has resolved to kill those whom he is enjoined to love, to bless, to do good to, to pray for, and to forgive as he hopes to be forgiven is not conceivably in a situation in which he can be at peace with himself. Anyone who has tried to apply this doctrine to a merely personal enmity will be aware of the enormous anguish that it could cause a national leader in wartime. No wonder that national leaders have ignored it for nearly two thousand years.

When people lose faith in leaders, when they flounder, people can also lose faith in the God their leaders profess and whose blessing they invoke. So what's at stake is not just the president's reputation but God's. As one pastor said, sometimes God needs some good lawyers, because God's been badly misrepresented.

38 Berry, *Sex, Economy, Freedom and Community*, 84.

"I am losing *faith* in how we are fighting this war. … I think Donald Rumsfeld needs to step down."

—Representative Christopher Shays, Chairman of the House [39]

"Ever-faithful God, in death we are reminded of the precious birthrights of life and liberty you endowed in your American people. You have shown once again that these gifts must never be taken for granted. … We seek your special blessing today for those who stand as sword and shield, protecting the many from the tyranny of the few."

—Secretary of Defense Donald H. Rumsfeld (September 14, 2001)

"We ourselves were well conversant with war, murder and everything evil, but all of us throughout the whole wide earth have traded in our weapons of war. We have exchanged our swords for plowshares, our spears for farm tools … now we cultivate the fear of God, justice, kindness, faith, and the expectation of the future given us through the crucified one … the more we are persecuted and martyred, the more do others in ever increasing numbers become believers." —Justin (martyred in 165 AD)

"Say to those that hate and curse you, You are our brothers!"

—Theophilus of Antioch

"Hate shall be rooted out from the earth. For I announce peace to you his saints, and all who hear it shall not fall in war … so put on the crown in firm alliance with the Lord. He brought me out of the depths of hell and gave me the scepter of his power to subdue the designs of the nations and bring down the power of the mighty, to wage war by his Word, and to win victory by his power." —Ode of Solomon

"Now we who once murdered one another not only refrain from all hatred of our enemies, we meet death cheerfully for confessing to Christ." —Justin

39 www.cbsnews.com/stories/2006/10/04/politics/main2064630.shtml?

201

What about Hitler?

In boundless love as a Christian and as a man I read through the passage which tells us how the Lord at last rose in His might and seized the scourge to drive out of the Temple the brood of vipers and adders. How terrific was His fight for the world against the Jewish poison.

—Adolf Hitler

What about Hitler? Folks often ask what Jesus would have us do in the face of Hitler, Saddam, or the genocide in Darfur. Shouldn't "we" intervene? (And who is "we" again?) No doubt the strongest argument for the sword is to use it to protect the innocent. It is tempting to think that there is a greater love than laying down our life for others, and that perhaps taking the life of someone to protect another person is the embodiment of that heroic love. But if ever there were a case for justified violence or "a just war," Peter had it when he picked up the sword to protect Jesus from the Roman soldiers coming to kill him. Jesus was laying down his life not for a country or nation or even his closest companions; he was laying down his life for sinners, evildoers, and enemies. He loved his enemies so much he died for them. That's love. After all, Jesus never said, "Greater love has no one than this: to kill those who oppress."

And we would say Dietrich Bonhoeffer[40] also had a strong case when he tried to kill Hitler and could very well have invoked God's blessing on his operation, but he did not. As one committed to the cross and to the nonviolent, nonpassive love of Jesus, Bonhoeffer felt a paralyzing conflict: what to do in the face of such evil as the Holocaust? Bonhoeffer remorsefully plotted the assassination of Hitler. In stark contrast to the invocation of blessing on violence that we hear today, Bonhoeffer made it clear that what he was doing was evil and sinful, but he felt left with no choice. He didn't ask God's blessing; he asked only for God's mercy. And

40 A German Christian in the 1930s who, along with many others, did not go along with the church's cooptation by the Third Reich.

he and his co-conspirators planted a bomb under Hitler's desk, hoping to rid the world of evil with their own hands.

The documentary film *Blindspot* presents the provocative, heart-wrenching memoir of Hitler's secretary, Traudl Junge. In it, she remembers the assassination attempt (on July 20, 1944). She recalls how the bomb exploded in such a way and at a precise moment that Hitler narrowly escaped. She says that after surviving the attack, Hitler was more convinced than ever before that God was protecting him and his mission (with a triumphant smile Hitler showed Mussolini the site of the bombing). It fueled his reign of terror and confidence in his mission. Violence galvanized his violence. Ms. Junge says that after the bomb attempt, "Any hopes for peace were lost." Hitler rolled forward with record fervor to "rid the world of evil." Another attempt to pick up the sword went haywire, not only fueling further bloodshed but costing our brother Bonhoeffer his own life as he was executed by the Nazis. Once again the cross lost, and the Devil laughed.

Hitlers don't come from nowhere. Some of the most brutal figures in history have come to power on the back of a silent, apathetic, and often supportive Church. Most of the slaughtering done throughout history has been done by people who sincerely believed they were promoting the good. Everyone thinks their wars are just, if not holy—Marxists, Nazis, the Khmer Rouge, Islamic terrorists, Christian crusaders.[41] The bloodstained pages of history are filled with people doing terrible wrong out of a deep sense of right. And sadly, many of the horrific acts of terror and violence throughout history have been backed by Scripture and a distorted Christian theology. We only need look to Hitler holding the Bible or the KKK's lynchings and flaming crosses.

"Thus I believe that I am acting in accordance with the will of the Almighty Creator: by defending myself against the Jew, I am fighting for the work of the Lord."

—Adolf Hitler, *Mein Kampf*

41 See Boyd, *Myth of a Christian Nation*, 84.

"All parties do wrong out of a sense of right."[42]

-1959 Saddam and five others recruited

What about Saddam Hussein? Saddam came to power backed by the leadership and prayers of leaders here in the US, with funds from money that says, "In God We Trust." We know that he had weapons because we have the receipts. If the church had been the church, we would have stood in the way of Hitler and the war, we would have stood in the way of Saddam as he gassed the Kurds and in the way of the US as they gave him the helicopters to do it with. If the church had been the church, we might not have had Hitler or Saddam.

Hussein and five others were supported by the CIA in coordination with the Egyptian Secret Service to assassinate Qasim. Although Qasim was wounded, the plot failed. Saddam, accidentally shot in the leg by one of his own, escaped to Syria and was later sent to Cairo. (1B2)

Too often we learn history through the lens of redemptive violence, memorizing dates of wars and battles. We've ordered history by the reigns of kings and presidents. But rarely do we remember how nonviolent movements have marked history and how the saints of the church have transformed societies and peoples. And we define news as acts of violence rather than the hidden acts of love that keep hope alive.

of the Interior for the new Ba'athist regime said, "we came to power on a CIA train". Ali Saleh Sa'adi, the Minister James Critchfield

But a common thread ties together the most horrific perpetrators of violence: they kill themselves. Violence kills the image of God in us. It's a cry of desperation, a weak and cowardly cry of a person suffocated by hopelessness. Violence goes against everything we are created for—to love and be loved—so it inevitably ends in misery and suicide, either literal or metaphorical.

-1970's Iraqi officers trained in U.S. on how to use chemical weapons
Answer 39 by the Department of Defense during the 1994 Senate hearing stated under oath that Iraqi Officers trained at the U.S. Army Chemical School until "the 1978-79 timeframe". Additional

When people succumb to violence, it infects them like a disease or poison that leads to their own death. Judas, the disciple who betrayed Jesus with a violent kiss, ended his life by hanging himself. After his notorious

42 James A. Aho, *This Thing of Darkness: A Sociology of the Enemy* (Seattle: Univ. of Washington Press, 1994), 12.

persecutions, Emperor Nero ended his story when he stabbed himself. Hitler gave suicide pills to his heads of staff and ended his life as one of the most pitifully lonely people to walk the earth. Columbine, the 2006 Amish school shooting, the 9/11 terrorist attacks, the Virginia Tech massacre—each ended with suicide.

-1982 Iraq removed from terrorist list, arms sold including chemical/ biological

Violence is suicidal. Suicide rates of folks in the military and those working the chambers of death row are astronomical; they kill themselves as they feel the image of God dying in them.

-1986 Iran Contra scandal breaks
The world becomes aware that the U.S. has been engaged in a policy of arming both Iran and Iraq, keeping the strength of both countries in balance and preventing either country from winning. Over one million people die during this eight year war. (1C2)

It's in moments like these violent times that grace looks so magnificent. It's in the shadow of violence that a victim's grace to a murderer's family shines so brightly, as in the aftermath of the Amish school shooting. It's even more scandalous to think of killing someone who kills, for they, more than anyone in the world, need to hear that they are created for something better than that.

We are reminded of a letter we got from someone on death row. He wrote to us to share that he was a living testimony against the myth of redemptive violence, the idea that violence can bring redemption or peace. This fellow on death row shared that the family of his victim argued that he should not be killed for what he did, that he was not beyond redemption, and as a result, he did not receive the death penalty for his crime. "That gave me a lot of time to think about grace," he said. And he became a Christian in prison. Another story of scandalous love and grace.

So even as we see the horror of death, may we be reminded that in the end, love wins. Mercy triumphs. Life is more powerful than death. And even those who have committed great violence can have the image of God come to life again within them as they hear the whisper of love. May the whisper of love grow louder than the thunder of violence. May we love loudly.

The Jesus way shows us that we need not battle violence with power and force, but with humility and revolutionary subordination. Violence eventually kills itself. Sometimes all the peacemakers need to do is battle violence with revolutionary patience and steadfast hope, for the universe bends toward justice and the entire Christian story demonstrates the triumph of love.

MILITARY INSISTS HIGH SUICIDE RATES DUE TO 'PERSONAL PROBLEMS'... NOT COMBAT

CBS News contacted the governments of all 50 states requesting their official records of death by suicide going back 12 years. They heard back from 45 of the 50. What they discovered is that in 2005 alone - (and again in 45 states alone) - there were at least 6,256 veteran suicides, 120 every week for a year and an average of 17 every day. [43]

43 More at http://alternet.org/waroniraq/68713/ and http://www.truthout.org/docs_2006/112607B.shtml

Hear the poignant words of US army veteran George Mizo, which were handed to us by one of his friends at a vigil for peace:

You, my church, told me it was wrong to kill

... except in war.

You, my teachers, told me it was wrong to kill

... except in war.

You, my father and mother, told me it was wrong to kill

... except in war.

You, my friends, told me it was wrong to kill

... except in war.

You, my government, told me it was wrong to kill

... except in war.

But now I know, you were wrong, and now I will tell you, my church, my teachers, my father and mother, my friends, my government, it is not wrong to kill except in war

... It is wrong to kill.

Dr. King knew it well.

You can wear down evil with love.

As one of the early Christians said, "The executioner's blade is dulled down by grace."

The Dangerous Meshing

The struggle between the church and the state is perhaps nowhere more painfully apparent than in soldiers who are trying to integrate their national and spiritual identities. In our communities here in Philly and Camden, we receive a lot of letters—letters from soldiers, from families who have lost their children in a war they never believed in, from parents whose kids came back from Iraq suicidal, depressed, addicted. Over and over we have gotten letters from soldiers who describe their crisis as a schizophrenia. One soldier said he is trying to serve two masters, the cross and the sword, and his arms aren't big enough to carry them both. Many military chaplains have felt this collision most poignantly and express the crippling sense that they are simply preparing soldiers to kill and helping them to recover from killing, without ever having space to question the killing itself, and many of these chaplains end up looking more like prophets than timid pastors who blindly accompany the war machine.

AWOL soldiers have mailed us their uniforms and dog tags in their attempts to strip themselves of the imperial branding, and they ask for our prayers.

After a Sunday service, one soldier met one of us at the altar to pray and confessed that he was on the ship that fired the tomahawk missiles into Baghdad. Now he was having a hard time living with that. We embraced, cried, and prayed for God to take that heavy yoke from his shoulders.

An older commander told me he had just risked his life for the American dream, and then said he no longer believed in that dream and was convinced that the world could not afford it, and that God had a better dream for the world than what he saw in Iraq. He went on to tell of how he had changed his way of living to almost obsessively cut out oil, plastics, and other luxuries.

To refuse to kill for patriotic reasons is to show that we actually take our identity in Christ more seriously than our identity in the empire.

Seneca spoke of venting one's fury: "We check manslaughter and isolated murders, but what of war and the much-vaunted crime of slaughtering whole peoples?"

"So very atrocious did that conduct now appear, which seemed at first to be doubted whether it was criminal at all."

—Pliny

"I would no more teach my kids military training than teach them arson, robbery, or assassination."

—Eugene Debs (American labor and political leader, 1855–1926)

"Every war ... with all its ordinary consequences ... the murder with the justifications of its necessity and justice, the exaltation and glorifications of military exploits, the worship of the flag, the patriotic sentiments ... and so on, does more in one year to pervert men's minds than thousands of robberies, murders, and arsons perpetrated during hundreds of years by individual men under the influence of passion."

—Leo Tolstoy

Idolatry is what we would sacrifice our children for.

Then There Is Logan

Logan wrote one of us a letter after returning from a tour of duty in Iraq, where he was a forward observer in the US army, a position on the front lines responsible for over 80 percent of the casualties on the battlefield. He had just been given a date of deployment for another tour of duty in Iraq. After six years in the military, he felt the collision of the cross and the sword and felt like he was trying to "serve two masters." With much prayer and counsel, Logan decided to file for conscientious objector status, and we decided to support him. He had fallen in love with the Jesus of the gospel, the hope of enemy-love, and committed himself to live that gospel. He was willing to die for it but knew he could not kill for it. So he told his commanding officers he would be glad to return to Iraq, but he would not be able to carry a weapon because he was a follower of Jesus.

Some of the officers cursed him out; others justified the war using Scripture. When Logan explained that he was willing to go to Iraq but would not be able to carry a weapon or fire a missile, they thought he was crazy. So they sent him in for a psych evaluation. Their hunch was correct—he was crazy. His condition was diagnosed as "maladjustment disorder."

REPORT OF MENTAL STATUS EVALUATION

For use of this form, see AR 635-200; the proponent agency is MILPERCEN

NAME	GRADE	SOCIAL SECURITY NUMBER
	E-5 SGT	

Pt is not deployable. He cannot carry a weapon. He is reporting that he is a Conscientious Objector and Objects to war.

SM meets DSM-IV diagnostic criteria for: Adjustment Disorder with Mixed Emotional Features, Major Depression Recurrent Moderate, and Anxiety Disorder NOS. These disorders are of sufficient severity that SM is not expected to adapt to the Army any further. However, the soldier is not a threat to himself or others.

He is not fit for duty and has failure to adapt to military and is non-deployable.

DO
Psychiatrist
Soldiers Assistance Center

He was discharged from the military a few months later. We reminded him that if he took a close look at church history, he would find himself in pretty good company.[44]

"If I am crazy, it's because I refuse to be crazy in the same way that the world has gone crazy."

—Peter Maurin
(farmer, teacher, and co-founder of the Catholic Worker community movement)

Still passionate about getting in the way of injustice, terror, and violence, Logan joined the Christian Peacemaker Teams and returned to the Middle East, spending time in Palestine and Israel doing the redemptive work of reconciliation. Now he lives with us here in Camden and continues to support other soldiers who feel the collision of the cross and sword. He is helping us create a resource we're calling Centurion's Purse for soldiers caught in the "economic draft"—the name Logan figuratively gives to the reality so many find themselves trapped in, feeling the financial pressure to join the military even as their consciences are deeply suspicious of or even opposed to the logic of redemptive violence. We wanted to share his story with you and told him we would be glad to protect his identity. He told us that we could use his story, but only under one condition—that we not change his name, for he is not ashamed of the gospel he professes.

Logan ended his first letter to us with the words of our beautiful sister Dorothy Day, prophetess of peace, saying, "Dorothy asks if the martyrs did not pray that 'love would overcome hate. That men dying for their faith, rather than killing for their faith, would save the world.' I think that has become my new 'war cry'; to love others, even if it kills me."

44 If it appears as though we are encouraging folks to leave the military, that's because we are. (Not Zondervan … just us, the authors of this book.)

The first letter Logan wrote us had these words:

> It was a time of great & exalting excitement. The country was up in arms, the war was on, in every breast burned the holy fire of patriotism; the drums were beating, the bands playing, the toy pistols popping; the bunched firecrackers hissing & spluttering; a fluttering wilderness of flags flashed in the sun... in the churches the pastors preached devotion to flag & country, and invoked the God of Battles beseeching His aid in our good cause.[45]

The other night a soldier called us on the phone (not that unusual these days). He said that he and his friend had just gotten back from Iraq, where a bunch of folks were passing around a copy of the book *The Irresistible Revolution*. His friend had been in a shooting conflict with some Iraqis, and he shot an older man. Now this twenty-year-old American soldier was having a hard time sleeping. But it wasn't the fact that he had killed the man that was keeping him up at night. It was the face of the man's son, a twelve-year-old boy, who had run out of the house, grabbed his dead father's gun, and started shooting at the US soldiers. So the soldier's friend shot the boy too.

What else could he have done? The soldier said it's absolutely maddening; people feel like they are turning into animals. And every time they point a gun in some young kid's face, they feel they're creating a terrorist. He said that our guns and wars are not making the world safer.

Another young soldier said there are days he feels like just walking into gunfire and dying without a gun in his hands, so that at least he could meet Jesus unarmed.

45 The beginning of Mark Twain's "The War Prayer," which upon his death remained unpublished because his publisher refused to print it. http://en.wikipedia.org/wiki/The_War_Prayer_%28story%29.

War Stories

Two soldiers go to war. One comes back and adjusts well, leaving it all behind. The other comes home with post-traumatic stress syndrome and cannot get the faces of the dead out of his mind. Which of them is crazy?

There's another young man, a decorated veteran of the 1991 Gulf War, who felt that the world killed the good in him. You might remember reading the letters he wrote home from the war. He told his family he felt like he was turning into an animal because day after day it became a little easier to kill. His name was Timothy McVeigh.

He came home from the Special Forces in the Gulf War, horrified, crazy, dehumanized, and became the worst domestic terrorist this country has ever seen. His essays cry out against the bloodshed he saw and created in Iraq: "Do people think that government workers in Iraq are any less human than those in Oklahoma City? Do they think that Iraqis don't have families who will grieve and mourn the loss of their loved ones? Do people believe that the killing of foreigners is somehow different than the killing of Americans?"[46] No doubt he had been deranged by the myth of redemptive violence. He bombed Oklahoma City in the hope that complacent Americans could see what "collateral damage" looks like and cry out against bloodshed everywhere, even in Iraq. Instead, the government that had trained him to kill, killed him, to teach the rest of us that it is wrong to kill. Dear God, liberate us from the logic of redemptive violence.

One of the people we have grown to admire is a man named Bud Welch. He lost his twenty-three-year-old daughter, Marie, in the Oklahoma City bombing. He says he went through a period of rage when he wanted Timothy McVeigh to die. But he remembered the words of his daughter,

46 Timothy McVeigh, "Essay on Hypocrisy."

who had been an advocate for reconciliation and an activist against the death penalty. She used to say, "Execution teaches hatred." It wasn't long before Bud had decided to interrupt the cycle of hatred and violence and arranged a visit with McVeigh's family. Bud says he grew to love them dearly, and to this day says he "has never felt closer to God" than in that union.

He decided to travel around the country, speaking about reconciliation and against the death penalty, which teaches that some people are beyond redemption. And he pleaded for the life of Timothy McVeigh. As he worked through his anger and pain and confusion, he began to see that the spiral of redemptive violence must stop with him. And he began to look into the eyes of Timothy McVeigh, the murderer, and see the image of God. He longed for him to experience love, grace, and forgiveness. Bud believes in the scandal of grace.

Eventually we have to say "enough". We repent and rethink the way our society has taught us to think.

Every gun that is made, every warship launched, every rocket fired signifies, in the final sense, a theft from those who hunger and are not fed, those who are cold and not clothed...This is not a way of life at all in any true sense. Under the cloud of threatening war, it is humanity hanging from a cross of iron.

Dwight D. Eisenhower, from a speech before the American Society of Newspaper Editors, April 16, 1953

34th president of US 1953-1961 (1890 - 1969)

"During times of war, <u>hatred becomes</u> quite respectable, even though it has to masquerade under the guise of <u>patriotism</u>."

–Howard Thurman, spritual advisor to Martin Luther King, Jr.

"Pray for them, and <u>resist</u> them."

–Fr. Dan Berrigan, S.J., referring to the responsibility of Christians to <u>government leaders</u>

"I am a soldier of Christ and it is <u>not</u> permissible <u>for me to fight</u>."

–St. Martin of Tours, 315-397

"On my knees I beg you to turn away from the paths of violence and to <u>return</u> to the ways of <u>peace</u>."

–Pope John Paul II

"Christians, instead of arming themselves with swords, <u>extend</u> their hands in <u>prayer</u>."–St. Athanasius

"<u>Murder</u>, considered a crime when people commit it singly, <u>is</u> transformed into <u>a virtue</u> when they do it <u>en</u> masse."

–St. Cyprian (200-258)

"If you enroll as one of God's people, <u>heaven is your country</u> and God your lawgiver."–St. Clement of Alexandria

"We have <u>grasped</u> the mystery of the atom and <u>rejected</u> the Sermon on the Mount."–General Omar Bradley

"Christ, in disarming Peter, disarmed <u>every</u> soldier."–Tertullian

Another Soldier Who Said "Enough"

Jesse arrived for boot camp at Fort Benning not sure what to expect. He was handed a gun and joined all the recruits marching in formation. As he marched, he internalized what he was training for, and the gun got heavier and heavier. Jesse felt a mysterious but clear whisper from God that God did not want him to kill or to carry a gun. The discomfort became more than he could bear, and he tried quietly to break formation to talk with the sargeant. Not so quick. "What the f*** are you doing, soldier?" the sargeant blasted.

Jesse said gently, "I need to talk with you. I have a problem."

"What the f***'s your problem, soldier?" he shouted in front of all the others.

With all hope for a quite private conversation squelched, Jesse told his sargeant, "As we were marching, I felt like God didn't want me to carry a weapon. I felt like I should love my enemies, and that means not killing them."

The sargeant fumed. "Get on your knees, soldier," he said. And he had the other soldiers march in a circle around Jesse. "Soldiers, do you want to see what a piece of s*** looks like? ... Left, right, left ... This is a piece of s***. Left, right ..."

On his knees, Jesse thought of how kneeling is a posture for prayer. He felt like insults and principalities and powers were swarming him. Humiliated and hurt, he could feel Jesus so near. The soldiers tore the cross from his neck. They ripped the flag from his uniform, insisting that he was unworthy to wear the red, white, and blue. He was handcuffed and taken into custody, branded as a deserter. In the holding area, his handcuffs were removed, and he was free to move about. Somehow he still had his cell phone. (Hmm.)

He decided to call for a cab and leave the rest in God's hands. Taxis move freely on and off the base, transporting soldiers, careful, of course, not to violate security. So Jesse left the area and hid in the bushes to wait for the cab. After what felt like hours, he saw it pull into the long drive.

When he hopped into the taxi, he was greeted by a lovely old Southern woman. "Hey there, soldier," she said. "Where you headed?"

"To the Greyhound station," Jesse said.

She saw where the patches had been torn from his uniform, and she said, "I ain't accusin' you of anything, but I'd better say that we're not allowed to transport no AWOL soldiers. I'm not sayin' you're AWOL. But if you are, you should know I ain't allowed to take you anywhere. And you should also know that soldiers are stationed to check for AWOL soldiers at the bus station."

Silence, and Jesse felt a moment of hopelessness, but then she continued. "So just in case you were AWOL, you would want me to take you by the Wal-Mart so you can get a change of clothes." And she smirked.

Jesse smiled. "Uhh, come to think of it, can we make a pit stop before the bus station? I need to swing by Wal-Mart."

They laughed as she pulled up to the Wal-Mart superstore, which to Jesse had never looked so appealing. With soldiers in uniform all around him, he ran into the store, knowing that he could be spotted easily and all would be ruined. He grabbed the first clothes he could find, darted to the checkout counter to buy them, and ran back to the getaway car outside. In the taxi, he squeezed into his new outfit, which was nowhere near the right size. He gave his new friend a hefty tip, made it safely onto his bus, and headed home. To Jesse it seemed like God did not want him to carry a gun and was able to make a way when there seemed to be no way out.[47]

My first allegiance is not to a flag, a country, or a man.

My first allegiance is not to democracy or blood.

It's to a king and a kingdom.[48]

47 This is a true story. Shortly after arriving in his small hometown in Illinois, Jesse found his face on wanted posters plastered around town. In a lovely act of revolutionary subordination, he turned himself in and was eventually legally discharged along with many other soldiers. Soon after that, he came to visit us here at the Simple Way.

48 Words from Derek Webb's lovely song "A King and a Kingdom."

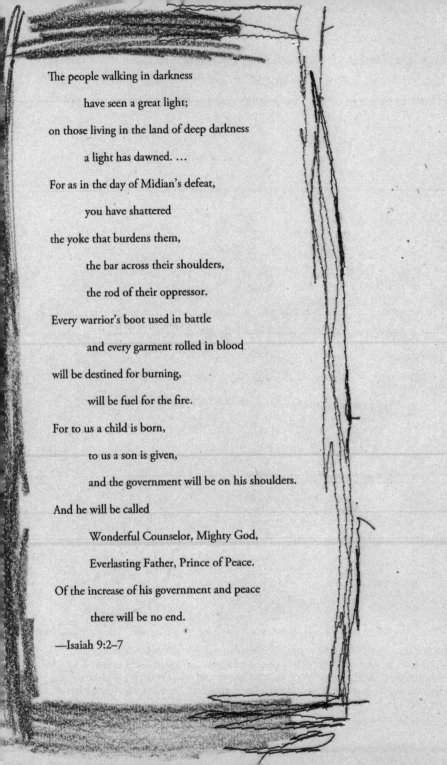

The people walking in darkness

    have seen a great light;

on those living in the land of deep darkness

    a light has dawned. ...

For as in the day of Midian's defeat,

    you have shattered

the yoke that burdens them,

    the bar across their shoulders,

    the rod of their oppressor.

Every warrior's boot used in battle

    and every garment rolled in blood

will be destined for burning,

    will be fuel for the fire.

For to us a child is born,

    to us a son is given,

    and the government will be on his shoulders.

And he will be called

    Wonderful Counselor, Mighty God,

    Everlasting Father, Prince of Peace.

Of the increase of his government and peace

    there will be no end.

—Isaiah 9:2–7

A Closing Confession

Sixty years ago, as a Catholic Air Force chaplain, Father George Zabelka blessed the men who dropped the atomic bombs on Hiroshima and Nagasaki. Over the next twenty years, he gradually came to believe that he had been terribly wrong, that he had denied the very foundations of his faith by lending moral and religious support to the bombing. Zabelka, who died in 1992, gave this speech on the 40th anniversary of the bombings. He left this message for the world:

As a Catholic chaplain I watched as the Boxcar, piloted by a good Irish Catholic pilot, dropped the bomb on Urakami Cathedral in Nagasaki, the center of Catholicism in Japan.

I never preached a single sermon against killing civilians to the men who were doing it ... It never entered my mind to protest publicly the consequences of these massive air raids. I was told it was necessary—told openly by the military and told implicitly by my Church's leadership.

I struggled. I argued. But yes, there it was in the Sermon on the Mount, very clear: "Love your enemies. Return good for evil." I went through a crisis of faith. Either accept what Christ said, as unpassable and silly as it may seem, or deny him completely.

For the last 1700 years the Church has not only been making war respectable: it has been inducing people to believe it is an honorable profession, an honorable Christian profession. This is a lie.

For the 300 years immediately following Jesus' resurrection, the Church universally saw Christ and his teaching as nonviolent. Remember that the Church taught this ethic in the face of at least three serious attempts by the state to liquidate her. It was subject to horrendous and ongoing torture and death. If ever there was an occasion for justified retaliation and defensive slaughter, whether in form of a just war or a just revolution, this was it. The economic and political elite of the Roman state and their military had turned the citizens of the state against Christians and were embarked on a murderous public policy of exterminating the Christian community.

Yet the Church, in the face of the heinous crimes committed against her members, insisted without reservation that when Christ disarmed Peter he disarmed all Christians.

Christians continued to believe that Christ was, to use the words of an ancient liturgy, their fortress, their refuge, and their strength, and that if Christ was all they needed for security and defense, then Christ was all they should have. Indeed, this was a new security ethic. Christians understood that if they would only follow Christ and his teaching, they couldn't fail. When opportunities were given for Christians to appease the state by joining the fighting Roman army, these opportunities were rejected, because the early Church saw a complete and an obvious incompatibility between loving as Christ loved and killing. It was Christ, not Mars, who gave security and peace.

Today the world is on the brink of ruin because the Church refuses to be the Church, because we Christians have been deceiving ourselves and the non-Christian world about the truth of Christ. There is no way to follow Christ, to love as Christ loved, and simultaneously to kill other people. It is a lie to say that the spirit that moves the trigger of a flamethrower is the Holy Spirit. It is a lie to say that learning to kill is learning to be Christ-like. It is a lie to say that learning to drive a bayonet into the heart of another is motivated from having put on the mind of Christ. Militarized Christianity is a lie. It is radically out of conformity with the teaching, life, and spirit of Jesus.

Now, brothers and sisters, on the anniversary of this terrible atrocity carried out by Christians, I must be the first to say that I made a terrible mistake. I was had by the father of lies. I participated in the big ecumenical lie of the Catholic, Protestant, and Orthodox churches. I wore the uniform. I was part of the system. When I said Mass over there I put on those beautiful vestments over my uniform. (When Father Dave Becker left the Trident submarine base in 1982 and resigned as Catholic chaplain there, he said, "Every time I went to Mass in my uniform and put the vestments on over my uniform, I couldn't help but think of the words of Christ applying to me: Beware of wolves in sheep's clothing.")

As an Air Force chaplain I painted a machine gun in the loving hands of the nonviolent Jesus, and then handed this perverse picture to the world as truth. I sang "Praise the Lord" and passed the ammunition. As Catholic chaplain for the 509th Composite Group, I was the final channel that communicated this fraudulent image of Christ to the crews of the Enola Gay and the Boxcar.

All I can say today is that I was wrong. Christ would not be the instrument to unleash such horror on his people. Therefore no follower of Christ can legitimately unleash the horror of war on God's people. Excuses and self-justifying explanations are without merit. All I can say is: I was wrong! But, if this is all I can say, this I must do, feeble as it is. For to do otherwise would be to bypass the first and absolutely essential step in the process of repentance and reconciliation: admission of error, admission of guilt.

Thank God that I'm able to stand here today and speak out against war, all war. The prophets of the Old Testament spoke out against all false gods of gold, silver, and metal. Today we are worshipping the gods of metal, the bomb. We are putting our trust in physical power, militarism, and nationalism. The bomb, not God, is our security and our strength. The prophets of the Old Testament said simply: Do not put your trust in chariots and weapons, but put your trust in God. Their message was simple, and so is mine.

We must all become prophets. I really mean that. We must all do something for peace. We must stop this insanity of worshipping the gods of metal. We must take a stand against evil and idolatry. This is our destiny at the most critical time of human history. But it's also the greatest opportunity ever offered to any group of people in the history of our world – to save our world from complete annihilation.

... an excerpt of a speech Father Zabelka gave at a Pax Christi conference in August 1985

Sometimes it's hard to know where to begin. None of us are free of the clutches of empire. But we believe in the mystery of confession (*sacrament* means "mystery"), that no matter what we have done, there is hope for redemption and restoration. The humility to confess mistakes and to wash people's feet is one of the marks that distinguishes the community of Jesus from the world of kings and presidents, who never confess anything they have done wrong unless they are caught in the middle of exploiting Bathsheba, Monica Lowinski, or Iraq.

Church history is also filled with movements of people who cry out to God that they are unholy, who identify and confess their sins—from Europe's Confessing Church to the US college revivals that began by humble confession of sins, by people beating their chests before each other and God. One of the most powerful things the contemporary church could do is to confess our sins to the world, humbly get on our knees and repent of the terrible things we have done in the name of God. In his book *Blue Like Jazz*, author Donald Miller tells the delightful story of how he and his friends dressed like monks and sat in a confessional booth on their notoriously heathen campus. But the great irony was that they were confessing their sins as Christians and the sins of Christendom to anyone who was willing to listen and forgive. A mystical, sacramental healing begins within us and could extend to the wounds of our world.[49] Perhaps the world would be willing to listen to a church on its knees, a church that doesn't pretend to be perfect or to have all the answers. As we move toward hope and imagination, let's begin with confession and call it like it is. We are in a mess. And it's not just the world that's in a mess. The calling and identity of the people of God in the midst of this world have become even more muddled.

But throughout the ages, beautiful saints have lived faithfully, giving us hope that a set-apart people can fascinate and bless the world.

49 During a recent gay-pride day, we were speaking at a congregation in the middle of the rainbow district and noticed that the Christian community there had done a similar stunt, setting up confessional tents where Christians could confess to bypassers the embarrassing things done to gay people in the name of Christ. They shared with us the incredible stories of redemption, the healing through tears and embraces born of this simple act of humility.

SECTION FOUR

A Peculiar Party

Christianity entered history as a new social order, or rather a new social dimension. From the very beginning Christianity was not primarily a "doctrine" but exactly a "community." There was not only a "Message" to be proclaimed and delivered, and a "Good News" to be declared. There was precisely a New Community, distinct and peculiar, in the process of growth and formation, to which members were called and recruited. Indeed, "fellowship" was the basic category of Christian existence.

—Georges Florovsky, "Empire and Desert:
Antinomies of Christian History"

This last section is a grand finale, like fireworks on the Fourth of July ... or we should say fireworks on Pentecost. We'll fire away snapshots of stories, reflections, and practical expressions of the peculiar politics of Jesus today.

that's the birthday of America

that's the birthday of the church

JULY 4

PENTECOST

Good News

Our president is not organizing another political party, nope ... not even running with Nader on the Green ticket. Jesus is forming a new kind of people, a different kind of party, whose peculiar politics are embodied in who we are. The church is a people called out of the world to embody a social alternative that the world cannot know on its own terms. We are not simply asking the government to be what God has commissioned the church to be. After all, even the best government can't legislate love. We can build hundreds of units of affordable housing (a good thing by the way) and people still might not have *homes*. We can provide universal health care and keep folks breathing longer (another nice move), but people can be breathing and still not truly be alive. We can create laws to enforce good behavior, but no law has ever changed a human heart or reconciled a broken relationship. The church is not simply suggesting political alternatives. The church is embodying one.

The idea that the church is to be the body of Christ is not just something to read about in theology books and leave for the scholars to pontificate about. We are literally to be the body of Jesus in the world. Christians are to be little Christs—people who put flesh on Jesus in the world today. You are the only Jesus some people will ever see. The promise of the church is this: none of us alone are Christ (that's blasphemy), but all of us together are Christ to the world (that's ecclesiology).

PUT ON JESUS

"Clothe yourselves with Christ." (Col. 3:12-17)

It's worth reiterating that the basis for living out the ethics of Jesus in this world is not that it *works* but that this is the way God is. We are not promised that everything is going to turn out perfect. Look at the cross. Look at how the story ends for the apostles. It is ugly. If there is anything we can learn from our history, as writer G. K. Chesterton says, it's that we are to be "completely fearless, absurdly happy, and in constant trouble." And in the end, love wins.

In an age of violence and terror, it's important not just to live well but to die well. We are not called simply to live like Christ, but we are called to die like Christ. And he died loving. The heroes of our faith (John the Baptist, Jesus, the apostles, Stephen, Ignatius, Maximilian Kolbe, Rufus and Zosimus, Perpetua and Felicitas,[1] all the way down to Tom Fox in our day[2]) are not war heroes but martyrs. Martyr means "witness," and the ripples that their deaths made are part of what spread the gospel of grace. They are not people who died killing but people who died loving and were slaughtered as they looked into the face of evil people and said, "God loves you."

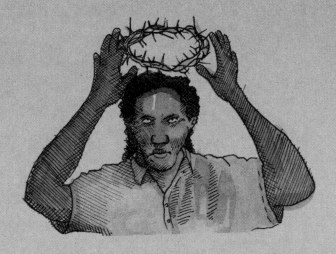

1 Our hope is to provoke some curiosity by throwing some unfamiliar names out there so we can discover new heroes. These aren't folks you study in world history or even in Sunday school for that matter. For more on the heroes of the church, turn to page 318.

2 See Thieleman J. van Braght, *Martyr's Mirror of the Defenseless Christians* (1660. Scottdale, PA: Herald Press, 27th printing 2006) and *Foxe's Book of Martyrs* for extensive coverage on the martyrs.

Looking Like Jesus

Remember when ole John the Baptizer sent his disciples to ask Jesus whether he was the one they were expecting and he didn't answer with a simple yes? Jesus instead told them to go tell John what they saw him doing. He knew that John could read the trail of crumbs. John knew that when lepers were healed, the blind saw, the dead rose, and the good news was preached to the poor, the one they were awaiting was indeed here.

What does our trail of crumbs look like? If someone asks if we are Christ-followers, can we say, "Tell me what you see"? Is there enough evidence to prove that we are taking after the slaughtered Lamb? What if they ask the poor around us? What if they ask our enemies? Would they say that we love them? Christians haven't always looked like Jesus. Perhaps the greatest barrier to Christ has been Christians who pronounce Jesus so loudly with their lips and deny him so loudly with their lives.[3]

In the South, we have a saying: "You are the spittin' image" of someone. Folks still speculate over how exactly the phrase originated, but I've heard it put like this. It's shorthand for "spirit and image." Spittin' image. (Go ahead and try it out; it won't hurt.) For us, it meant more than just that you *look like* that person. It goes beyond just appearance to include character and temperament. It means that you remind people of that person. You have their charisma. You do the same things they did. In the truest sense, Christians are to be the spittin' image of Jesus in the world. We are to be the things he was. We are to preach the things he preached and live the way he lived. We are to follow in the footsteps of our rabbi so closely that we get his dust on us.

3 A recent survey of young adults who are "familiar outsiders" to Christianity showed that the three most common perceptions of Christians by onlookers are that we are anti-homosexual (an image held by 91 percent of the folks surveyed), judgmental (87 percent), and hypocritical (85 percent). How sad that the very things that Jesus scolded the religious elites around him for are the very things for which Christians are now known. We have a major image problem. To hear more about this study by the Barna research team, check out the book *Unchristian* (Baker, 2007) by our friends David Kinnaman and Gabe Lyons.

We are to remind the world of Jesus. The criterion for whether something is a manifestation of the kingdom of God is the person of Jesus. Does it look like him?

"Be imitators of God" (Eph. 5:1)—that word *imitate* derives from the same word as *mimic*, like a mime.

What Do You See?

It is the Christians, O Emperor, who have sought and found the truth, for they acknowledge God. They do not keep for themselves the goods entrusted to them. They do not covet what belongs to others. They show love to their neighbors. They do not do to another what they would not wish to have done to themselves. They speak gently to those who oppress them, and in this way they make them their friends. It has become their passion to do good to their enemies. They live in the awareness of their smallness. Every one of them who has anything gives ungrudgingly to the one who has nothing. If they see a traveling stranger, they bring him under their roof. They rejoice over him as over a real brother, for they do not call one another brothers after the flesh, but they know they are brothers in the Spirit and in God. If they hear that one of them is imprisoned or oppressed for the sake of Christ, they take care of all his needs. If possible they set him free. If anyone among them is poor or comes into want while they themselves have nothing to spare, they fast two or three days for him. In this way they can supply any poor man with the food he needs. This, O Emperor, is the rule of life of the Christians, and this is their manner of life.

—Aristides 137 AD

Those godless Galileans feed our poor in addition to their own.

—Emperor Julian

The Issues

As I (Shane) was growing up in East Tennessee, my political worldview was carefully crafted by Bible Belt culture. I had all kinds of views on the hot-button political issues. But mostly I had ideologies, which aren't very compelling, even if they are true. I've learned from conservatives and liberals that you can be politically correct and still be mean.

I can remember ripping liberals up in debates on homosexuality. But I didn't know anyone who was gay or who felt like talking to me about it (which is understandable). Years later I met a fellow in college who shared with me that he was attracted to other men and that he had grown to feel that God had made a mistake when God created him. Far from finding any sense of community or intimacy in the church, he was alone and confessed that he wanted to kill himself. I thought that if this brother cannot find a home in the church, who have we become? I marveled at the complexity of the struggle to understand our sexuality, a complexity I couldn't understand until the issue took on a face and had a story and cried tears.

We would do much better to create communities in the church in which people can find intimacy and love than to split congregations over issues. Christians should stick to replicating the sacrificial love of Jesus toward gay people and trust that this loving service will do more to transform people than laws ever could. Besides, the contradictions in evangelicalism are clear. Take divorce, for example, a sin Jesus spoke clearly about. The divorce rate of evangelical Christians now surpasses that of the rest of the population in the United States. Evangelicals are getting divorced, and gay folks are wanting to get married, and religionists keep accusing homosexuals of destroying the family. Yikes. If we truly had a church in which people could love and be loved, we would transcend so many divisive issues and be free to become the people God has created us to be.

"We can live without sex,

but we cannot live

without love."

there are plenty of folks who have a lot of sex but very little love, and
ty of others who never have sex at all but experience a great deal of

continued to wrestle with complex human and political issues, I
olved myself to one thing: the starting point must be that the church
place where we can grapple with difficult questions with grace and
nility. And I believe that, even more important than thinking identically
every issue, we must learn to disagree well. Our ability as a church
disagree well is as powerful a witness to the larger society as our
formity on every issue.

Political Misfits

It's easy to have political views—that's what politicians do. But it's much harder to embody a political alternative—that's what saints do. The greater challenge is right living, not merely right thinking. In Jesus we meet not a presentation of ideas or a new political platform but an invitation to join up, to become part of a movement, of a people that embodies good news.

Political embodiment means that we become the change that we want in the world, not just lobby politicians to change things for us. It means that we must take the responsibility that our political views demand of us. Not many of us have seen people, much less a political party, who are ready to enact the change they want in the world.

Those who would like to see abortion grow rarer and become nonexistent had also better be ready to take in some teen moms and adopt some unwanted babies. To be pro-life in our neighborhood means we have to figure out how to come alongside a fourteen-year-old pregnant girl. This is why we loved Mother Teresa so much. Mother Teresa embodied her politics. She didn't just wear a T-shirt that said, "Abortion is homicide." She loved moms and unborns so much, she could say with integrity, "If you don't want to have the baby, you can give it to me." Which is why everyone called her Mother.

Nor have we seen a political platform with a consistent ethic of life—and by that we mean not simply being pro-birth but being pro-life, and recognizing that life doesn't begin at conception and end at birth.

Just because our gospel gets political doesn't mean it gets political on the empire's terms. The question isn't whether are we pro-life but how do we consistently honor life? One of the most important questions for the church today isn't whether Christianity is political but *how* is Christianity political? And hopefully Jesus and the biblical narrative have given us some good tools for political mischief.

Cultural Refugees

If we take a close look at the identity crisis of the church in our day, we might say that Christians, surrounded by weapons of mass destruction and in a world run on greed, are aliens in a strange land. We are in exile, struggling to live the love of God in a strange world. But this is not new: exile is a familiar theme in the biblical narrative. As we retraced in this book the shape of Israel's history, from the exodus to the temptations of power and statehood, we did not talk much of Israel's later history: exile in Babylon.[4] Israel's attempt to create a powerful nation, through kings and temples, had finally crumbled. The warning of 1 Samuel 8 finally made sense. They had been plundered and carried off to distant lands, gradually spreading all throughout the known world. It is from this time of exile that we today can draw some of our greatest lessons. While the Israelites lived as slaves in a foreign land, the spirit of despair was foreboding. But in that time, the prophet Jeremiah spoke a word of encouragement.

> This is what the Lord Almighty, the God of Israel, says to all those I carried into exile from Jerusalem to Babylon: "**Build houses** and **settle down**; **plant gardens and eat what they produce. Marry and have sons and daughters**; find wives for your sons and give your daughters in marriage, so that they too may have sons and daughters. **Increase in number there**; do not decrease. Also, **seek the peace and prosperity of the city** to which I have carried you into exile. **Pray to the Lord** for it, because if it prospers, you too will prosper."

4 Around 586 BC, the southern kingdom (Judah) fell to the Babylonians. The northern kingdom (Israel) fell even earlier, during the 700s BC.

HOW CAN WE SING ZION'S SONG

IN A FOREIGN LAND?

By the rivers of Babylon we sat and wept when we remembered Zion. There on the poplars we hung our harps, for there our captors asked us for songs, our tormentors demanded songs of joy; they said, "Sing us one of the songs of Zion!" How can we sing the songs of the Lord while in a foreign land?

—Psalm 137:1–4

The people of God were tied up in Babylon, but they were not to grow homesick for Jerusalem and hope to eventually re-root there. God's blessing is not about land. Rather, through the exhortations of Jeremiah, they lived in a paradox of home and homelessness: "Every foreign land can be home; every homeland is foreign."[5] They were aliens and strangers as they were spread throughout the earth by violent chaos, and yet they made themselves at home with the Creator, who walked with them everywhere. The whole point of their calling as a set-apart people became clearer. They would be sprinkled like salt throughout the earth, blessing its various places of residence with their homes, gardens, children, and peace. They would seek the peace of wherever they landed. This is the point of the last section of this book: the peculiarity of the church is not for its own sake but for the sake of the whole creation, for the cities and neighborhoods in which we find ourselves.

5 John Howard Yoder, *The Jewish-Christian Schism Revisited* (Grand Rapids: Eerdmans, 2003), 79.

The people of the exodus, whether in Babylon or in this land we call America, are not simply offering the world a better empire. They are building another society, offering the world another strange and upside-down "empire." And that's what gets you in trouble. Living an alternative vision for society can be a lonely thing, which is why community is at the center of it all. Creating a contrast society demands a collective imagination to create rituals and celebrations other than the festivals of the Caesars. That's why there are so many Jewish holidays. They remind them, and us, of the Story from which we come.

Consider the Amish, who understand well what it means to be a "colony of heaven," people who are living as strangers in a foreign land, resident aliens on the earth.[6] It's easy to imagine the questions of young Amish children growing up: "Mom, why can't we have an Xbox?" "Dad, why do we dress like this?" "Why don't we have cars?" And you can almost hear the parents explain, "Other children may do those things, but you are special. You are different; you are Amish. You have a different story and live in a different way from other people in this world." Christianity is an invitation to be part of an alien people. Get ready for the neo-Amish. It's time for another movement of Anabaptists.

The reason we are not to be *of* the world is so we may be *for* the world. As our brother Rodney Clapp says so well, we are still to "eavesdrop on the world" even as we create a new one, and practice the art of selective engagement and sanctified subversion. We are cultural refugees. The beautiful monastics throughout church history were cultural refugees; they

> Christianity is not a matter of persuasive words. It is a matter of true greatness as long as it is hated by the world.
>
> —Ignatius 110 AD

6 We are drawing here from the work of Stanley Hauerwas and William Willimon, *Resident Aliens* (Nashville: Abingdon, 1995).

ran to the desert not to flee from the world but to save the world from itself.

We talk a lot about how the church's mission is to create a new culture, a culture in which it is easier for people to be good. Let us not forget that the word *cult* comes from the same root from which we get *culture*. So while we are not waiting for a UFO landing, preparing for a mass suicide, or stockpiling weapons, we are indeed forming an alternative culture. It is not simply a counterculture reacting to the dominant culture. We are forming a new culture, a society in contrast to the dominant one. And in many ways it's much broader and more sustainable, much less tribal than nationalism and much less dangerous than the cult of civic religion that is infecting the church. And the imperial cult is suspiciously closer to those infamous cults that stockpile weapons and await their suicidal fate while fortifying themselves against any truth that would set them free from the illusions that are killing them. And the only reason God's cultural refugees seem so peculiar is because of how far the world has moved from God's dream for it. We should live in ways that don't make sense without God. God's people look strange in a rebellious and fallen world.

For our biblical ancestors, the law set them apart from the world they came from—peculiar ways of living, eating, dressing. God also gave them laws for caring for the poor, the land, aliens, and immigrants. Much of the law was a warning: "If you do not do this, you will end up like Egypt." Today things are a little different. If it's not circumcision or eating kosher that sets us apart, what marks us? Wouldn't it be beautiful if people asked questions like, Why do they have homeless folks coming into their homes? Why don't they watch television? Why are they so nice to people who ask questions like this?

What if we could say to our kids, "You are different; you are a Christian." We are a contrast society, not just a hip counterculture. What marks us as different must be more than something external or superficial; it must be a peculiar way of living. The New Testament speaks of the circumcision of the heart, cutting away the things of the culture, keeping ourselves from being "polluted by the world." Preserving the distinctiveness of the kingdom of God has always been the most important and most difficult task for the church.

Much of the world now lies in the ruins of triumphant and militant Christianity. The imperially baptized religion created a domesticated version of Christianity—a dangerous thing that can inoculate people from ever experiencing true faith. (Everyone is a Christian, but no one knows what a Christian is anymore.) Our hope is that the postmodern, post-Christian world is once again ready for a people who are peculiar, people who spend their energy creating a culture of contrast rather than a culture of relevancy. If we are to be relevant to the world we live in, we must be relevant nonconformists.[7]

7 For more on relevant nonconformists, check out the heroes of the church on page 318 and throughout your Bible.

Every culture has particular ways of eating. Some folks eat with chopsticks; others sit on the floor. In India we ate with our right hands. How do Christians eat? Christians eat with poor folks, with the outcast, the marginalized, and the excluded—all who were never invited to anyone else's party. Ours is a different kind of party. It's more like a divine banquet than another political program. Society's misfits are our people, our "constituency."

There's an old story of a bishop whose cathedral was about to be robbed. The bandits demanded the "treasures of the church." So the bishop went into the shelter and gathered up the poor, saying, "These are the treasures of the church." The bandits left empty-handed that night.

Luke 14: "When you throw a banquet do not invite your friends … invite the poor."

Gospel: "The king said to the servant, go into the streets and bring any who will come."

241

We are resident aliens.

Politics for Ordinary Radicals

Talking about peculiarity often raises the question of whether Christians can hold certain jobs. As activist-theologian Brian Walsh once said, "A Christian can hold any job. But if they act as Christians, they will simply need to be ready to be fired within a few weeks." Especially if they are commander-in-chief of the largest military in the world. We should be more concerned about identifying the radical spirit of love that must permeate every disciple's journey than about making a list of kosher Christian jobs.

The other day we met a robotics engineer who used to make robots just to impress people. But then he started thinking about his purpose in this world and God's dream for the world. He's still a robotics engineer, but of a different kind. He designs robots to dismantle land mines so kids in countries like Afghanistan can play without worrying about getting blown up. Before the robots came, many of the land mines were being dismantled by little kids who were paid next to nothing and often had their hands blown off. He's a missional robotics engineer, disarming the world for Jesus.

Another friend of ours is a massage therapist. She could be making $100 an hour giving massages to rich folks. But she says there are plenty of massage therapists who do that. She lives near the poor and homeless. She knows plenty of people whose feet are their transportation, and she is friends with women involved in sex trafficking who walk the red-light district all night long. These people have tired, sore feet and no massage therapist to offer them services ... until now. Every week, she opens her home to them, washes their feet with the most delicate and deliberate touch, and gives them the best foot massages money can't buy.

We met a married couple who was deeply disturbed about the conflict between Israel and Palestine, but they weren't sure how to stop just complaining about the way things are and start living into what could be. So they just went there. They are business entrepreneurs, so as they built relationships with the Palestinian people, they saw the need for jobs. They started a fair-trade T-shirt company that employs nearly a hundred Palestinians with dignity and hope. It may not be what their parents expected them to do with an Ivy League business degree, but they make it possible to imagine another world in the Holy Land.

Then there's a group of jewelers in the United Kingdom, many of whom had been business folks in the world's market economy. The jewelry industry is notoriously wicked, often called the "blood diamond" market, responsible for significant human suffering around the world as workers shed blood, tears, and their very lives mining gems and precious metals that they can't even afford to buy. And many of these business folks in the UK found their faith colliding with the industry—you know, the ole can't-serve-God-and-mammon thing. Rather than just abandon the industry, they decided to try transforming it—"practicing resurrection," as we like to say. They traveled to Bolivia, Colombia, and across Africa, finding the people who work in the diamond industry. They built personal relationships with them and pioneered an incredible jewelry business called Cred. As we met in their store in England, one of the founders said to me, "Can you imagine the feeling of satisfaction when you put your wedding band on and know that from the moment it was mined till it goes on your finger, every worker was treated with dignity and respect?" And his wife is a theologian, so she puts into words the theology and philosophy that drive their vision. Actions like theirs give such integrity to the gospel we preach. Having encountered the sacredness of Jesus and of their global neighbor, they are a different breed of jewelers now.

Another group of friends thinks it's a scandal that we spend so much money on water. Sales of bottled water are estimated to be between $50 and $100 billion (US) annually and increasing approximately 7 to 10 percent annually. In 2004, sales were approximately 154 billion liters (41 billion gallons). It's a strange irony that folks in countries with cheap, readily accessible drinking water spend enough money on bottled water to provide water for the rest of the world. Yikes. So several friends started a company that sells bottled tap water at festivals and concerts and uses the profits to dig wells and provide water access to the world's 1.2 billion people who are dying of thirst. Brilliant.

We can start changing people's mindset. Instead of asking young people, "What are you going to do when you grow up?" ask them, "Who are you becoming?" The question is not whether you will be a doctor or a lawyer but what kind of doctor or lawyer you will be.

These are everyday miracles, the political lives of ordinary radicals. These are political and social and economic miracles. And miracles are different from marvels. Empires and corporations are good at marvels. Remember, in the desert Satan tempted Jesus to turn stones into bread to feed himself. But he refused. He refused to use his miraculous power to marvel people into the kingdom. He worked his miracles not to shock and awe or to feed his own mouth but to feed the masses. So we might not be able to turn water into wine, but if we can help the two billion people who are dying of thirst find water, that is a miracle. Then maybe Jesus will whisper to us on the day of judgment, "When I was thirsty, you gave me something to drink." And perhaps an even greater miracle than walking on water is walking on this war-torn earth for peace.

Very truly I tell you, all who have faith in me will do the works I have been doing, and they will do even greater things than these, because I am going to the father.
                                                    --John 14:12

Vagrant Campaigning (No SUVs or Secret Service)

In the mountains of New York lives one of those peculiar communities of Christians who know what it means to be resident aliens. In the 1930s, they were kicked out of Germany because they were Christian pacifists, unwilling to allow the influence of the Third Reich into their classrooms. They were political misfits, speaking against Hitler and against the war, and they welcomed everyone who suffered from the violence. As they moved from country to country, many of them ended up in the mountains of New York. They educated their kids, teaching them how to live "off the grid" of the empire. They ran a business making medical equipment for folks with disabilities. They generated much of their own energy, managed their own sewage, explored green building methods, grew their food and meat, and formed a culture of peace shaped by Christian discipleship.

Having spent years developing a peculiar life, some of them came to feel that they had lost contact with the very world Jesus came to save. They did foreign missions, reached out to their neighbors, and ran a publishing house that put out some great books (Plough Publishing). But they had a sense that they were to be *in* the world even as they were not of it, that they were not simply to live a life of integrity isolated in the hills. They wondered whether there was anything more they could do to heal the wounded society around them. They looked to the gospels and recalled how Jesus sent his disciples into the world, two by two. Jesus didn't create an outreach committee, start a social justice group, or formulate a five-year strategy for evangelism. Risky and crazy as it may seem, the early revolution was spread by vagrant evangelists who were sent out with no money or extra clothes, who were maybe even barefoot.

And so it was decided. The next morning they sent out (probably with shoes—how luxurious!) from their community and from other affiliated communities about three hundred people on foot with no money or resources other than their love and service to the world. Pairs of women slept in parking garages as they looked for places to serve. Pairs of men walked the streets, ready to love their neighbors. Some made their way down to hurricane-battered Louisiana. Others found themselves serving in addiction-recovery communities. Unlike popular forms of "evangelism," which are often infused with a sense of superiority and condescension, they adopted the appearance of homeless vagrants, fragile and dependent on the hospitality of others. Their engagement with the world was not triumphant or "relevant." It was peculiar and vulnerable, like a king washing feet.

This community recognized that Jesus calls us to be peculiar but also engaged in the world we find ourselves in. We are to be relevant nonconformists. We are to develop countercultural habits and norms (the Sermon on the Mount) and live them in the midst of an insane world. Much of the church, however, in its search for relevance, falls in love with the world, its methods of communication, and its patterns of consumerism, and sacrifices holy nonconformity for the sake of cultural relevancy. But for the first little campaign of Jesus, there was no mortorcade or SUVs or Secret Service, just a bunch of barefoot ragamuffins sent out in pairs with a vision for changing the world.

TRAMPLE

If salt loses its

saltiness,

what is it worth?

Good Pattern for God's Good Creation

Recognizing the connection between war and oil, resources and global conflict, some folks have begun exploring alternatives. We know folks who have organized their lives in such a way that their homes are located where they can walk to work or take public transportation. Others have made their bikes more comfortable to use for daily transportation and capable of carrying groceries. One community even has a laundry machine that operates off of a stationary bicycle. The radical character of these decisions can't be celebrated enough. These people have chosen to reduce not only their personal costs and the amount of gas they burn but also their participation in the vast, international, wasteful system of processing and transporting (and fighting for) fuel before it even makes it to a car. (And hey, less energy is spent on finding the best new diet or exercise video.)

The community that sent out three hundred people on foot embodies an alternative. Among other things, they made a radical decision regarding the youth in the community. Because petroleum supplies are finite and will become (along with water) one of the major sources of conflict in this century, the community told their fifteen-year-olds that they couldn't get their driver's licenses until they could build a vehicle that runs on something other than fossil fuels.[8]

We have a community here in Philly called New Jerusalem. It's a recovery community for folks who struggle with drug and alcohol addictions. More than fifty folks live at New Jerusalem; many of them have been homeless and jobless. They know that their own healing is connected to the healing of the world. Folks at New Jerusalem have a sign on the wall that reads, "We cannot fully recover until we help the society that made us sick recover." In Philly, more than two hundred thousand jobs have left

8 This challenge led their youth to successfully create a mesquite-burning pickup truck.

the neighborhoods, so we have to get creative. One of their projects for practicing resurrection is a grease co-op. They gather used vegetable oil from around the city and have a little greasel station where they convert it to biodiesel. We have cars that run on used oil and homemade biodiesel, pointing us toward the hope of a post-oil era. New Jerusalem provides jobs for formerly homeless folks in a business that radiates with the hope for another world that rises from a desperate love for our God. Maybe people will ask, "Why do they run their cars off used veggie oil?" And we can say, "Because we are Christians."

Others are learning to create houses that are in harmony with creation. Some have covered their roofs with grass and plants, reducing cooling and heating costs, extending the life of their roofs and retaining water that would otherwise drain into overburdened street sewers. Others are completely rethinking environmental design so that our economies are not just less bad (like hybrid cars—though admirable in their own way) but positively healthy and generative (like a car that creates drinking water).[9] And this whirlwind of prophetic imagination we're blasting you with here is not just some addendum to our book, an attempt to fit in another "issue." Rather, the entire story of the people of God—from Adam, to Israel, to Jesus, to the church—has presupposed the claim that "the earth is the Lord's and everything therein." This great planet isn't just a boring lump of secular earth but *a divine miracle, a creation!* Any Christian politics that doesn't presume this is missing out on God's gift.

9 Though a bit more optimistic about technology than we might be, William McDonough and Michael Braungart are thinking these thoughts in *Cradle to Cradle: Remaking the Way We Make Things* (New York: North Point, 2002). For the more humble Luddite side, see anything by Wendell Berry.

Practicing Resurrection

There is a lot of talk about global warming and environmental issues these days. Here in the concrete jungles of Philly and Camden, we talk a lot about practicing resurrection, or making ugly things beautiful. We try to use the trash of a disposable society. We do a fair amount of dumpster diving, and at most of our potlucks you can find food labeled "vegetarian," "vegan," or "rescued" (meaning it came from the trash). In our gardens, you'll find old refrigerators serving as compost bins, veggies growing out of toilets and tires, and gutted computers and TVs converted into flower pots.

One of the most revolutionary practices you can participate in is growing your own food. Some of the kids here in the city see tomatoes growing in our gardens and they can't believe their eyes. "You can't eat that," they say, and we laugh and say, "Oh yes; that, my dear, is a tomato. They aren't made in factories. They are God's miracles." How can we fully love the Creator when we've grown so far from the creation?

But the church can do more than just grow its own food. Aiding the farmers in our local bioregions is a way to reduce dependence on long distance food transport and enjoy knowing where higher quality food comes from. Community supported agriculture (CSA) is one way to support local farmers. CSAs connect those of us who know little about the food we eat with the farmers and land that produce it. Consumers participate in a CSA farm by purchasing "shares" of the crop yield, thereby supporting small farms whose existence is threatened by gigantic agribusinesses. Congregations that catch on and create their own "congregation supported agriculture" are signs of hope for us today. As this renewed agrarian practice grows in the church, we will come to see that it's not so much that the community supports agriculture as it is that agriculture supports community. If we return to the helpful dictum of "reduce, reuse, recycle," we will remember that green consumption needs to be checked by *less* consumption. The question becomes not just how to accumulate more, but how to covet less.

Setting the Captives Free

It has been said that if you want to gauge the health of a society, look at its prisons. Here in the US we have the largest prison-industrial complex in the history of civilization. More than two million citizens are in prison, largely for crimes related to economics and the drug economy.[10] In fact, a few years ago, as welfare "reform" laws were being passed, a city official was asked, "How is Philadelphia preparing for the welfare cuts?" The official answered, "We are building four new prisons." Many Christians have begun to ask, in light of Jesus' emancipation proclamation ("I have come to set the captives free"), what place prisons have within the kingdom of God. We have many friends who know that God wants more than punitive justice and have begun beautiful projects of restorative justice, bringing victims and offenders together to listen to one another, ultimately trusting that God is a God of reconciliation.

One of the most beautiful stories we know of setting captives free is of a prison chaplain we met overseas. He was working in a maximum security prison and was overwhelmed with the hopelessness of it all. But when he looked at the history of prisons, he found that they were never meant to warehouse people in dungeons of despair but were to provide a space away from society where offenders could repent, or rethink how they were living, and be restored to society. That's why prison rooms were called cells; prisons were to be monasteries of sorts where people could be with God in solitary confinement.

10 It is worth noting that the thirteenth amendment of the Constitution reads, "Slavery or involuntary servitude is illegal ... unless the person is convicted of a crime." Now one in three African-American men is in prison or under judicial constraint. And corporations can hire prisoners to work for far below minimum wage. The prison-industrial complex is one of the fastest-growing industries. Slavery did not end; it only changed. Thankfully, Jesus declares that he has come to set captives free. For more on this, check out our friend Mark Lewis Taylor's book *The Executed God: The Way of the Cross in Lockdown America* (Minneapolis: Augsburg Fortress, 2001).

This chaplain got a vision from God of turning the prison into a monastery. So he began thirty-day silent retreats with ten men at a time. On these retreats, the men become like a family of monks. They confess sins. They contemplate the passion of Christ. (The cross is located in the waste room of the prison, so the men go to be with Jesus, think on the sins of the world, and smell the stench of it all around them.) Then they experience cleansing and burn their lists of sins. (And for some, it's quite a bonfire.) Then they turn their jail cells into monastic cells; each cell has an altar in it. The hell is transformed. And the prisoners become monks.

God's Streets

A few years back, our friends in Chicago were having some hard times. On the one hand, crime was out of control. Cars were being stolen, drugs were everywhere, and street violence had trapped the neighborhood in fear. The police were not very helpful. They had become notorious for misconduct, racism, and brutality. So our friends at Lawndale Community Church began praying and conspiring. They decided to put some flesh on their prayers and to organize their own security team. There's an amazing group of folks in Lawndale called Hope House—men in recovery from substance addictions, men who are familiar with the streets and with the uglier side of police violence. They organized themselves, got some bright security vests, and stationed themselves on the street corners, where they would work shifts throughout the night. With a little creativity and courage, and with fresh eyes and prayerful hearts on every corner, the ugliness of the streets and of the police was neutralized. Love, especially when it's organized on every corner, really can drive out fear.

Living with Old People

In its worship of all things new and hip, US culture has sacrificed its relationship with the elderly and infirm. And most of the church has done exactly the same, putting older people into nursing homes and retirement centers. One community we have encountered has taken another path. They take care of people from the cradle to the grave. One time when I visited this community, one of its elderly folks was dying. His grandson had taken off work for a few months to take care of him and push him around the community in his wheelchair. His grandpa still made appearances at the community business, where he took his time putting together easy pieces for its manufacturing process and shared his time-tested wisdom with anyone around. At other times, when members were nearing death, everybody in the community would gather outside their window to sing them songs.

Another couple of our friends, Darin and Meeghan, grew to love an elderly lady named Guinn, whom they had met in the projects of Omaha. Guinn was afflicted with Alzheimer's and had no friends or family to care for her. As the government began to tear down affordable housing, Darin and Meeghan were faced with a difficult question: What is going to happen to Guinn? As they prayed and struggled, they tried everything they could think of to help Guinn live independently for as long as possible, as she wished. It started out with simple things, such as having meals together and doing her laundry while they talked. It progressed to helping her bathe at their home, setting up her daily medication for her, taking her to appointments, and managing her financial affairs. After a lot of work, it became clear that it was no longer the best option for Guinn to live on her own. Darin and Meeghan took part in the tough decision to help her move from independent living to a country nursing home. As Meeghan cleaned out Guinn's apartment, she came across an old, weathered 3 x 5 card that read, "Don't put me in a nursing home," signed in small print "Guinnevere G. Collins."

Darin and Meeghan wrestled with what it meant to be family to Guinn, who had no kids and never married. Eventually, they became the answer to their own prayers, adopting Guinn. Now they have lived together for more than four years. It isn't always easy. Guinn's sickness has gotten much worse. She's a wild and eccentric old diva (she used to be an aspiring actress), so every moment is an adventure as she tries to remember where she is. Every hour she asks, "Is this the Alps? Are we in England?" and sometimes Darin and Meegs will let her choose her adventure for the day or the hour. They have helped her find ways to continue to paint and make art. And she makes them smile as she tells dirty jokes and looks for her boyfriends and does her little booty-shake boogy when she gets excited. A little while back, Darin and Meegs had a child, and now Guinn comes to life as she holds little Justice. And Darin, Meeghan, and Justice will help Guinn make the transition from this world with a smile on her face and a family around her.

Give to Uncle Sam What Is Uncle Sam's

It's hard to know what Jesus would do about paying taxes if he were a citizen in the ole US of A, where nearly half of every tax dollar (the same dollars that say "In God We Trust") goes to the war machine. And yet the more you look at the eerie similarities between the Roman Empire and the American Empire, the more you get some idea of what he might do. Like the Roman Empire, the American Empire is loved by some and hated by others, but feared by everyone. And scholars estimate that Rome's military expenditures, like the US's, were also around 50 percent of the budget. So if the IRS came to Jesus, what would he do? Pull the money out of a fish's mouth? What if we can't pull that one off (or don't have a lake nearby)?

Christians all over the empire are living with the same prophetic creativity as Jesus did. Many folks live so far below the poverty line that they never even show up on Uncle Sam's radar screen. Is it lawful to pay taxes? Jesus' answer might be, "Live in simplicity, and there won't be anything for Uncle Sam to take from you." Many Christian communities, such as Reba Place in Chicago, live off the grid to such an extent that the government has a category for them known as an "apostolic order" under section 501d3 of the government code! They just don't know what to do with these Jesus freaks!

The idea of war tax resistance has emerged in fresh ways in this era of military building. One of our favorite approaches to taxes, which is employed by many Christians in the US, is to send a letter to the IRS along with a check for a portion of the taxes owed and a receipt showing that the sender has donated the amount that would have gone toward weapons to a nonprofit doing the work of the kingdom of God. Usually such letters applaud the use of tax money to benefit the poor

and the common good (which is about half of all tax receipts)
but lets the government know that as people of the gospel,
we are peacemakers and cannot contribute to the destruction
of life. Deeply disturbed by the amount of money going
toward weapons, many Christians are unable to support such
expenditures, just as the early Christians could not burn incense to
Caesar.*

May the one who pulled money from the mouth of the fish guide
us in revolutionary subordination to
our Caesars.

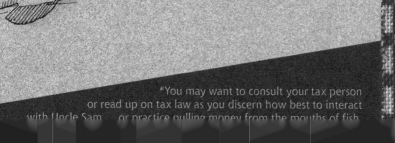

*You may want to consult your tax person
or read up on tax law as you discern how best to interact
with Uncle Sam ... or practice pulling money from the mouths of fish.

Make Stuff

One of the ways we can embody a new economy and politics is by making our own stuff from the scraps of the empire. In our communities, we are able to make many of the things we need. We have friends who make shoes from tires. We have lovely bags made from curtains, using seatbelts and bike tires for straps. When we drink from our mugs, we know where they came from, because we made them. Each creation is a small act of resistance to the corporate global economy. It's also a lovely way to bond with each other as we make candles or paper. Shane and his mom make clothes together each winter (perhaps helping to fulfill his mom's wish for a little girl). As a wedding gift, they made pants for the men in Chris and Cassie's wedding. These are

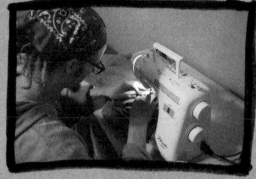

things that give meaning to the work of our hands, substance to our days, since we are created in the image of an artistic God.

For Gandhi, the spinning wheel was the symbol of the movement to nonviolently counter the British occupation and colonization of India in the early twentieth century. Making their own cloth was a way of saying, "We don't have to be dependent on the society that is oppressing us." We will march to the sea and get our own salt. We will grow our own food, and sew our own clothes. They were no longer dependent on the king's economy. In fact, folks said you could tell how broadly the

revolution had spread because people were wearing homespun clothing
even in the government buildings and in parliament!

A story goes that Gandhi went off to an important
meeting with British royalty. He arrived wearing his
usual rags, the typical attire of India's poor.
  On the way, a news reporter stopped him and noting
     his clothes said, "Why didn't you wear more clothing,
knowing you were going to meet the king?"
                        Gandhi said to him with a smile,
     "I knew he'd have enough clothes for both of us."

Besides, it's fun to make stuff. We had a youth group write us to let us
know they had begun making their own clothes together and were having
a blast. It had created a sense of community in ways that no Disneyland
trip ever could. And it was their little way of "protestifying" against the
abuse of overseas workers that breaks the heart of our God. Another
youth group said they had taken their kids out in the cotton fields to pick
cotton so that they could remember their ancestors, and so that they could
begin to think about the hidden faces behind our way of life. As the kids
got their hands dirty and scratched up, had the sun's heat beating on their
sweaty bodies, and felt the soreness of their backs the next day, they had
new eyes to see the people laboring all over the world to make the things
we buy and dispose of.

We visited one college where the Young Republicans and the social justice
club had become quite polarized. In a beautiful gesture of grace, they
got together to find common ground. While there wasn't much they
could agree on ideologically, politically, or socially, they could agree that
homeless people shouldn't freeze on the streets. So they began making
blankets together and taking them to the streets. Something mystical
can happen in the course of acting together that transcends words and
ideologies—people who do not agree on ideas can create common
ground in the act of loving. And frankly, the folks on the street probably
couldn't care less who the students voted for in the last election.

A Real Security Plan

The rain forests of Belize are not an easy place to farm. Farmers there work hard to till and nourish nutrient-poor soil. Most agricultural fertility is locked in the huge leaves of the green canopy, having been rapidly cooked out of the soil by the rainforest heat and humidity. The scurrying ants carry away for their own purposes any leaves that would enrich the soil.

So their farming is an uphill battle. They irrigate their crops with precious water dripping from pinholes in hoses running along their rows of carrots, lettuce, and other greens. They travel by way of horses and run their sawmill with them. Certainly, they have very little monetary wealth and don't need much. Their hard, co-operative work and skill is their wealth.

Nevertheless, armed bandits at times steal what money they have. A robber recently came into their community while they were away, broke into their houses, and took their money. The police found this man and imprisoned him. In response, the farming community did two things: (1) they printed money that is useless in the national economy and useful only in their farming village, removing the incentive to steal from them, and (2) when the robber was released from prison, they found him and built him a house. Without a doubt, this thief was "converted."

While the most obvious realities of this story are the farmers' nonviolence and creativity, we must see what makes their nonviolence possible. Certainly, belief in Jesus' teachings is at the root of their obedience and creativity. However, believing in Jesus often looks different from actually following him. A multitude of "sold-out" Christians say they "just want to do what Jesus taught," but we wouldn't suggest testing their commitment by striking them on one cheek and waiting for them to turn the other. For most people, too much comes in the way of doing what Jesus did and taught. Economic and social factors (which take time and effort to nurture) can either help us or hinder us in doing what Jesus taught.

A major factor in this community's response to violence and theft is communal economic strength. It's not that they are rich in any worldly sense. But the farmers' economic lives are structured in such a way that their community gets them through trials. They live with confidence in the face of conflict because the community has proven itself able to withstand living with less. They understand that they are not alone. Because their survival comes not from making money but from sweat, acquired skills, and communal work, they do not fear theft. They know how to make a living without making money off of somebody else. They can make their own lumber, build their own houses, make their own clothes, and grow their own crops. Because they do not store up treasures on earth, they are not tempted to kill the intruder. They can pray, "As we forgive those who trespass against us," because they know how to work to absorb a transgression.

Our individuated lifestyle of single-family dwellings, a car per person, and a house full of "my" stuff purchased cheaply from China makes it harder to follow Jesus, even for those with the best of intentions. When your house is built on sand, you waste energy keeping it from being knocked over. In the farmers' case, strong community economics makes theft easy to overcome. Free from the economic fear of being toppled by the enemy, they can focus outwardly on the harder task of redeeming their enemy. You cannot follow Jesus socially (in relation to your enemy) if you are not following Jesus economically.

The Third Way of Jesus

Criminologists teach that one of the quickest ways to diffuse violence is by doing the unexpected. Those who commit violence depend on the predictability of their victims. When their victims do something that surprises them, it throws the whole plan out of whack. Jesus is always doing weird things in the midst of conflict. When the men are about to stone the adulteress, he bends down and draws in the dirt, and eventually they all drop their stones. There's that time when the soldiers come to arrest Jesus, and Peter pulls out a sword and cuts off a guy's ear. Jesus rebukes him, and then grabs the dude's ear and puts it back on. That must have been a little awkward for everyone, especially the soldiers. (How do you arrest a guy who just put your buddy's ear back on?) Jesus' theological stunts and prophetic imagination surprise and disarm. They make people laugh and catch folks off-guard, even folks who wish they could hate him.

We catch another glimpse of this disarming grace in the musical *Les Miserables*, in which a priest allows a vagrant, Jean Valjean, to stay in his home, only to find himself knocked unconscious and his home robbed. The next day, the authorities catch Jean Valjean and drag him before the priest, telling him that Valjean claimed the priest gave him the silver goods in his bag. And the priest instinctively, beautifully, says, "I am so thankful you have come back, because you forgot the candlesticks." As the authorities release Jean Valjean, the priest whispers in his ear, "With this, I have ransomed your soul."

Sounds good—musicals can do that for you—but it's not that easy. When someone stole our power drill (and we all knew who), we didn't run after the person with the drill bits, calling, "Hey, my friend, you forgot these." We're more inclined to teach a lesson of justice than a lesson of love.

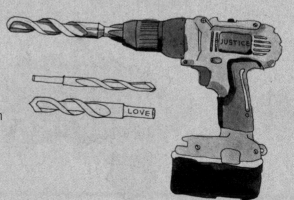

Love takes courage. One of the neighborhood kids who hangs out at our house all the time came up to us one day very upset because one of the bullies in his school was picking on him. We told him, "Rolando, that means you get to show him how friends treat each other. He must not know what love and friendship feel like, so you get to teach him." And Rolando said, "Aww man, love is so hard."

> Love is a harsh and dreadful thing to ask of us, but it is the only answer.
>
> —Dorothy Day

263

Bustin' Out a Can of Grace

Kassim, a great kid who lives in our neighborhood, is eleven, and his mom doesn't let him out a lot. He's the sort of gentle kid you never want to see lose his innocence and trust or have his heart grow hard. He likes cooking with us, gardening, getting beat at Othello, even cleaning the house or doing homework.

One time Kassim and I (Shane) were walking to the post office, a walk I take several times a week. We were walking down a narrow side street, and some teenage guys started following us. You could just feel the mischief brewing, and the group grew from two young men to four to eight, until there was a little mob of sorts. They started calling out some names, throwing rocks and sticks, trying to stir up trouble. It's always hard on the spot like that to know what Jesus would do. I told Kassim, "Let's go say hi." He looked at me skeptically. We turned back and walked toward them, knowing full well that if we had run, we probably would have made it to the post office. "Hey, I'm Shane. And this is my friend Kassim. We live around the corner," I said with my hand out. They weren't really sure what to do with that. A couple of them shook my hand and introduced themselves. Others snickered. One or two refused the handshake. We said, "Nice to meet you guys," and headed back on our walk.

With the wind taken out of their sails a bit, they regrouped and continued to build momentum toward a brawl. They ran after us, throwing some rocks and bottles, and I noticed two of them now carried broomsticks from the trash. We picked up the pace a bit, and then I looked at Kassim and said, "No, don't run." We turned back, and before we knew it, one of them had clocked Kassim on the side of the head with a stick. I said firmly, "Why would you do that? We haven't done anything to hurt you." They laughed. Then they started hitting me with a broomstick until it broke over my back. At this point I decided to bust out a can of holy anger. I looked them in the eyes and said as forcefully as I could, "You are created in the image of God ... every single one of you. And you were made for something better than this. Kassim and I are followers of Jesus and we do not fight, but we will love you no matter what you do to us." That wasn't exactly what they expected or hoped for. They looked at each other, startled a bit. For the first time they were quiet. And then they scurried off in every direction.

I'll never forget what Kassim said afterward. "Shane, why am I taking boxing lessons?" We laughed at the irony of it, having just experienced a prime chance to implement his mad skillz. I asked Kassim what he thought would have happened if he had chosen to fight. "It would have been ugly," he said. "They might have been bloody, and we probably would have been real bloody." No one would have left any nicer, that was for sure.

I asked Kassim if he thought Jesus was happy with how we acted. He thought about it, and then nodded with a smile. I told him that, honestly, I wasn't sure what Jesus would have done if he were in our place, but there are two things I know Jesus would not have done. He would not have fought. And he would not have run. I told him Jesus might have thought of something else, or he might have done something weird to throw them off, as he often seemed to do—like writing on the road with sidewalk chalk, "You are better than this," or maybe pulling candy from a pigeon's mouth for them—but I thought that Jesus was happy with how we acted, that we were good representatives, good witnesses, of Christ to them. Not only did we refuse to hit, but we refused to hate. Kassim agreed, and then we prayed for them together. And finally, as he was leaving, Kassim reminded me that each of those boys had to go to bed thinking about what they did that day, and so did we.

I'm not sure about those other boys, but Kassim and I both slept well that night … and woke up a little sore but happy the next morning. Hopefully Kassim's mom will let him come out of the house again.

Like King David

One time when I (Chris) was down in Belize, the farmers played a trick on me. I had asked if I could take a ride on a horse, and they saddled one up for me. I got on, and before long, he had disobeyed all of my requests, running as fast as possible. When I returned to the farmers, I could tell they had given me one of the more volatile horses. I forgave them anyway.

One of the farmers said, "We didn't always have that horse. He's new."

"Where is the old one?" I asked.

"Some *banditos* came into our community and stole him. We could tell he didn't run away; we found him already tied up in the nearby woods."

"You found him ..." I said. "Umm ... if you found him, why is he not here?"

"Oh," he said, "we cut the mane and the tail and left the hair there with the horse."

"What? I don't understand," I said.

He was also a little confused. He looked at the group I was with. There were seventeen of us. We had come to Belize to study abroad. We were a pack of clean, spunky Christian college students who looked like we'd come straight from Minnesota.

"Aren't you all Christians?" he asked, trying not to give offense.

"Sure we are," someone in the group said.

"Well …" he said. "Haven't you all read the Bible?"

We all nodded and assured him that we believed that the Bible is the inspired Word of God.

He said, "Well, if you are familiar with the Bible, you might recall the story of David and Saul in the cave. Saul was tracking David to kill him, and they both ended up in the cave. David could have killed Saul in the dark, but he showed him mercy and love by simply cutting the edge of his cloak, unbeknownst to Saul. Saul figured it out later."

Our ever-so-Christian group still didn't understand why they didn't take back

their horse, which I'm sure was worth as much as a car to them. We all silently looked around the group, waiting for the punch line.

He said, "If that doesn't make sense, you might be familiar with Jesus. Right?" He described how Jesus taught his followers to deal with evil by overcoming it with good. Jesus taught and showed us how to love our enemies, our new farmer friend told us.

Lydia

In the early days of the Simple Way, a young woman from Brazil named Lydia was living in the community. She was petite, and, like many of the women in our community, she was a fireball—sassy, bold, somehow able to be both gentle and direct. One day as she was traveling on the train, a fellow sat down next to her and pulled a knife. "Listen carefully," he said, "here's what's gonna happen. You are going to hand me your bag, get off at the next station, and not say a word." She looked at him unflinchinchingly. "My name is Lydia," she said winsomely, firmly, "and I am from Brazil." The man stared at her blankly, taken aback. She continued, "My bag is filled with photos and addresses of my family and those mean a lot to me but will do you no good. I'd imagine what you want is money. There is no money in my bag, However, I have some money in my pocket, so here's what we'll do. I'll get out my money, give you twenty dollars, you get off at the next station, and we won't say a word." And it worked.

Practicing Forgiveness

Randomly, we saw one of those World's Best Video clips a while back. One of them captured a hockey game in which one of the key players went for a shot, and then everything went crazy and erupted into a brawl. This player was famous for his gentle spirit and love for the game. He hated it when players fought, so when the fight broke out, he pulled aside. And as it escalated, he decided to create a distraction, so he ripped his gear off and started streaking the hockey rink. As you can imagine, the fight didn't last long.

"Okay, that's great," you say, "but what if you live in Darfur, where hundreds of thousands of people have been mercilessly slaughtered and more than two million have been displaced by violence?"

We have a friend named Celestin who grew up in Rwanda during the genocide when about a million people were mercilessly killed. In the middle of that madness, Celestin became a pastor and felt God calling him to teach tribal reconciliation to the Hutus and Tutsi during the conflict. Forgiveness wasn't very fashionable, and he landed on the hit list of both tribes because he called them to repent of their violence. He was beaten again and again and saw some of his closest friends tortured and killed. At times he was angry, confused, heartbroken, but he never ceased preaching about the nonviolent Jesus. In December 1998, militants came into the village and killed more than seventy people in Celestin's congregation and village, including Celestin's father. And yet he continued to preach the gospel of reconciliation, with blood on all sides. Eventually one of the relatives of the soldiers who killed Celestin's church members surrendered his life to Christ, put down the sword, and took up the

cross. Now that person is the caretaker for Celestin's aging mother, as an act of repentance. That's the gospel of grace.[11]

These are the stories that don't make the news. But these are the stories that change the world. The ripples from one soldier's conversion are immeasurable, and their potential to disarm a conflict is mystical. We are no longer talking about an eye for an eye and a bomb for a bomb but about how one person committed to enemy-love can transform an entire conflict.

11 This fellow, along with Celestin, now serves on the ALARM Rwanda board working to end the violence. Celestin continues his work for reconciliation, training Muslim community leaders and Christian pastors in peacemaking. At the time we were writing this book, Celestin dropped us an email from a training camp in Uganda with these words: "Only the cross, not nationalism or patriotism, is the common ground for divided communities."

Fighting with Fruit

In the midst of this Iraq war, people in the US have become polarized, and hatred and anger often seem to dominate, no matter which side you are on. Friends at the Camden Houses did something beautiful. They each dressed in sackcloth with one of the words of the fruit of the Spirit sewn on it—love, joy, peace, patience, kindness, goodness, faithfulness, gentleness, and self-control—fruit that most revolutions are starving for. And then they walked into the middle of the war protests, a witness of the Spirit to both the warmongers and the Bush bashers. That's the sort of thing that makes us laugh and nudges us all a little closer to God.[12]

When I (Shane) spoke to a congregation not long ago, it turned out that one of their young men was headed to Iraq soon. After my sermon on peacemaking, the pastor spontaneously asked me to pray for the soldier.

12 The women in several of the communities in Philly organized a similar witness at a march for women's rights that had attracted a counterdemonstration by pro-life activists. They went to build bridges and talk with people on both sides.

What was I to pray? I prayed the fruit of the Spirit, slowly naming them one by one, and asked that God would help those things to live in him. The young recruit came up to me afterward with tears in his eyes and said that was exactly what he needed to hear, because those were not things being instilled in him in the army. I told him that if he felt the fruit of the Spirit could not survive in him in the military to let us know and we would help him get out.

When we talk about peacemaking and the "third way of Jesus," people inevitably ask bizarre situational questions like, "If someone broke into your house and was raping your grandmother, what would you do?" We can't exhaustively troubleshoot every situation with a nonviolent "strategy,"[13] but what we can do is internalize the character and spirit of Jesus. We can meditate daily on the fruit of the Spirit and pray that they take root in us. Then we can trust that when we encounter a bad situation, we will act like Jesus.

At one festival, I was asked after a talk, "What would you do if you lived in Darfur and had a gang of young men running at you with machetes?" I thought such a strange question deserved an equally far-out answer, so I said, "I'd take off all my clothes and run around like a chicken, squawking wildly and pecking at the ground with my mouth." I figure the chicken response is about as likely to disarm a mob of young hooligans as my trying to fight them. Either response would be ugly, but I'd opt for the former. I've already decided that the next time I get jumped, I'm going to turn some backflips and act like a ninja. Or I might just get on my knees and start speaking in tongues. Either seems as likely to hold promising results. At any rate, these aren't solutions for the tragic situations of brothers and sisters in areas like the Sudan. Without a doubt, protecting the innocent is one of the strongest arguments for redemptive violence. A bunch of folks running around like naked chickens is not a solution to the crisis there. But the story of my friend Celestin is. After all Jesus, didn't say, "Greater love has no one than this, to kill to protect the innocent."

13 John Howard Yoder gives this question thorough treatment in his book *What Would You Do?* (Scottdale, PA: Herald Press, 1992).

Getting in the Way: Christian Peacemaker Teams

Unless we are prepared to risk injury and death in nonviolent opposition to the injustice our societies foster, we don't dare even whisper another word about pacifism to our sisters and brothers in those desperate lands. Unless we are ready to die developing new nonviolent attempts to reduce international conflict, we should confess that we never really meant the cross was an alternative to the sword. Unless the majority of our people in nuclear nations are ready as congregations to risk social disapproval and government harassment in a clear call to live without nuclear weapons, we should sadly acknowledge that we have betrayed our peacemaking heritage. Making peace is as costly as waging war. Unless we are prepared to pay the cost of peacemaking, we have no right to claim the label or preach the message.

—Ron Sider (speaking at the Mennonite World Conference, 1984)

Amish for Homeland Security

Do you remember how the Amish responded to the act of terror in their school, when a gunman killed five Amish children in 2006? Our friend Diana Butler Bass wrote an article pontificating what the world would look like if the Amish had led us after September 11.[14] Consider their response to the murders, a response that fascinated the world. Within the first week after the shootings, the Amish families who had suffered such terror responded in four ways that captured the world's attention. First, some elders visited Marie Roberts, the wife of the murderer, to offer forgiveness. Then, the families of the slain girls invited the widow to their own children's funerals. Next, they requested that all relief money intended for the Amish families be shared with Ms. Roberts and her children. And finally, in an astonishing act of reconciliation, dozens of Amish families attended the funeral of the killer.

Diana goes on to share that she talked with her husband about the spiritual power of these actions, commenting, "It is an amazing witness to the peace tradition." And her husband looked at her and said passionately, "Witness? I don't think so. This went well past witnessing. They weren't witnessing to anything. They were actively *making* peace." Her article ends with these words, as she reflected on that truth:

> Their actions not only witness that the Christian God is a God of forgiveness, but they actively created the conditions in which forgiveness could happen. In the most straightforward way, they embarked on imitating Christ: "Father, forgive them; they know not what they do." In acting as Christ, they did not speculate on forgiveness. They forgave. And forgiveness is, as Christianity teaches, the prerequisite to peace. We forgive because God forgave us; in forgiving, we participate in God's dream of reconciliation and shalom.

14 This article originally appeared on the God's Politics Blog (www. godspolitics.com), presented by *Sojourners* and Beliefnet. Excerpt quoted with permission.

Then an odd thought occurred to me: What if the Amish were in charge of the war on terror? What if, on the evening of Sept. 12, 2001, we had gone to Osama bin Laden's house (metaphorically, of course, since we didn't know where he lived!) and offered him forgiveness? What if we had invited the families of the hijackers to the funerals of the victims of 9/11? What if a portion of the September 11th Fund had been dedicated to relieving poverty in a Muslim country? What if we dignified the burial of their dead by our respectful grief? What if, instead of seeking vengeance, we had stood together in human pain, looking honestly at the shared sin and sadness we suffered? What if we had tried to make peace? So, here's my modest proposal. We're five years too late for an Amish response to 9/11. But maybe we should ask them to take over the Department of Homeland Security. After all, actively practicing forgiveness and making peace are the only real alternatives to perpetual fear and a multi-generational global religious war. I can't imagine any other path to true security. And nobody else can figure out what to do to end this insane war. Why not try the Christian practice of forgiveness? If it worked in Lancaster, maybe it will work in Baghdad, too.

Well said sista', a lovely addition to the campaign.

Jesus for president and the Amish for Homeland Security.[15]

Amen.

15 For more reading on the beautiful redemptive love practiced during this tragedy, check out *Amish Grace: How Forgiveness Transcended Tragedy* by Donald Kraybill, Steven Nolt, and David Weaver-Zercher (San Francisco: Jossey-Bass, 2007).

Bearing a Cross

If the cross—willingly suffering at the hands of the powers—is such a central message to the Gospels, the church will need to reconsider its political worldview. The cross wasn't a politically triumphant "reclaiming Israel for God" or a prideful assertion of Israel's privilege in the world. Rather the cross is the sign of God's humble way in the world: instead of ruling the world through a sword, God would wash its feet with a towel.[16] The crucifixion story is not only about Jesus' suffering love. The biblical story carries us from believing in Jesus to imitating him. We join him in his way of the cross. "But thanks be to God, who always leads us as captives in Christ's triumphal procession and uses us to spread the aroma of the knowledge of him everywhere. For we are to God the pleasing aroma of Christ among those who are being saved and those who are perishing. To the one we are an aroma that brings death; to the other, an aroma that brings life" (2 Cor. 2:14–16).

How astounding it is that Jesus' "triumphal" procession is his bloody crawl to his torture and execution. Jesus didn't consider the way of the cross something he simply accomplished for the sake of others' salvation, but he insisted, "You cannot be my disciples unless you too pick up your cross and follow me." In addition to Jesus' commonly ignored teachings in the Sermon on the Mount, Jesus also taught nonviolence when he said, "I send you out as sheep among wolves." Jesus knew that his followers would face threats to their lives. But nowhere did Jesus teach that his followers should turn into wolves when they run into other scary wolves. He himself was killed like a sheep by wolves. By freely accepting crucifixion, he demonstrated what a sheep among wolves looks like. Refusing to become like the wolves to defeat the wolves, Jesus revealed that God, being love, chooses a different path—to suffer evil to overcome it.

16 A phrase put into circulation through Stanley Hauerwas.

A deep fellowship of the suffering (Phil. 3:10) grows among those who carry the cross, a fellowship based on the joy that comes from faith in a God who is overcoming the ways of the world. Suffering is a way to see God. The martyrs embody for us the story of Jesus. They become the body of Christ.

As Paul wrote to the people in Philippi, "In your relationships with one another, *have the same attitude of mind Christ Jesus had*: who, being in very nature God, did not consider equality with God something to be used to his own advantage; rather, he made himself nothing by taking the very nature of a servant, being made in human likeness. And being found in appearance as a human being, he humbled himself by becoming obedient to death—even death on a cross! Therefore God exalted him to the highest place and gave him the name that is above every name, that at the name of Jesus every knee should bow, in heaven and on earth and under the earth, and every tongue acknowledge that Jesus Christ is Lord, to the glory of God the Father" (Phil. 2:5–11, emphasis added).

Let's not get the wrong idea about imitating Jesus. We are not all called to imitate Jesus' homeless nomadicism, his life as a tradesman, or other aspects of his life. The only thing all Christians are called by the New Testament to imitate is Jesus' taking up his cross. Christians are people who are "crucified with Christ."[17] Christ died so that we might live. Now we are to die so that Christ might live.

And we must be cautious not to abuse the idea of "bearing our cross." The cross is too easily turned into a religious metaphor for any of our hardships. But the Bible never waters down the cross into a mere symbol that can make us feel more spiritual by wearing it around our necks. No,

---

17 "Every strand of New Testament literature testifies to a direct relationship between the way Christ suffered on the cross and the way the Christian, as disciple, is called to suffer in the face of evil" (John Howard Yoder, *The Original Revolution* [Scottdale, PA: Herald Press, 2003], 57).

the cross is the execution tool of the state that killed Jesus and countless insurgents. And it is the place where Jesus faced and overcame violence with love. How ironic when someone gets a tattoo of Jesus on the cross but has no problem with religiously condoning violence. Too often a cross is placed in a house to signify respectability, symbolically saying, "Hey, we're good people." "The cross of Calvary was not a difficult family situation, not a frustration of visions of personal fulfillment, a crushing debt, or a nagging in-law; it was the political, legally-to-be-expected result of a moral clash with the powers ruling [Jesus'] society."[18] There are plenty of biblical motifs to counsel, soothe, and care for people in their troubles, but the cross is not one of them.

To say that the cross is the way of salvation is not to say, "Seek persecution and suffering." The fellowship that comes from suffering is not group masochism. It is not suffering, per se, that is great. Certainly, suffering has led many not to love but to hatred and bitterness. And the Bible clearly counsels against thinking that any kind of trial is meaningful (1 Peter 2:18–21; 3:14–18; 4:1, 13–16; 5:9; James 4:10).[19] Rather, it is *love* that is great, and it's in the midst of suffering and violence that that light shines brightest.

Jesus' telling his disciples to take up their cross was like asking those young revolutionaries to pick up their handcuffs, because they were about to get into trouble.

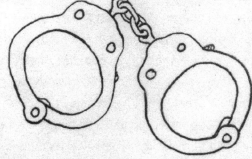

18 John Howard Yoder, *The Politics of Jesus* (Grand Rapids: Eerdmans, 1994), 129.
19 Ibid.

Practicing Revolutionary Patience

Immediately following the Al Qaeda attacks of September 11th, President George Bush proclaimed, "Our responsibility to history is already clear: to answer these attacks and rid the world of evil."

In this speech (and countless speeches like it throughout history), history seems to play the role of God. It is the transcendent judge and mysterious entity to which we owe a moral responsibility. Not only do we owe it our obedience, but also history can actually call on us. This history-god of the state necessarily replaces the supposed God of many of those running the United States: Jesus Christ. The government is teeming with self-proclaimed Christians whose goal is to rid the world of evil. But they cannot obey Jesus and satisfy the state. Jesus was detestable to the state in his day, and he is detestable to our state today. His teachings are impossible for the state to ever follow. What state would ever say, "Do not resist the evil person," or, "Turn the other cheek"? Indeed, for a Christian to participate in ridding the world of evil, one must replace Jesus with the history-god of the state.

or GET READY TO LOSE THEIR JOBS

The problem with this history-god is that it has no described nature or character. When it calls, how does it call? Does it always call us to the same type of action? Does history prefer love over vengeance or mercy over justice? Christians must discern between the voices competing for their allegiance. Is history's voice the same as Jesus'? Does it call us to do the same things Jesus did? And whose history are we talking about? Considering that history has recently called the US to execute disastrous wars in Afghanistan and Iraq, resulting in the deaths of hundreds of thousands of civilians, we can know that this is not the voice of the shepherd who calls his sheep to love their enemies.

President Bush's speech also promoted the popular goal of ridding the world of evil. This goal is not new. The ostensibly good intention to rid the world of evil, ironically, is associated with some of the most evil and tragic events in history. Even, Osama bin Laden's stated goal, more or less, was to rid the world of evil.[20] Three thousand people were killed in the tragedies of 9/11 in the hope of destroying evil.

Another example is the United States' ill-advised avenging of those attacks in Afghanistan and Iraq. If killing three thousand innocent civilians is a heinous evil, then the US has inflicted more evil upon the world than Al Qaeda could ever imagine inflicting. In the summer of 2006, reports were released informing the public that the conservative death toll of fifty to sixty thousand innocent civilians killed in Iraq is vastly understated, and that the estimate of 654,965 is much more appropriate and conservative.[21] (This is not to say that if these wars had killed several thousand fewer people it would have been acceptable for Christians to join in. It simply shows that violent attempts to rid the world of evil will never achieve anything remotely close to that goal, much less receive God's blessing.) Imagine the terror and evil of an attack two hundred times the devastation of 9/11. The people of Iraq have experienced nothing less. Ridding the

20 Hence, the attacks were directed at the two places Al Qaeda sees world evil operating from: the Pentagon and the centers of world trade. In a video, purportedly of bin Laden, released on October 29, 2004, bin Laden stated (proving that he too wants to rid the world of evil), "While I was looking at these destroyed towers [by a US-aided Israeli bombardment] in Lebanon, it sparked in my mind that the tyrant should be punished with the same and that we should destroy towers in America, so that it tastes what we taste and would be deterred from killing our children and women. ... If Bush says we hate freedom, let him tell us why we didn't attack Sweden, for example. It is known that those who hate freedom do not have dignified souls" (BBC, "Excerpts: Bin Laden Video," October 29, 2003).

"I say to you, Allah knows that it had never occurred to us to strike the towers. But after it became unbearable and we witnessed the oppression and tyranny of the American/Israeli coalition against our people in Palestine and Lebanon, it came to my mind" (Al Jazeera, full transcript of speech by bin Laden delivered November 1, 2004).

21 See *Lancet Medical Journal*'s "Mortality after 2003 Invasion of Iraq: A Cross-sectional Cluster Sample Survey," *The Lancet* 368, no. 9545 (October 21, 2006): 1421–28.

world of evil by violent means only creates and sustains evil. This is the point of Jesus' politics. The parable of the weeds and the wheat is among the clearest illustrations we have of how Jesus deals with the evil of the world.

Cutting against our scientific modes of thought, *hope in God* is an essential part of Jesus' politics on ridding the world of evil. As the parable of the weeds and wheat illustrates, Jesus understood the destruction of evil to be not in human hands but in God's hands. Though such an understanding could be abused in a number of ways, we can't get around the fact that Jesus' nonviolent dealing with evil is founded on an eschatological hope. Jesus had faith in how God ultimately deals with the world.[22] We must also point out that all views (including the most atheistic) have their own take on how things ultimately get worked out in the world.

The New Testament view of God's ultimate dealing with the world is Jesus' second coming. Jesus has been known as the "one who is coming into the world." Christians claim he embodies hope of the wonderful world to come. He represents the coming justice for the world. Christians claim that all of the hopes for saving (or "healing") the world are satisfied through the coming of the expected one. Jesus came, he healed, he lived the kingdom, and he was killed. And yet, even when the one who is awaited finally comes, hope and expectation are not quelled. Expectation is again raised: *Christ will come again.* To have this hope is to politically apply the parable of the weeds: don't pull out the weeds but wait until the harvest.

22 The popular definition of *eschatology* must be broadened to include this present life, not simply the end of the world. John Yoder writes that eschatology is a "doctrine of what is ultimate" (Yoder, *The Original Revolution*, 52), and, "The *eschaton*, the 'Last Thing,' the End-Event, imparts to life a meaningfulness which it would not otherwise have. ... This is what we mean by eschatology: a hope which, defying present frustration, defines a present position in terms of the yet unseen goal which gives it meaning" (53). Yoder goes on to distinguish eschatology from the fashionable moneymaking work of "apocalyptics," which speculates on dates and the shape of things to come: "[E]ven when an apocalyptic type of literature occurs [in the Bible], its preoccupation is not with the prediction for the sake of prediction, but rather with the meaning which the future has for the *present*" (54).

The practical point of the second coming is not to look up at the sky in expectation (1 Thessalonians is written largely against this misguided hope) but to live in a certain way. The second coming imparts political and practical meaning and shapes the way we view the world.

Hope for the second coming is not just about hope *in* Jesus; it is about having a hope *like* Jesus'. His hope in God is on display in his parable of the weeds: trusting that God will sort out the evildoers. Living in hope of God's coming to us purifies us, for we live not impulsively or rashly but with the sense that matters are ultimately in God's hands. "Leaving things in God's hands" is an often abused and quaint phrase that many seem to think means "don't bother with doing anything, because Jesus will come someday and undo all your work anyway." Or even worse, some might say, "Let things get worse in the world, then Jesus will come back even sooner."

"Leaving things in God's hands" should rather be used to mean "do what Jesus did." Follow Jesus' example without regard for whether you are effectively "changing the world." Jesus demonstrated what it means to leave things in God's hands. So if we want to know what it means for us to trust in Jesus, we should ask what it meant for Jesus to trust in God.

For it is commendable if you bear up under the pain of unjust suffering because you are conscious of God ... When they hurled their insults at him, he did not retaliate, when he suffered, he made no threats. Instead he entrusted himself to him who judges justly. --I Peter 2:19,23

Trusting in God made Jesus nonviolent. If we don't understand *how* Jesus believed in God, we make our belief *in* Jesus misguided.[23]

Thomas Merton wrote that when the church thinks it's in charge of the direction of history, it changes the essence of the hopeful Christian prayer from "Lord, come quickly" to "Give us more time."[24] This is why one cannot practically believe in the second coming and also take up arms. When we take up arms, we not only disobey Jesus' teachings, but we foolishly think that we can effectively change the course of history through force. We falsely think that violence will soon end with *this* act of violence, just as it was thought that World War I would be "the war to end all wars." We think, "The perfect world is just around the corner. We just got a pious man in office, have killed a good share of the essential evildoers, and have set up a few good governmental systems." This is like praying "give us more time."[25] And whether it's pursued by "the establishment" or by zealous liberationists, the desire to be "authors of history" ultimately ends in hubris, unending conflict, and the victimization of others. Instead of trusting in the command to love our enemies, we insist that having the right people take office to direct the right bombs to fall in the right places is a more effective way to deal with evil. We can't be peaceful now, we say. So give us time to rid the world of evil; eventually it will work. After thousands of years, we haven't learned that violence begets only violence.

---

23 Another phrase (among hundreds) that would normally be confused for abstract religious jargon but has real-world meaning is found in Hebrews 13:5. Oddly enough, the thought that God will never leave us or forsake us is meant to help us resist greed.

24 Thomas Merton, *Conjectures of a Guilty Bystander* (New York: Doubleday, 1965), 124.

25 "*Build* the kingdom," a popular phrase among Christians, borders on this dangerous and disappointing hope. The kingdom Jesus spoke of can't be dragged into the world but only can be accepted and nurtured in humble faith, hope, and love.

As much as we might balk at its mysticism, the central political prayer and hope of Christians is, "Lord, come quickly; may your kingdom come."

Jesus humbled himself and didn't take charge by force. He is the mover of world history as a lamb, not a conqueror. To be a Christian is simply to follow suit. We are to live as Christ lived, to die as Christ died, to resist evil as Christ resisted evil. In the film *Romero*, which documents the struggle of the people of El Salvador during the 1970s and '80s, there is a scene in which Archbishop Romero, priest and martyr among the poor of El Salvador, speaks to one of his fellow clergy as they try to navigate the way of Christ through a tumultuous revolution:

ROMERO: "You're a priest. You believe in God
        and the power of love. You used to pray."

ZEALOT REVOLUTIONARY PRIEST: "I still do."

ROMERO: "Then why are you carrying a gun?"

What to Do with Kings Gone Wild?

excommunicate (eks-kuh-myoo-ni-keyt), **v.**
  "to exclude a baptized Christian from taking part in
  communion because of doctrine or moral behavior
  that is adjudged to offend against God or the Christian
  community"

One of the kids who lived with us here at the Simple Way was a little ball of fire named Bianca. One of her favorite things was to get body-slammed on the couch. Whenever I (Shane) needed to discipline her, all I had to say was, "If you continue to do that, I will not body-slam you for an entire week." It worked better than I could have imagined. And every time I disciplined her, it was not to place burdensome restrictions on her but to keep her from doing something that could badly hurt her or someone else.

Since one of the most precious treasures of the church is the gift of community, one of the most powerful disciplines of the church is isolation from community, the denial of communion. Excommunication has a harsh ring to it. It conjures up visions of judgmentalism, exclusion, cultlike weirdness, and political incorrectness. It has been deeply distorted and abused in church history (even in recent church history—like when the Baptist congregation in the South tried to excommunicate church members who did not vote for Bush). But compared with preemptive bombings, state-sanctioned execution, and sending folks into lifelong exile in places where they'll die alone, the church's most extreme act of discipline—excommunication—seems quite tame and reasonable, even redemptive when properly understood. The need for some sort of restorative justice is particularly urgent when we consider the scandalous sins of leaders within the church in both recent and ancient history. This era of sloppy Christianity and timid politeness demands that we rediscover this hidden treasure, which has led to the restoration of even the worst backslider, the most dangerous heretic, or the most influential hypocrite who might otherwise threaten the health of Christ's body in this world.

In 389 there was an uprising in Thessalonika that resulted in the death of the Roman army commander stationed there. Emperor Theodosius, a practicing Christian, gave the brutal order for a general retaliation in which seven thousand Thessalonians were herded into the imperial games and slaughtered. Ambrose, who was the bishop of Milan and the emperor's pastor, wrote a beautiful letter to Theodosius articulating a deep longing for reconciliation and expressing the firm resolve to exclude him from communion. Ambrose expressed painfully his obligation to excommunicate Theodosius, for to allow him to participate in the liturgy and in communion without reconciliation would be a sign of contempt for God. Ambrose met Theodosius at the door of the church and forbade him to enter, saying, "Submit to the exclusion to which God, the Lord of all, wills to sentence you. God will be your physicist, and God will give you health." The emperor did penance for eight months, then offered a public confession before the people during the Christmas celebration of 390, whereupon he was reconciled to the community with a grand celebration.

One thing that became clear to me (Shane) when I was in Iraq is that what's at stake today isn't just America's visibility and reputation but Christ's reputation and the identity of the Christian disciple. I heard Iraqi people, even Iraqi Christians, call the leaders of the US "Christian extremists" in the same tone that we hear people in the US talk about "Muslim extremists." One Iraqi woman said, with tears in her eyes, "Your government is declaring war and asking God's blessing, and that is the exact same thing that my government is doing. My question is this: what kind of God would allow this?" She found herself quite distant from that God, and she went on to say that she had been to America and met so many beautiful Christians who had an incredible faith, much more healthy and vibrant than what Iraqis saw on the news. She knew that our Christianity has more to offer than the violence they saw, and she ended the conversation longing for that Christianity, saying, "What ever happened to the God of love and the Prince of Peace?"

So the public confrontation of public figures who have visibly misrepresented Jesus is an important practice of our faith. It is a way of saying, "When you do that, it's not just your reputation that is at stake, but mine ... and our God's."

Excommunication is never to be imposed on people outside the covenant of Christian faith, and it is never to be used to expose private sins. Scripture gives clear guidelines on how Christians are to restore someone who is living in ways that hurt themselves or others. We are to talk with them one on one. If that doesn't work, we are to talk with them before a small group of caring friends. If that doesn't work, we are to bring it before the community of grace to try to figure out how best to love and support the fellow struggler. However, for those in public positions whose acts affect an entire population, their confession and reconciliation should also be made public. More is expected, which is no doubt why Dr. King's harshest words in his "Letter from the Birmingham Jail" were written to the clergy, of whom he expected much more, and likewise why Jesus reserved language like "brood of vipers" for the religious and political elite, not for folks who were floundering in their brokenness.

The excommunicated have already put themselves outside of the body. Excommunication is less of a forced isolation than a recognition that a member of the church has already isolated themselves from the community; they have stepped outside of the teaching of Christ. If a Quaker joins the army, she's chosen not to be a Quaker anymore. And of course, in the case of the church, discipline is critical not only to protect the person "in sin" and others from the ill-effects, but also to protect the identity and credibility of the community. The beautiful thing about the church is that we are a people of grace, and mercy triumphs over judgment. So excommunication is never the end we hope for.

Excommunication at least temporarily and provisionally makes clear what is and is not the body of Christ. It's a quarantine of sorts, isolating a part that has grown sick to restore it to health and save the body from infection. This discipline has its roots in Old Testament concepts for maintaining the identity and purity of a people set apart as a visible sign of God's salvation for the world. It's helpful to see it as a way to quarantine someone whose unhealthy patterns endanger the health of the larger body, just as Jesus often described sin as an infection or as yeast that leavens the whole batch of dough. But the promise is that we have a Physician.

Repentance and confession safeguard the witness of the church. Paul warns that it is a desecration of the unity of the body when the well-fed come to the communion table with the hungry, or when the tortured and the torturer drink from the same cup. It's no wonder Jesus prays that we would be one as God is one, right after warning that the world will hate us and the things we stand for.

The Gates of Hell

There's a lot of bad theology out there. Some folks tell us we shouldn't worry about caring for creation since it's all going to burn soon anyway. Other folks have a fatalistic view that the world stinks, so we just need to prepare people to die. But we are convinced that Jesus came not to prepare us to die but to teach us how to live. The kingdom of God is not just something we hope for when we die but something we live "on earth as it is in heaven." And we're not willing simply to promise the world that there is life after death when the world is asking, "Is there life before death?" We are thankful for heaven, but we are not willing to stand by and watch people live through hell to get there. So let's talk about hell for a minute.

We figure anytime you are about to talk about hell, it's good to start with a joke, so here goes … It was a busy day in heaven as folks waited in line at the pearly gates. Peter stood as gatekeeper, checking each newcomer's name in the Lamb's Book of Life. But there was some confusion because the numbers weren't adding up. Heaven was a little overcrowded, and a bunch of folks were unaccounted for. So some of the angels were sent to investigate. And it wasn't long before two of them returned. "We found the problem," they said. "Jesus is out back, lifting people up over the gate."

We remember as children hearing hellfire and damnation sermons. We had a theater group perform a play called *Heaven's Gates and Hell's Flames*, in which actors presented scenes of folks being ripped away from loved ones only to be sent to the fiery pits of hell, where there is weeping and gnashing of teeth, and we all went forward to repent of all the evil things

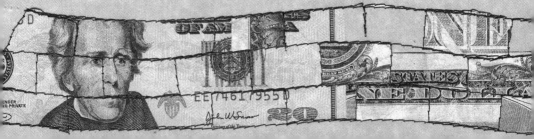

we had done over the first decade of our lives, motivated by the fear of being "left behind." The preacher literally scared the hell out of us.

But have you ever noticed that Jesus didn't spend much time on hell? Really there are only a couple of times when he spoke of weeping and gnashing of teeth, of hell and God's judgment, and both had to do with the walls we create between ourselves and our suffering neighbors. One is in Matthew 25, where the sheep and the goats are separated, and the goats who didn't care for the poor, hungry, homeless, and imprisoned are sent off to endure an agony akin to that experienced by the ones they neglected on this earth. And then there is the story of the rich man and Lazarus, a parable Jesus tells about a rich man who neglects the poor beggar outside his gate. In this parable, the gate becomes an unbridgeable chasm separating the rich man not only from Lazarus but also from God. The rich man is no doubt a religious man (he calls out to "Father" Abraham and knows the prophets), and undoubtedly he has made a name for himself on earth, but he is now a nameless rich man begging the beggar for a drop of water. And Lazarus, who had lived nameless in the shadows of misery, is now seated next to God and is referred to by name. Lazarus is the only person in all of Jesus' parables who is referred to by name, and his name means "the one God rescues." God is in the business of rescuing people from the hells they experience on earth. And God is asking us to love people out of those hells.

Hell is not just something that comes after death but is something many are living in this very moment: 1.2 billion people groan for a drop of water each day; more than thirty thousand kids starve to death each day; and thirty-eight million folks are dying of AIDS. It seems ludicrous to think of preaching to them about hell when we would do better sitting at the

well asking them for a little water. We see Jesus spending far more energy loving the hell out of people, and lifting people out of the hells in which they are trapped, than trying to scare them into heaven. And one of the most beautiful things we get to see in community here in Kensington is people who have been loved out of the hells they find themselves in— domestic violence, addiction, sex trafficking, loneliness.

C. S. Lewis understood hell not as a place where God locks people out of heaven but as a dungeon that we lock ourselves into. So we hold the keys to liberation from our own captivity. With this perspective, we gain new insight when we look at the parable of Lazarus or hear the brilliant words with which Jesus reassured Peter that "the gates of hell will not prevail against you." As adolescents, we understood that to mean that the demons and fiery darts of the Devil will not hit us. But lately we've done a little more thinking and praying, and we have a bit more insight on gates. Gates are not offensive weapons. Gates are defensive—walls and fences we build to keep people out. God is not saying the gates of hell will not prevail as they come at us. God is saying that we are in the business of storming the gates of hell, and the gates will not prevail as we crash through them with grace.

People sometimes ask if we are scared of the inner city. We say that we are more scared of the suburbs. Our Jesus warns that we can fear those things which can hurt our bodies or those things which can destroy our souls, but we should be far more fearful of the latter. Those are the subtle demons of suburbia. As Shane's mother says, "Perhaps there is no more dangerous place for a Christian to be than in safety and comfort, detached from the suffering of others." We're scared of apathy and complacency, of detaching ourselves from the suffering. It's hard to see until our 20/20 hindsight hits us, but every time we lock someone out, we lock ourselves in. Just as we are building walls to keep people out of our comfortable, insulated existence, we are trapping ourselves in a hell of isolation, loneliness, and fear. We have "gated communities" where rich folks live. We put up picket fences around our suburban homes. We place barbed wire and razor wire around our buildings and churches. We put bars on our windows in the ghettos of fear.[26] We build up walls to keep immigrants from entering our country. We guard our borders with those walls—Berlin, Jerusalem, Jericho. And the more walls and gates and fences we have, the closer we are to hell. We, like the rich man, find ourselves locked into our gated homes and far from the tears of Lazarus outside, far from the tears of God.

Let's pray that God would give us the strength to storm the gates of hell and tear down the walls we have created between us and those whose suffering would disrupt our comfort. May we become familiar with the suffering of the poor outside our gates, know their names and taste the salt in their tears. Then when "the ones God has rescued," the Lazaruses of our world—the baby refugees, the mentally ill wanderers, and the homeless outcasts—are seated next to God, we can say, "We're with them." Jesus has given them the keys to the kingdom; maybe they will give us a little boost over the gate.

The gates of the kingdom will forever be open.

And in the New Jerusalem, the great city of God,

"on no day will its gates ever be shut." REV. 21:25

26 A few years ago, the house of our friend's family caught on fire. Their house was so locked up and fortified with deadbolts and bars on the windows that the kids could not escape, even through a window, and all of them died, in part because they had so effectively locked themselves in.

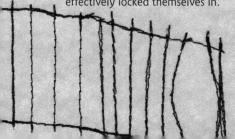

Revolutionary Subordination

In a world of power battles, it's tempting to "take the power back" in a fist-in-the-air revolution, yelling out in street protests, "Whose streets? Our streets!" But if Jesus ever had a fist in the air, it had blood on the wrist.[27]

In an age of injustice, the just may find themselves in jail. There have been so many times over the years that we've bumped into laws that contradict and collide with God's dream, and we've had to consider how to engage them with revolutionary subordination and prophetic imagination, remembering that we follow the one who pulled coins out of fish's mouths and knocked over tables in the temple.

Many years ago, Philadelphia passed laws that made it illegal to lie down on the sidewalk or sleep in the parks, and even to feed the homeless. So what is a Christ-follower to do? We are to love our neighbors as ourselves with imagination. So we gathered in the parks and served communion (which was pushing the envelope). We continued the breaking of bread by bringing in pizzas, and we eventually ended up sleeping in the park. We were fined hundreds of dollars and taken to jail (over and over), the whole time simply practicing revolutionary subordination. And what we did called the laws into question. We even had police officers show up in court to argue that the charges (which they themselves had charged us with) should be dropped because the laws were bad. Eventually a judge challenged the constitutionality of the charges, saying, "If it were not for people who broke unjust laws, we wouldn't have the freedom that we

27 Thanks to our friends at Jesus Radicals for their logo. Check out jesusradicals.com.

have. That's what this country's built on, from the Boston Tea Party to the civil rights movement. We'd still have slavery." He said we were not criminals but freedom fighters and dropped all of the charges against us. And we caught a glimpse of what it must have felt like for Paul and Silas to have the prison walls fall down (Acts 16:26). And we knew that Jesus meant it when he said, "If the world hates you, keep in mind that it hated me first" (John 15:18), but "I have overcome the world" (John 16:33). In fact, we remember thinking that if the world does not hate us, perhaps we should question whether we are really a part of another kingdom. And of course the prayer "forgive us our trespasses" has a new ring to it when you're sitting in jail charged with trespassing.

Since that time, we've heard about all sorts of holy mischief happening around the country where groups of Christians have resisted similar anti-homeless laws with an imagination and a courage that must make Jesus proud. One city made it illegal for people to possess shopping carts, the assumption being that they were stolen. But then many folks lost their only means to carry their groceries home, to get their laundry to and from the laundromat, or to collect metal for recycling. In a gentle act of creative resistance, one Christian community bought a bunch of shopping carts and gave them out, engraving the names of the recipients on them so they could not be accused of stealing. That's beautiful.

In Atlanta, homeless folks were being arrested for public urination in a city with no public restrooms. Our friends at the Open Door Community organized a demonstration called Pee for Free with Dignity, marching to city hall carrying toilets and asking for public restrooms. And it worked. Certainly this wouldn't have happened had they not been nice. That's what revolutionary subordination looks like.

To this day, I (Shane) hold on to a little saying of Dr. Martin Luther King's that I had with me the day I was in court after our pizza party in the park: "There is nothing wrong with a traffic law which says you have to stop for a red light. But when a fire is raging, the fire truck goes through that red light, and normal traffic had better get out of its way. Or when a man is bleeding ... the ambulance goes through those red lights at top speed. There is a fire raging ... for the poor of this society. Disinherited people ... are bleeding to death from deep social and economic wounds. They need brigades of ambulance drivers who will have to ignore the red lights of the present system until the emergency is solved."[28]

Certainly Dr. King and the heroes of the civil rights movement are exemplary of revolutionary love and subordination. Here's a brother who would look into the faces of police officers and jailers and still see the image of God. One of our friends who was an old civil rights organizer recalls marching down the streets and seeing a racist white man spit into the face of one of the marchers, and the marcher looked into his eyes and said, "I love you." As she told that story another man shared about a woman pushing her two babies down the street in a carriage and the same thing happened to her. She looked into the eyes of that man who spit on her and said, pointing to her babies, "Would you like to do that to them too?" He was startled and disarmed and walked away like a dog with his tail tucked between his legs.

28 Martin Luther King Jr., *The Trumpet of Conscience* (New York: Harper and Row, 1968).

> To our most bitter opponents we say: "Throw us in jail and we will still love you. Bomb our houses and threaten our children and we will still love you. Beat us and leave us half dead, and we will still love you. But be ye assured that we will wear you down by our capacity to suffer. One day we shall so appeal to your heart and conscience that we shall win you in the process, and our victory will be a double victory."
>
> —Dr. Martin Luther King Jr., "The American Dream"

During the Vietnam War, groups of Christians in the US planned prophetic actions to voice dissent about the war and express hope for another world. They burned draft cards and went onto military bases with household tools to beat on the war machines, enacting the Scripture in Micah and Isaiah: "my people will beat their swords into plowshares." In a courtroom filled with supporters, one such protester was asked by the prosecuting attorney, "Did you drive the van that carried the defendants?" Silence. "Answer the question. Did you drive the van?" the lawyer asked. Someone stood up in the courtroom and said, "I drove the van." Then another stood: "I drove the van." And another. "Order in the court!" the judge bellowed, hammering his gavel. Before long, dozens were standing in the courtroom, proclaiming, "I drove the van." That is revolutionary subordination.

The group with which I (Shane) went to Iraq, Voices in the Wilderness, was fined $20,000 for violating US/UN sanctions on Iraq because we brought simple medications and other necessities into the "enemy" country. We paid the fine. But in order to expose the tremendous devastation of the sanctions, we paid it in Iraqi dinars. The pile of dinars equivalent to twenty thousand US dollars in 1991 with which we paid the fine was now worth around eight US dollars in 2005. (Of course, the US government didn't get the joke.)

At one point, the intentional community in Philly was told that the way we live is a violation of city laws. In a culture driven by the detached nuclear family, extreme individualism, and obsession with home ownership and entitlement, Christian community itself goes against the grain. City officials informed us that because we had many unrelated people living under the same roof, we were violating a "brothel law." We were officially branded as a Christian brothel! Here's the great humor of God: when we were brought before the court and the zoning board, the name of the person representing the city was a guy named Jesus. And our lawyer was Jewish, so every time we went to court, he would throw his hands in the air and say, "Oh boy, here we go to face Jesus again, and he's causing us all this trouble!" Luckily, our Jewish lawyer beat Jesus in court.

These men who have caused trouble all over the world have now come here. ... They are all defying Caesar's decrees, saying that there is another king, one called Jesus." --Acts 17:6-7

Laws enforced by the sword control behavior but cannot change hearts, no matter how sharp the sword is. The redemption of the cross does what laws and bullets and bombs can never do—bring transformation of evildoers and enemies.

—Greg Boyd, *Myth of a Christian Nation*

History is filled with subversive heroes, such as Oscar Schindler and Harriet Tubman, and even Hollywood tells their stories in moving films like *Schindler's List* and *Hotel Rwanda*. Sometimes we just have to discover the stories that we are in danger of losing, stories that don't always make the news. Sure, it's easier to build a memorial than to build a movement, and we're always better at bronzing our saints than following them, but we have to remember the stories of people who have lived and died well.

Take, for example, Franz Jägerstätter (1907–43). Franz, a husband and the father of three children, refused to serve in the military when he was drafted by the Nazi regime. Although advised by his parish priest and local bishop that his duty was to serve his country and care for his family, Jägerstätter firmly believed that to participate in the war was to cooperate with evil, and he held that belief as a voice in the wilderness, even after the Nazi's put him in jail. After a military trial, he was beheaded on August 9, 1943. In 2007, he was declared a martyr of the church and beatified as a saint, a hero for all of us who hope to have a church of conscientious objectors to the wars of kings and presidents.[29]

"Franz reminds us of the danger of distorting the cross of Jesus. After all the Nazi swastika that he denounced is only the cross contorted, deformed, and bent from its original form." — the words of a priest in Philadelphia on the day of Franz's beatification, referring to a wood sculpture on the altar that showed Franz busting through a swastika

29 While writing this section, I (Shane) spoke at Notre Dame University the week of Veteran's Day and stayed with a kid who had dropped out of the campus ROTC military training program. This young man had been banned from campus due to his active counter-recruitment antics, and he taught me about the powerful story of a saint who was a deep inspiration for him—Marcellus the Centurion. Marcellus left the army of Emperor Diocletian in 298, saying, "I serve Jesus Christ the eternal King. I will no longer serve your emperors. ... It is not right for a Christian to serve the armies of this world." Sentenced to die by the sword, he prayed for God to bless his executors, and then he was killed. Now, in beautiful irony, his bones and relics are buried beneath the basilica altar there at Notre Dame. They sure chose the wrong saint to bury on their campus if they ever hoped to have a thriving ROTC! My ROTC dropout friend now works with the Catholic Peace Fellowship, which has created a great resource for guerilla peacemakers on their website: catholicpeacefellowship.org.

Alternative Economics

So we are convinced that God didn't mess up and either make too many people or not enough stuff to go around. We believe in an economy of abundance, a theology of enough.

There's that time when Jesus was preaching to the masses and they got hungry. When the disciples brought this to Jesus' attention, he told them to go ahead and feed them. But the disciples couldn't think outside the matrix of the empire's economy and complained about how much money it would cost to feed everybody. So Jesus stepped in, but not with triumphal power (the stones-to-bread temptation). He didn't rain down bread from heaven. He just asked the people to give him what food they had with them. He took the humble offering of a kid's lunch—a few loaves and fishes—and fed the masses, and basketsful were left over. God's still in the work of taking whatever we have and working with that to work miracles.

Consider these glimpses of divine providence:

About twenty years ago, there was a little congregation of about four hundred folks that didn't have a ton of money. The pastor had an accident, and he didn't have any health insurance, so the congregation decided to pool their money to cover his medical bill. It all worked out so well that the pastor ended up saying, "If you can do that for me, we can do that for each other." So they did. They created a common fund to cover any medical needs that arose in the congregation. Now I (Shane) am a part of that community, which has grown to over twenty thousand people.[30] Every month we get a newsletter that tells us who is in the hospital and how to pray for them. And I know that my money is going directly to meet the needs of brothers and sisters. Over twenty years, we have paid more than $400,000,000 in medical bills. What a beautiful embodiment of a political alternative.

And that is good news to the poor, to the forty-seven million folks in the US who don't have health insurance, to the nearly nine million uninsured children.[31] One of those children was a little girl here on Potter Street named She-She, who died of asthma a few years ago simply because she didn't have adequate medical care. If our good gospel is not good news to the poor, it is not the gospel of Jesus.

30 See christianhealthcareministries.org.
31 The National Academy of Sciences reports that each year, more than eighteen thousand people die prematurely in the US because they lack proper medical care.

Relational Tithe

Another embodiment of alternative economics is a group called Relational Tithe. Church father Ignatius said that if our church is not marked by caring for the poor, the oppressed, and the hungry, then we are guilty of heresy—and a new reformation is long overdue. Some of us who were pretty discontent with how the church was embezzling money belonging to the poor to build buildings and pay staff began to dream again what it would look like to reimagine tithes and offerings, which God intended to be instruments of a redistributive economy. We considered how the early church brought their offerings and laid them at the feet of the apostles to be redistributed to folks as they had need. And we came up with something beautiful and small—the relational tithe.[32]

Relational Tithe is a network of reborn friends around the world organized like little cells in a body taking care of each other. All offerings and needs are brought before the community and shared, just like they were in the early church. But unlike the early church, we have a blog and can wire money across the globe. We pool 10 percent of our income into a common fund. Regularly, the needs of our neighborhoods and villages are also brought before the community, and we meet them as we are able. Meanwhile, we are building relationships that tear through the economic walls that formerly divided us, from economists to homeless folks, all the time trusting that we can do more together than we can do alone. Together, we've helped friends get cars, kept friends' utilities on, created new jobs, sent kids to summer camps, thrown birthday parties, and sent people on their first vacations. And it all happens through relationships. No one is giving or receiving who is not grounded in sincere friendships. After the tsunami hit in 2004, two folks from the RT went to Thailand and brought before the community the needs of people they met there. We helped repair fences and boats and playgrounds, and even got a write-up

32 See relationaltithe.com.

in the *Bangkok Post*, one of Thailand's most prominent papers. That sounds like God's vision for a human family with a divine wallet.

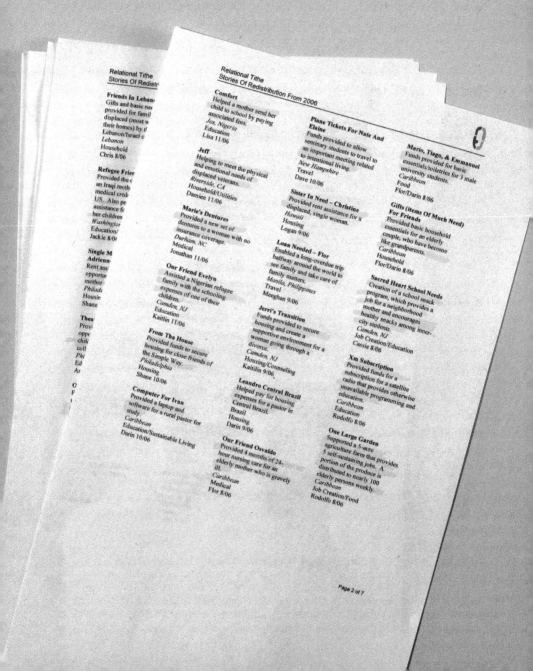

A Village of Interdependence

A few years ago, we did another little experiment in alternative economics.
We gathered hundreds of folks from around the country on a farm in
Tennessee for a little shindig we called PAPA Fest. Don't so many of the
Christian festivals and conferences seem infected by the empire's market
and celebrity culture? We tried to do things a little differently. We created
a gift economy that allowed the festival to be essentially free, but every
person offered their gifts and sweat to pull it off. We created a bartering
economy using PAPA Hours; folks would trade hours of work—doing
everything from filling water jugs and cooking meals to teaching workshops
or providing childcare—for cloth currency that they could trade in the
village. And then we had a barn where folks could trade in their PAPA
Hours and get books and CDs, massages or crafts, or even blueberries and
chickens. US currency was invalidated and made powerless there.[33] In the
mornings, we had workshops that were deep and philosophical, discussing
theology, economics, and peacemaking. And in the afternoon, all the
workshops were practical—workshops on sewing, bike repair, canning,
circus skills, and gardening. Everyone was able to participate in the
village. We'll never forget seeing Shane's uncle, who doesn't have much
to do with anything that smells religious, taking some nuns fishing. It was
a great image of the kingdom. One of the most beautiful things was that
we pulled the whole thing off for a few thousand dollars and created an
environment of empowerment where people's gifts were celebrated. It
was a beautiful alternative to the many conferences where we pay large
amounts of money to passively attend sessions being taught by folks who

33 As we planned PAPA Fest, we were honored to have a fellow named Paul Glover
advising us on alternative economics. He helped to create a bartering economy in
Ithaca, New York, that has pioneered the idea using Ithaca Hours (STATS). They began
by listing the various services that folks were willing to trade alongside a list of things
people needed and everything bubbled up out of that. Not only did he give us advice
but he came down to the festival and helped us pull it off.

are being paid lots of money to preach a gospel that tells us to sell all we have and be with the poor. It was one of those times when you catch a little glimpse of the kingdom and of a world where it is easier for people to be good to each other.

In a lovely poem titled "Mad Farmers Liberation Front," Wendell Berry stated that every day we should do something that doesn't compute. "As soon as the generals and the politicos can predict the motions of your mind, lose it." Love and gifts are the premiere actions situated outside of the system.

The teaching of the church is, basically, the church herself, as the sign and the beginning of this renewed community. The verbal proclamation of the message is merely the articulation of the community's self-consciousness.

—Nicholas Lash, "His Presence in the World"

Another World Is Possible

Sister Margaret is one of our wisest—and wildest—elders. Some years back, she and some other Christians felt moved by the Spirit to enact some of the prophecies in the Bible. They drew their own blood, which they planned to pour on the war machines as a symbolic lament of the bloodshed they create. And they had a bag full of hammers and other tools with which to begin the conversion of the things of death into the things of life. Then they showed up for a tour of a navy ship. Sister Margaret was designated to carry the tools, since she was the older nun, the least suspicious. It's hysterical to hear her so innocently tell the story of how she just went through the strict security with metal detectors and bag checkers, praying and trusting God. As she went through the checkpoint, her bulky bag got stuck on the gate, and a guard came to her aid. He took the bag from her and lifted it through the security check, and then he helped Sister Margaret, who just thanked him over and over like an innocent granny. They went onto the boat and began climbing up the ladders, up to the top of the ship. There they poured their blood onto the side of a Tomahawk missile launcher. She said it looked like a giant star. Then they prayerfully began beating on the hollow metal of the launcher. The sound of each hit of the hammer seemed to echo across the entire creation. It was sacramental. It was as if time stopped. They continued to hammer together, thud after thud reverberating. Sailors began to surround them—confused, paralyzed. Officers told the nuns to lay face down with their hands above them on the deck. And they gladly obeyed. It reminded Sister Margaret of the times the sisters would lie prostrate, face down, with outstretched hands in prayer before God. As they lay there, it began to rain, and Sister Margaret says it was like God was crying.

One thing that's clear in the Scriptures is that the nations do not lead people to peace; rather, people lead the nations to peace. There's a beautiful text in both Micah and Isaiah where the prophets say that the people will beat their swords into plowshares and their spears into pruning hooks. And it ends by saying that nations will not rise up against other nations, and they will not study war anymore. Peace begins not with nations but with the people of God. It is people who humanize the nations, people who follow the Human One that Daniel spoke of rising from the beasts, the Son of Man the gospels proclaim. The end of war begins with people who believe that another world is possible and that another empire has already interrupted time and space and is taking over this earth with the dreams of God. Those dreams begin with people of faith and hope who are audacious enough to be certain of what they do not see. We believe so much that we cannot help but start enacting the prophecies. We believe despite the evidence, and we watch the evidence change.

What if we got our best scientists to figure out a plan for converting all our B-52s into tractors?

What if people began to prayerfully take household tools onto military bases and beat the war machines into farm tools?

It has been done. And it will be done again.

We are people who believe in conversion. We believe things can be transformed into new creations.

THIS VIOLENCE IS FOR A WORLD THAT HAS LOST ITS IMAGINATION
— Manager of a Baghdad hospital

Conversion

It's a shame that a few conservative evangelicals have had a monopoly on the word *conversion*. Some of us shiver at the word. But conversion means to change, to alter, to make something look different than it did before—like conversion vans or converted currency. We need conversion in the best sense of the word—people who are marked by the renewing of their minds and imaginations, who no longer conform to the pattern that is destroying our world. Otherwise we have only believers, not converts. And believers are a dime a dozen nowadays. What the world needs is people who believe so much in another world that they cannot help but enact it.

Then we will start to see some true conversion vans that run on veggie oil instead of diesel. Then we will see some converted homes that run on renewable energy, power their laundry machines with stationary bicycles, and flush their toilets with dirty sink water. Then tears will be converted to laughter as people make their machine guns into saxophones or police officers use their clubs to play baseball.

BREAK THE CROWNS, BUT LEAVE THE HEADS UNHARMED.

We Need New Celebrations

> Scripture isn't just something to
> "apply" in the world but is something
> to be performed like a symphony,
> a ballet, or a circus.

A couple of years ago, two things happened. First, we won a lawsuit over police misconduct in New York City. The police had been arresting homeless people for sleeping in public, and charging them with disorderly conduct. Hundreds of folks rallied to bring attention to this situation, and many of us slept outside to express our feeling that it shouldn't be a crime to sleep in public. I (Shane) was arrested one night as I slept. Through a long legal process, I was found not guilty, and then I filed a civil suit of wrongful arrest, wrongful prosecution, and police misconduct. And we won, in addition to a legal precedent, around ten thousand dollars. But we figured the money didn't belong to me or to the Simple Way but to the homeless in New York for all they endure. It was their victory.

The second thing that happened was that after our study of biblical economics, we were given an anonymous gift of ten thousand dollars, money which had been invested in the stock market and now was being returned to the poor.

So twenty thousand dollars was enough to stir up the collective imagination. What would it look like to have a little Jubilee celebration today? The idea rippled far beyond the Simple Way, and before long, friends from all over were thinking about it, with smiles on their faces. Where should we have it? Where else but on Wall Street, in the face of the world's economy? We also decided that this was not a one-time celebration but an ancient celebration, going back to Leviticus 25, and an eternal celebration of the New Jerusalem. We decided to send one hundred dollars to a hundred different communities that incarnate the spirit of jubilee and

Jubilee on Wall Street

the economics of love. Each one hundred dollar bill had "love" written on it. And we invited everyone to Wall Street for the jubilee.

After months of laughter and dreaming, it really happened. It was a big day. And we were ready (though we still had butterflies in our bellies). About forty people brought all the change they could carry, more than thirty thousand coins in bags, coffee mugs, briefcases, and backpacks. Another fifty people would be meeting us on Wall Street. A dozen "secret stashers" ran ahead hiding hundreds of two-dollar bills all over lower Manhattan—in parks, napkin holders, phone booths. At 8:15 we started trickling into the public square in front of the main entrance to the New York Stock Exchange. We deliberately dressed to blend in; some of us looked homeless (some were), others looked like tourists, and others business folks. Word of the redistribution had spread throughout New York, and nearly a hundred folks from the alleys and projects had gathered. We had choreographed the celebration like a play production, making Wall Street the stage of our theatrics of counterterror. At 8:20, Sister Margaret, our seventy-year-old nun, and I stepped forward to proclaim the jubilee.

"Some of us have worked on Wall Street, and some of us have slept on Wall Street. We are a community of struggle. Some of us are rich people trying to escape our loneliness. Some of us are poor folks trying to escape the cold. Some of us are addicted to drugs, and others are addicted to money. We are a broken people who need each other and God, for we have come to recognize the mess that we have created of our world and how deeply we suffer from that mess. Now we are working together to give birth to a new society within the shell of the old. Another world is possible. Another world is necessary. Another world is already here."

Then Sister Margaret blew the ram's horn (like our Jewish ancestors used to) and we announced, "Let the celebration begin!" Ten people stationed on balconies above the crowd threw hundreds of dollars in paper money, filling the air. Then they dropped banners which read, "Stop terrorism," "Share," "Love," and "There is enough for everyone's need but not enough for everyone's greed—Gandhi."

The streets turned silver. Our "pedestrians," "tourists," "homeless," and "business people" began pouring out their change. We decorated the place with sidewalk chalk and filled the air with bubbles. Joy was contagious. Someone bought bagels and started giving them out. People started sharing their winter clothes. One of the street sweepers winked at us as he flashed a dustpan full of money. Another guy hugged someone and said, "Now I can get my prescription filled."

It worked. We had no idea what would happen.[34] We knew it was dangerous, intentionally bringing God and mammon face to face. But this is precisely what we have committed our lives to. It's risky, and yet we are people of faith, believing that giving is more contagious than hoarding, that love can convert hatred, light can overcome darkness, grass can pierce concrete ... even on Wall Street.

34 The police had come in full force but were quite disarmed by the fun (hard not to smile at bubbles and sidewalk chalk). One of them later told me he was ordered to "get rid of them," but he couldn't tell who "they" were. Laughing, he said next time we have a jubilee, we could do it outside his station.

It's parties like this that help tear down
the walls and Wall streets. Remember old Jericho,
where God's people surrounded the gates of the
city and toppled it not with power and
weapons
but with LITURGY, DANCING, AND WORSHIP.

Sometimes all we need is a divine celebration.
A holy party can tear down the walls and Wall Streets
of an empire.

Die to the world by
renouncing the madness
of its stir and bustle. God
created nothing evil. It
is we who brought forth
wickedness. Those who
brought it about can also
do away with it again.

—Tatian

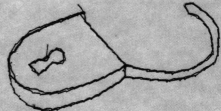

We Need New Language

The apostle James writes that the way we speak controls our lives. In the same way that you are what you eat, it's true that you are what you say. Our language changes the way we view the world. In section 2, we talked about how the kingdom of God implies a new citizenship, giving Jesus' followers a new identity. If our citizenship is in heaven, this truth should change the way we talk. The word *we*, if a person is truly born again, will refer to the new people into whom a Christian has been born: the church. Christians can no longer refer to "our troops" or "our history" because of their new identity. Fabricated boundaries and walls are removed for the Christian. One's neighbor is not only from Chicago but also from Baghdad. One's brother or sister in the church could be from Iran or California—no difference! Our family is transnational and borderless; we are in Iraq, and we are in Palestine.[35] And if we are indeed to become born again, we will have to begin talking like it, changing the meaning of *we, us, my,* and *our.* We see the question of whether we should intervene in a case like Hitler in a whole new light when we change our allegiance and language: **the resounding answer is _yes_: we, the church, should certainly help and intervene—but _as Christians_.**[36]

Another practice is to avoid the language of hype. "Engaging culture" is a big goal for Christians these days. And the best way to do this, so the logic goes, is with the style of the culture at large. We'll need some websites to change the world, and so we'll need some catchy titles, phrases, and images to create "a movement." And of course any good movement has T-shirts, hip words, bumper stickers, and slogans (oh, yes, and wrist bands).

35 Consider the fact that there are more Palestinian Christians than there are Israeli Christians. We can't help but see the world differently when we have family suffering from war and poverty.

36 The final scenes of the film *The Mission* poignantly illustrate this point. Hoping to protect an indigenous mission-village from colonialism and the slave trade, two priests differ over how best to help the villagers: by fighting or by suffering with them nonviolently as Christians? "Help them, yes, but *as a priest*" is the call.

Christians often think something is meaningful only if it has some title, if it gets publicity on television, or if it shapes some national agenda or legislation. (Since we're publishing a book, we have, of course, entered into this process, though with considerable trepidation. Have mercy on us.)

The world of hype waters down the complex, nuanced, and demanding aspects of living as a Christian. Farmer and author Wendell Berry has avowed not to join movements—yet another hip word for Christians these days—for many reasons, and they are good ones. He writes that movements "too easily become unable to mean their own language, as when a 'peace movement' becomes violent. ... They almost always fail to be radical enough, dealing finally in effects rather than causes. Or they deal with single issues or single solutions, as if to assure themselves that they will not be radical enough."[37]

It will be a great and arduous task for us Christians to relearn how to talk without the oversimplifications and slogans of the world. But doing so can't just be some side project, as if the economic practices of biking and local agriculture are the only practical applications of alternative economics. Our mouths control the rest of our bodies and our imaginations, and so we must watch our language.

37 Wendell Berry, *Citizenship Papers* (Washington, DC: Shoemaker and Howard, 2003), chap. 5.

We Need New Rituals

It is no easier to identify a true Christian than it is to identify a true America. So we need ways to create a real sense of belonging as Christians. We need to remember that there are people all over the world singing the same songs, praying the same prayers, all part of this transnational community we call the church. Just as there are no true Americans apart from America, there are no Christians apart from the church.

One of the church's peculiar practices is communion, or the Lord's Supper or the Eucharist. The early Christians were accused of being cannibals because they talked of eating flesh and drinking blood together. The most important dimension of the mystery of communion is what our Catholic friends have taught us: you are what you eat. When we take the wine and bread and eat it, we are digesting Christ—or an even better way of understanding it is that when we are digested into the body of Christ, we are made into a new creation. Performing the Eucharist with a community makes us into the body of Christ. As often as Christians take the common elements of bread and wine, they re-member themselves into Jesus. In the Eucharist, we don't just remember Jesus in general, we remember his suffering. The bread is a *broken* body and the wine is poured like *shed blood*. If you are what you eat, the Eucharist is indeed the act of uniting yourself with the one who lovingly suffered at the hands of his enemies. If you ritually cross yourself (like Catholics do), you are stamping upon yourself the sign of the cross; you are identifying with Jesus' suffering love. Those who ingest and become one with the suffering body of Christ all together become the Body of Christ.

The practice of the Eucharist or communion is a radically political act. Check out this snapshot of the church on the border between the US and Mexico. From the evening of December 16 through the evening of the 24th, the Mexican Church celebrates the feast of Las Posadas, remembering Mary and Joseph's journey from Nazareth to Bethlehem in their search for sanctuary. Christians in both the US and Mexico observe this holiday as time of insight into our contemporary struggles for sanctuary and issues of immigration. On these evenings, Christians gather on both sides of the fortified border fence, sing songs, hear each other's stories, and recite the liturgy of Mary, Joseph, and the innkeeper. The border patrol and minutemen stand by in skeptical consternation. After the liturgy, both sides shower each other with candy thrown over the fence, and eat tamales and drink champurrado (Mexican hot chocolate), and pass ribbons of hope through the holes in the fence.[38] These folks have begun to embody a borderless Eucharist.

While Congress is paralyzed in debates over immigration and border issues, we will continue to celebrate communion across the fences and walls and gates and artificial borders of nations. We will not wait for Congress to tell us how to treat immigrants. We already have a Bible that tells us how, and a Savior who shows us.

> The church's task is neither to destroy nor to maintain ethnic identities, but to replace them with a new identity in Christ that is more foundational than earthly identities.
>
> —Manny Ortiz,
>   pastor in North Philadelphia

38 Much of the insights from this section come from the Bartimaeus Cooperative Ministries newsletter (December 2006) and Ched Meyers (especially his article "Epiphany under Empire: Remembering Resistance," published in *America* in January 2007).

We Need New Heroes

In the church, we celebrate martyrs and saints, not warriors and conquistadors. The church has a rich history of celebrating particular people. While the US might celebrate Christopher Columbus, the church celebrates the lives of saints on feast days. And we cannot forget to honor even our contemporary martyrs. Let us set aside in the church a day for Tom Fox, who went with Christian Peacemaker Teams to Iraq and was killed as he sought peace. Another recent martyr is Dorothy Stang, a seventy-three-year-old nun from Ohio who was assassinated in Brazil in 2005 for her prophetic resistance to corporate interests' pillaging of the rain forests. We need new heroes and sheroes. We need to be about discovering lost relatives and forgotten ancestors.

Who are your heroes? Here are a few for you to consider.

Felicitas and Perpetua

Felicitas and Perpetua lived in North Africa in the beginning of the third century. Felicitas was Perpetua's slave, but they both converted to Christianity and became sisters and dear friends. They were jailed together for their faith. Felicitas was eight months pregnant when she was thrown in prison. And Perpetua, a twenty-two-year-old mother, nursed her newborn baby in prison while her father begged them to renounce their faith (even just in word) so they could come home. There was an imperial edict against killing pregnant women, so they remained in prison for a while, awaiting their martyrdom. Two days after Felicitas gave birth, Felicitas and Perpetua were fed to the beasts during the imperial games and are said to have given each other a kiss of peace as they met their deaths together.

Maximilian Kolbe

Maximilian Kolbe was a Polish priest who provided shelter for thousands of Jews in his friary and was an active voice against the violence of his world. He was arrested by the German Gestapo and imprisoned in Auschwitz, where he was prisoner number 16670. When a fellow prisoner escaped from the camp, the Nazis selected ten other prisoners to be killed in reprisal. As they were lined up to die, one of the ten, Franciszek Gajowniczek, began to cry, "My wife! My children! I will never see them again!" At this, St. Maximilian stepped forward and asked to die in his place. His request was granted. He led the other men in song and prayer as they awaited their deaths on August 14, 1941. He was canonized in October 1982. There is a statue of him outside Westminster Abbey in London. An incredible footnote to his story is that Maximilian had also lived in Japan and founded a monastery on the outskirts of Nagasaki. Four years after his martyrdom, on August 9, the atomic bomb was dropped on Nagasaki and his monastery miraculously survived. Maximilian's feast day, when Christians around the world celebrate his life and sainthood as a hero of the church, falls one week after Nagasaki Day. Each year, we spend the week reflecting on the best and the worst that human beings are capable of.

Martin of Tours

Martin of Tours was born during the troubling time of Constantine's crusades. He was born four years after Constantine's legendary conversion to Christianity, when Christians were exchanging the cross of Jesus for the sword of the empire. Into this world of "holy war," Martin was born. He was named after Mars, the god of war. His dad was a veteran, in fact a senior officer, of the Roman Army. And like many of our kids, Martin entered the service as a young teenager to fight the crusades of the empire.

And then there was an interruption. Outside the gates of Amiens in modern-day France, Martin had a human encounter that would forever change him. He met a scantly-clad beggar and was deeply moved with compassion. With very little to give away, he took off his military cloak and cut it in half, giving half to the beggar. Then he laid down his arms, saying, "I am a Christian, I cannot fight." Later he would be taken to jail, insulted, and persecuted for deserting the army.[39]

BROTHER JUNIPER

On a different note, consider Brother Juniper, one of the crazier brothers of St. Francis in Assisi. He was always getting in trouble for his foolery. On one occasion, Brother Juniper was left in charge of the cathedral by the caretaker. (Not sure what he was thinking.) Some beggars came to the door asking for food and money. Juniper had little to offer, but he mentioned that there were some silver bells in the cathedral they could have, since it was God's house. So he helped them with that. When his superior,the bishop, got word of this, he scolded Brother Juniper. Legend has it he yelled so loudly that he lost his voice. Brother Juniper, feeling remorse for having angered him so badly, made some porridge that night to take to the bishop. He carefully carried it by the light of a candle to the bishop's house. When his superior answered the door, he was irate, having been awakened from his slumber. He wanted nothing to do with Juniper's gift. So Juniper, with the innocence of a child, asked the bishop if he would mind holding the candle so Juniper could eat the porridge before it got cold. At this point, the bishop was so taken aback, he fell apart with laughter at the absurdity of this simpleton. He held the candle, and they finished the porridge together. Oh, Brother Juniper, what a simpleton.

---

39 The feast day of St. Martin of Tours, when Christians around the world celebrate his life, is November 11, which, interestingly enough, is when Americans celebrate Veteran's Day. So as patriots remember the veterans of war, the church is remembering the veterans of peace.

BASIL OF RUSSIA

One of the great holy fools of the church was a man named Basil, a bona fide saint in the Orthodox Church. He was quite a troublemaker, often wandering the streets as a vagrant and a beggar, wearing nearly nothing at all. There are tales of him destroying the merchandise of dishonest tradesmen at the market on Red Square. And yet there are also stories of him kissing the cornerstones of the mansions of the rich, praying for their conversion. Basil was one of the few prophets who dared confront the evils of Russian tsar Ivan the Terrible. Ivan was notorious for an iron-fisted reign sprinkled with religious devotion. In the midst of Lent, when many Russians keep a rigorous vegetarian fast, Basil finagled his way in to the tsar to deliver a gift. He brought a giant, bloody slab of raw beef with a message: "Why abstain from meat when you are shedding the blood of your people?" Unbelievable. The tsar, whose infamous wrath was feared throughout the land, dared not lay a hand on Basil. He is said to have even offered gifts to the naked saint of the streets in admiration of his foolish devotion to God, gifts which Basil in turn gave to the poor.

If Jesus is our president, then the saints are his cabinet, which, we must say, is hard to beat.

WHO ARE YOUR HEROES?

And here are a few more...
we have to keep
discovering lost ancestors

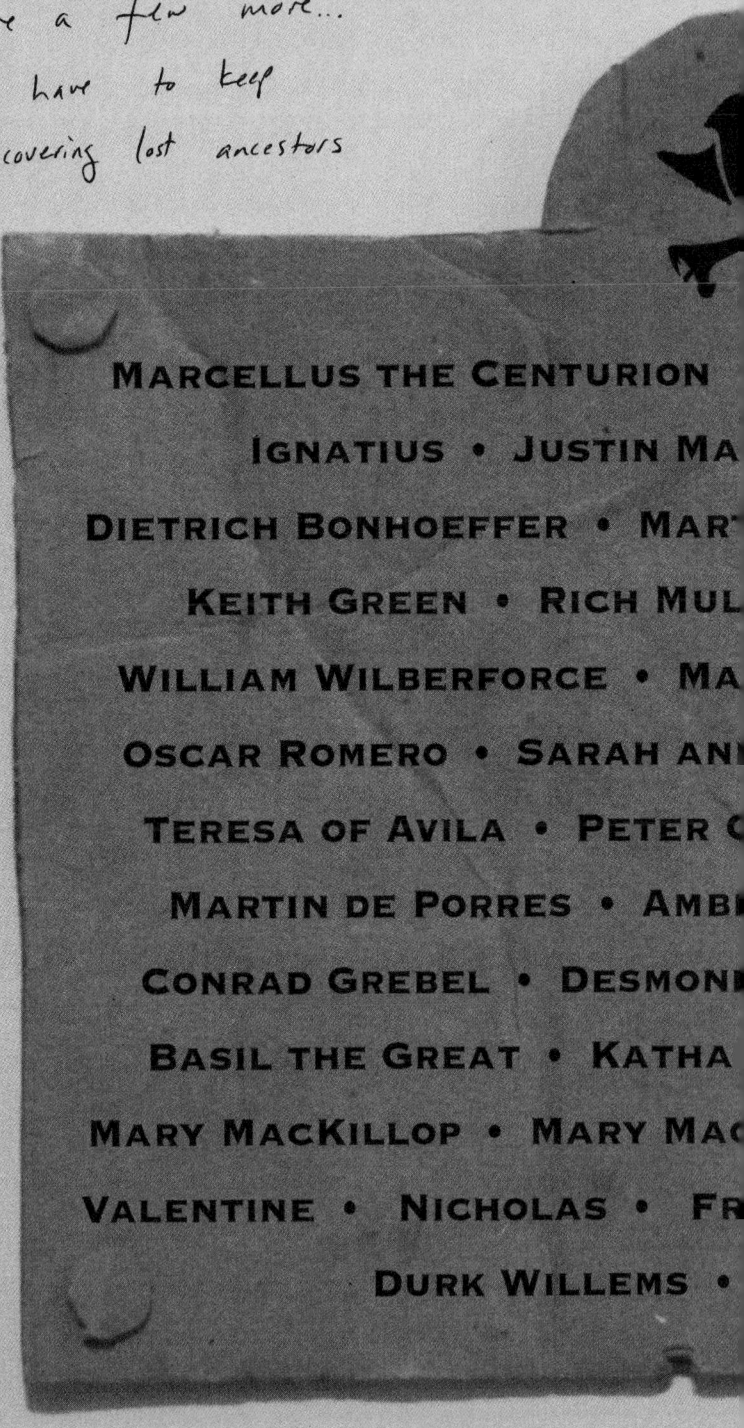

MARCELLUS THE CENTURION

IGNATIUS • JUSTIN MA

DIETRICH BONHOEFFER • MAR

KEITH GREEN • RICH MUL

WILLIAM WILBERFORCE • MA

OSCAR ROMERO • SARAH ANN

TERESA OF AVILA • PETER C

MARTIN DE PORRES • AMB

CONRAD GREBEL • DESMON

BASIL THE GREAT • KATHA

MARY MACKILLOP • MARY MAC

VALENTINE • NICHOLAS • FR

DURK WILLEMS •

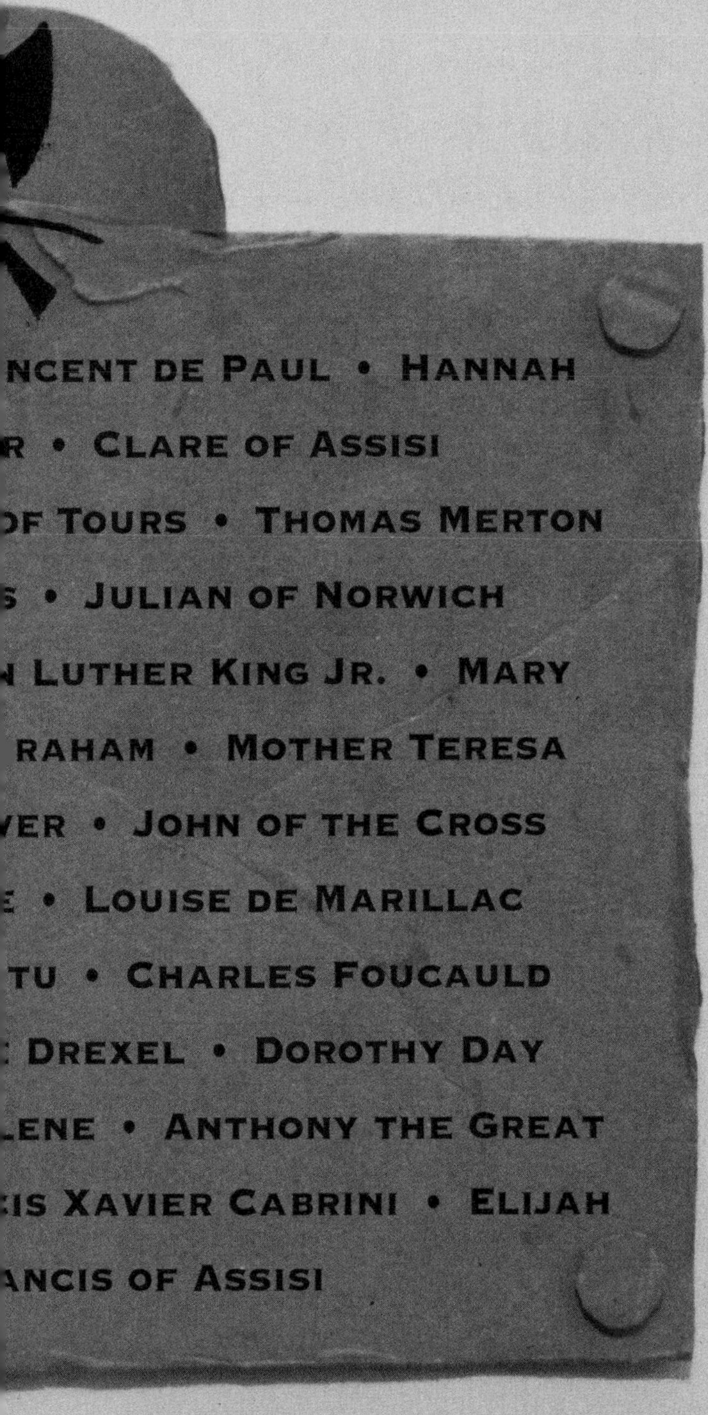

NCENT DE PAUL • HANNAH

R • CLARE OF ASSISI

OF TOURS • THOMAS MERTON

S • JULIAN OF NORWICH

N LUTHER KING JR. • MARY

RAHAM • MOTHER TERESA

VER • JOHN OF THE CROSS

E • LOUISE DE MARILLAC

TU • CHARLES FOUCAULD

DREXEL • DOROTHY DAY

LENE • ANTHONY THE GREAT

CIS XAVIER CABRINI • ELIJAH

ANCIS OF ASSISI

Keep adding names to the list. And keep
creating feast days and holy holidays to
remember their lives.

We Need New Songs

Come now and join the feast,

from the greatest to the very least.

Come now and join the feast,
right here in the belly of the beast.

Cops and soldiers, you can come too,

just lay down your guns and come on through.

Rich people get rid of your stuff
and poor people there will be enough.

Mighty ones come down from your thrones.

And little ones you are not alone.

Come on patriots, you can bring your flags.
We're washin' feet and we'll need some rags.

--From a worship group named PSALTERS

e Need New Liturgy

t as America has her liturgy[40]—singing the national anthem or placing
r hands over our hearts or twenty-one-gun salutes—we as a church
ed new rituals and a liturgy to give people a sense of belonging and
votion, of an identity that runs deeper than nation.

Our Father, who art in heaven
I pledge allegiance to the flag

Thy kingdom come, thy will be done
and to the republic for which it stands

e need ways to make the gospel visible in the world. One of the ways
e do that is by remembering on Good Friday the suffering and passion
f Christ. For many folks that means walking through the events of
hrist's final hours, often referred to as the stations of the cross. It's easy
o do this in a vacuum, though, forgetting the world in which Jesus lived
nd depoliticizing his crucifixion. And it's tempting to detach the cross
rom the world we live in, missing the full meaning of what it means
to follow our Savior and take up our crosses. Sometimes innovative
worship services that stimulate the senses or use good multimedia just
aren't enough. So we take the liturgy to the streets. Our friends began
organizing the stations of the cross outside of the headquarters for
Lockheed Martin, the world's largest weapons contractor. At each
station, we read Scripture and remember the suffering of Jesus, but we
connect that to the suffering of our world, where Christ aches in "the
least of these." With each station, we slowly enter the property of
Lockheed. Finally, we end up at the cross, on our knees remembering
the broken body and blood of our Lord. And then folks are taken to
jail, where they continue their contemplation.

40 *Liturgy* means "worship," as well as "public work." Worship is more than
just what happens on Sunday morning. It is learning to live. We have included in
this section a beautiful litany.

Litany of Resistance and Confession

One: Deliver us, O God.

All: Guide our feet in the ways of your peace.

One: In humility, we ask.

All: Hear our prayer. Grant us peace.

One: In humility, we ask.

All: Hear our prayer. Grant us peace.

One: Lamb of God, you take away the sins of the world.

All: Have mercy on us.

One: Lamb of God, you take away the sins of the world.

All: Free us from the bondage of sin and death.

One: Lamb of God, you take away the sins of the world.

All: Hear our prayer. Grant us peace.

One: Today we pledge our ultimate allegiance to the kingdom of God.

All: We pledge allegiance.

One: To a peace that is not like Rome's.

All: We pledge allegiance.

One: To the gospel of enemy-love.

All: We pledge allegiance.

One: To the kingdom of the poor and broken.

All: We pledge allegiance.

One: To a king who loves his enemies so much he died for them.

All: We pledge allegiance.

One: To the least of these, with whom Christ dwells.

All: We pledge allegiance.

One: To the transnational church that transcends the artificial borders of nations.

All: We pledge allegiance.

One: To the refugee of Nazareth.

All: We pledge allegiance.

One: To the homeless rabbi who had no place to lay his head.

All: We pledge allegiance.

One: To the cross rather than the sword.

All: We pledge allegiance.

One: To the banner of love above any flag.

All: We pledge allegiance.

One: To the one who rules with a towel rather than an iron fist.

All: We pledge allegiance.

One: To the one who rides a donkey rather than a war horse.

All: We pledge allegiance.

One: To the revolution that sets both oppressed and oppressors free.

All: We pledge allegiance.

One: To the way that leads to life.

All: We pledge allegiance.

One: To the slaughtered Lamb.

All: We pledge allegiance.

One: And together we proclaim his praises, from the margins of the empire to the centers of wealth and power.

All: Long live the slaughtered Lamb.

One: Long live the slaughtered Lamb.

All: Long live the slaughtered Lamb.[41]

We need a renewing of our minds so that we do not conform to the patterns of this world.

God is in the work of liberating our imaginations from the clutches of the empire and market.

41 For a full litany that we have used and invite you to use or adapt, check out

We Need New Eyes

Being a Christian is not about having better vision but about having new eyes.

We Need New Holidays

Every sturdy society has created its own calendar according to its own values. For some time now, Western civilization has used the Julian and Gregorian calendars, which are influenced largely by the Roman Empire's traditions ("August" referring to Augustus Caesar and "January" referring to the god Janus, etc.). The United States' civil religion uses this calendar, mixing in its own set of holy days, most notably its date of inception (July 4) and its remembrances of human sacrifice (Memorial Day and Veterans Day). Consumer culture always threatens to monopolize the feast days when the church remembers saints like St. Nicholas, St. Valentine, and St. Patrick, turning them into little more than days to buy stuff in the name of cultural idols like Santa, the Easter bunny, and green leprechauns. Too often we have forgotten the lives of the people for whom these days are named.

But if we in the church are going to take our citizenship in heaven seriously, we must reshape our minds by marking our calendars differently. We must remember the holidays of the biblical narrative rather than the festivals of the Caesars, and celebrate feast days to remember saints rather than war heroes and presidents. Instead of thinking of our inception as July 4th, we would be best served to know that *our* inception as the church was at Pentecost. (Our fireworks should go off a few months earlier than America's.) And instead of commemorating people's sacrificing themselves in order to kill for their country, we will find a deeper and more powerful observance in the Christian holiday of Good Friday, the day when Jesus willingly died for everyone in the world, even his enemies, instead of killing them to "change the world." Or consider the holy day of Epiphany, when the church celebrates the civil disobedience of the magi, who, coming from outside of Caesar's realm, honored a different kind of king and sneaked away from the violent Herod. And one of the lesser known holidays is the Feast of the Holy Innocents (December 28), when the church remembers Herod's genocide of children in his attempt to root out any would-be incumbents. On such a day, we take in the harsh truth that there was and still is a political cost to the incarnation of God's peaceable love.[42] Such a holy feast day of mourning provokes our own political memory to communally and publicly remember the Iraqis (around one million) who have died since the US invasion in 2003. On such a day, we don't consider those deaths to be the necessary sacrifice of "collateral damage"; we consider their deaths to be the acts of our contemporary Herods.

We learn history by studying wars and violence; we organize it by the reigns of kings and presidents. But in Jesus, we reorder history. We date it from his visit to earth and examine it through a new lens, identifying with the tortured, the displaced, the refugee, and the revolutions on the margins of empires.

One congregation decided to do things a little differently one Christmas. They took out all of their fancy decorations and put manure on the floor of the sanctuary, so that when people came, some of them in their best attire, they had nowhere to sit but in a pile of poop. But people will never forget that Christmas. And they will never forget the Christmas story, the fact that our

42 See Meyers, "Epiphany under Empire." John Yoder writes, "'Peace' is not an accurate description of what has generally happened to nonresistant Christians throughout history. … Nor does Christian pacifism guarantee a warless world" (Yoder, The Original Revolution, 53).

Savior was born into the stench of this world, born in a rank manger in the middle of a genocide.[43]

One of our other favorite holidays is Buy Nothing Day, the biggest shopping day of the year. We find it deeply troubling that consumer activity peaks annually around the birthday of our Lord. So we head to the malls with a circus of antiheroes, celebrating that there are other ways to share love than by spending money. One year we gave away free pizzas in the mall, and several of us were arrested for such a subversive act. We were told that you cannot give away food in the food court; you can only sell food. So we were handcuffed and taken into custody to the mall security office. They took snapshots of us and posted our pictures on the wall, right next to the other notorious criminals. (The most common crime seemed to be asking for money.) We were given a "ban and bar" from the mall, and officially became part of the Mall's Most Wanted. No doubt Jesus probably got a similar ban and bar after the table-flipping incident in the temple. We were much more well behaved.

In seeking a different way for our communities to mark time, we've created a calendar that celebrates the birthdays of different communities and other related times. We labeled Resurrection Sunday, Easter, as "President's Day." Small steps like this creatively guide us toward a renewed mind not shaped by the patterns of the world.

43 For another project reclaiming Christmas from the corporate machine check out the Advent Conspiracy. This little project started by some friends of ours has now snowballed into an international movement "restoring the scandal of Christmas by worshipping Jesus through compassion not consumption." Their website says it like this: "While we are not living under Herod's reign, there is another empire of consumerism and materialism that threatens our faithfulness to Jesus. Jesus brought with him such an extraordinary Kingdom that is counter-culture to the kingdoms of this world" (adventconspiracy.org).

Vote the Rock

It's election year and once again poor people are running ... for their lives.

—Gil Scott Heron, poet and troubador of the civil rights era

As the 2004 presidential election campaign heated up, we wrestled with the question of voting—whether to vote, who to vote for, how much significance to give the act of voting—while everyone from Fox News to MTV's Rock the Vote seemed to assume that voting was the most significant act of one's life. Having seen the devastating effects of the war in Iraq, the deception surrounding its escalation, and the list of recent sins of the US government, it seemed that the voting slogan "Anybody but him" might be appropriate. But as the debates between Kerry and Bush raged on, it became apparent that both believed in the redeeming effects of violence. As Kerry needed to prove himself strong and uncompromising, his shtick seemed to be, "I'm not a wimp; I want to make the largest military appropriations in world history!" As we heard this, the political dissonance between being a Christian and a citizen of the US became more unmistakable. Christian politics (like the Sermon on the Mount) not only are alien to the requirements of becoming a president but are detestable and would be laughed out of the debate (if not worse).

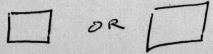

Some of us began to think that if God had wanted us to vote, God would have given us some better options to choose from (wink).

With people's faith in kings and presidents at an all-time low, the greatest challenge may be that folks want to disengage and have nothing to do with politics at all—especially folks in a generation that has more faith that Bono can change the world than that the next president can. But we want to offer another option. We want to redefine what it means to vote.

The distinctly kingdom question is not about how we should vote but about how we should live. The decision we make in each future election is no more important than how we vote every day. We vote every day for companies, for people, and we put money toward "campaigns." We need to think of the faces behind the scenes. Who are the masters and Caesars that we pledge allegiance to by the way we live and through the things we put our trust in? We vote every day with our feet, our hands, our lips, and our wallets. We are to vote for the poor. We are to vote for the peacemakers. We are to vote for the marginalized, the oppressed, the most vulnerable of our society. These are the ones Jesus voted for, those whom every empire had left behind, those whom no millionaire politician will represent.

And when it comes to voting for candidates, we can use the same prophetic imagination we've explored in this book. One community we know of was working among immigrants and undocumented people. They had very little hope in "the system," and many of them did not vote in national elections. But they realized that a degree of so-called "privilege"[44] protected them from the consequences of their disengagement. Their social status allowed them the luxury of not voting, certainly a troubling

44 We say "so-called" privilege because for many of us from backgrounds of the inherited wealth and power that comes from our ethnicity, gender, or geography, we find it anything but a privilege to also inherit a legacy built around the slaughter, enslavement, and abuse of other peoples.

situation when we look at folks who fought and went to jail for the right to vote. So here's what they did. They paired up with their immigrant friends, who did not have the right to vote. They created forums for educating one another on important political issues. And then they asked their friends who *they* wanted to vote for in the election, and voted on their behalf, acting, in a sense, as a voice for the voiceless. There's another intentional Christian community that is composed largely of Caucasian folks who have relocated to a poor African-American neighborhood in North Carolina. They have decided to be good listeners and learners. One of the ways those who are not originally from the neighborhood have submitted themselves to their indigenous neighbors is by asking them who they think would be good to have in office, and casting their votes alongside of theirs.

Remember what Ruth said to Naomi after years of partnership: "Where you go I will go, and where you stay I will stay. Your people will be my people and your God my God. Where you die I will die, and there I will be buried" (Ruth 1:16–17).

There are endless ways to engage politically. We just need imagination and courage. We need to insist on not settling for anything short of the politics of the cross and the kingdom of our God. When our options seem to limit us to choosing the lesser of two evils (or the evil of two lessers), then we must not put our faith in anything short of God, or we will be sadly disappointed by even the best things this fallen world has to offer, especially in a world of contradictions like "holy wars" and "smart bombs." Sometimes voting may be little more than attempting to lessen the impact of the empire—less of a vote for something and more of a vote against something we know to be out of line with God's dream. And perhaps for others, rocking the vote may mean going to the booths and writing in our Candidate, because he doesn't seem to be on the ballot.

APPENDIXES

We realize there is much more to say, and much left to wrestle with. This book easily could have become four separate books. As the Sermon on the Mount shows, Christian politics must be woven with discussion of prayer, sexual ethics, anger, worry, fear, and so on—the connections are endless. But to keep things manageable, we cut out lots of content. We realize for some folks the appendix of a book is like the appendix of the body (you could just as well live without it), but there are a number of important tangents that warrant more attention.

There are two appendixes that we hated to cut but are available on our website, jesusforpresident.org. The other two we have left here for your reading enjoyment, like dessert. "Appendix 3: Subordination and Revolution" addresses one of the most significant and long-standing shortcomings in the history of biblical interpretation and offers some reflections on reconciling our book with Romans 13. And "Appendix 4: Litany of Resistance" is a litany of prayer that we created with the help of Christian peacemaker Jim Loney and theologian Brian Walsh. We hope that it's helpful for you to use or adapt for public gatherings, and we thought it a beautiful way to end the book—in prayer. Enjoy.

Appendix 1

How the Creation Story Deepened Israel's Identity As Set Apart and Anti-Imperial

See jesusforpresident.org

Appendix 2

Mohammed for President? Pluralism and Uniqueness

See jesusforpresident.org

Appendix 3

Subordination and Revolution: What about Romans 13?

This appendix has been shortened. For the unabridged version, see jesusforpresident.org

If we are aliens and strangers to the powers of the world, how do we relate to those powers? It makes sense that two of the longer New Testament passages on relating to the powers are coupled with even longer passages on nonconformity. The popularly misquoted Romans 13 is surrounded by exhortations to *not* conform to the patterns of the world, to love one's enemies, and to overcome evil with good. The passage in 1 Peter 2:13ff. on submitting to authority is woven into a larger tapestry about Christians living as aliens and strangers to the ways of the world. So before we hastily jump to the conclusion that these passages support Christian war or violence, we must understand what they actually say and their placement in overarching New Testament themes.

Because of space limitations, we'll address only Romans 13 in this book. Let's start by reading Paul.

Let everyone be subject to the governing authorities, for there is no authority except that which God has established. The authorities that exist have been established by God. Consequently, whoever rebels against the authority is rebelling against what God has instituted, and those who do so will bring judgment on themselves. For rulers hold no terror for those who do right, but for those who do wrong. Do you want to be free from fear of the one in authority? Then do what is right and you will be commended. For the one in authority is God's servant for your good. But if you do wrong, be afraid, for rulers do not bear the sword for no reason. They are God's servants, agents of wrath to bring punishment on the wrongdoer. Therefore, it is necessary to submit to the authorities, not only because of possible punishment but also as a matter of conscience.

This is also why you pay taxes, for the authorities are God's servants, who give their full time to governing. Give to everyone what you owe: If you owe taxes, pay taxes; if revenue, then revenue; if respect, then respect; if honor, then honor.

—Romans 13:1–7

We'll note some talking points about this text.[1]

(1) To study any text with an appropriate sympathy, one must give it the benefit of the doubt before judging it. One must allow the text to be "innocent until proven guilty." This means we must assume that the author (in this case, Paul) is intelligent enough not to contradict himself or herself. If there is coherence in Paul's thought, then we can use his clear passages to illuminate passages that are harder to understand. Granting this, we

---

1 It would be hard to cite all of the places where John Yoder has influenced these short observations. His remarks in *The Politics of Jesus* (especially the chapter "Let Every Soul Be Subject") have thoroughly influenced our understanding. Readers would do well to go beyond our sketch and read his work and the works from which he draws.

can assume that Paul's point in Romans 13 harmonizes with the rest of his politics. Without this initial sympathy, we might fail to understand a text. The critical eye, squinting with distrust, cannot see clearly.

And it's a disservice to an author to reconcile apparent contradictions in different texts by "balancing" them, concluding, for example, that "Christians need both a violent side and a peaceful side." Others simply write off Romans 13 as either a later compromise in Paul's originally radical politics, or another author's later addition to a largely nonconformist epistle. But what if, instead of having two contradicting points, Paul had a single point? Let's assume that nowhere in Romans 13:1–7 is Paul saying anything that contradicts what he says at the end of the previous chapter:

✳✳✳✳✳✳✳✳✳✳✳✳✳✳✳✳✳✳✳✳✳✳✳✳✳✳✳✳✳✳✳✳

Bless those who persecute you; bless and do not curse. … Live in harmony with one another. … Do not repay anyone evil for evil. Be careful to do what is right in the eyes of everyone. If it is possible, as far as it depends on you, live at peace with everyone. Do not take revenge, my dear friends, but leave room for God's wrath, for it is written: "It is mine to avenge; I will repay," says the Lord. On the contrary: "If your enemy is hungry, feed him; if he is thirsty, give him something to drink. In doing this, you will heap burning coals on his head."

Do not be overcome by evil, but overcome evil with good.

—Romans 12:14–21

✳✳✳✳✳✳✳✳✳✳✳✳✳✳✳✳✳✳✳✳✳✳✳✳✳✳✳✳✳✳✳✳

(2) Note that the text says God orders "*all* authority." As we asked before, what would this text sound like to a German Christian under Hitler's rule or an Iraqi Christian under Saddam's rule? It is easy to blindly use this text to support some militaristic adventure of Constantine or the United States and assume its divine sanction, but this overlooks the fact that "all" must

include *all* authorities: Nero, Domitian, Pilate, Mao Tse-tung, Saddam Hussein, Hitler's Third Reich, and so on. Also, there is no place in the text where these authorities, under the right conditions, are considered divinely inspired (therefore worthy of obedience) or, not meeting some criteria, are considered divinely condemned (therefore worthy of disobedience). The text does not give ordination only to democratically elected governments, but includes dictators!

When certain governmental standards (which have been imported into this text from elsewhere) are not met, some Christians like to introduce an exception: "We must obey God rather than men." But this phrase was intended not to provide an exception to the rule but to serve as a clue to the overarching politics of the people of God: they always obey God rather than men, *and* they always subordinate to all authorities.

That God establishes all authority does not mean that God approves of all authorities. The point is rather that God is to be considered greater than, not equal to, all the powers of this world. Even the best democracy in the world isn't worthy of allegiance, for God is sovereign even over it. "Established" here means that God orders the powers, as a librarian orders books but doesn't necessarily approve of their content. After all, Paul speaks of a government that "rewards the just," but he also has extensive experience with persecution under its rule, and John of Patmos later refers to the powers (in Revelation 13) as the great whore. That God "ordered" pagan Assyria to chastise Israel (Isaiah 10) is similar to Paul's point. Isaiah made no hint that God approved Assyria or the violence it used, but Israel was to trust that, in their suffering, they were not outside of God's sovereignty. Jesus echoed this belief when he declared to Pilate, "You would have no power if it were not given to you from above," while obviously acknowledging Pilate's abuse of this power. Or remember back to when Israel demanded a king despite God's warnings of what kings would do to them, and "in God's anger God gave them a king." And now we ask God to save us from ourselves and our kings and presidents.

(3) Because Paul gives no conditions for a disciple to be subordinate to the authorities, we see he is talking about something deeper than disobedience or obedience. Paul, in fact, did not use the word *obey* (which would imply the sense of bending one's will). He used the word *subordinate*, which means that you simply consider yourself *under* their *order*. This word is not about patriotism, pledging allegiance, or any affection for the powers. Paul isn't trying to convince unpatriotic Christians to pledge better allegiance. Rather, Paul's problem is the opposite: he must convince Christians, who are not conforming to the patterns of this world, not to overthrow the government![2] Paul is helping disciples understand the futility of such endeavors, encouraging them to keep on the path described in Romans 12 (and all of Jesus' life and teaching), and not fly off into a new and hopeless project of vying for power. As Paul makes clear in chapters 9 through 11, Gentiles need to see themselves not as participants in the political dramas of upheavals and revolutions but as part of the set-apart people of God which were begun through Abraham and Sarah.

Subordination is not simply a helpful spiritual caveat to remind the Christian to stay humble. It's a necessary safeguard against violence and power. It's difficult to find a time in history when the revolutionary, through violence and coercion, doesn't become a new oppressor. As we mentioned in chapter 2, Jesus knew this was the case in his people's recent history with the Maccabeans. Thus Jesus rejected the Zealots' goal to "take the power back" from Herod or Pilate. Paul too is rejecting the Zealots' impulse and opting for revolutionary subordination. As with Tolkien's Lord

2 A few years before, Priscilla and Aquila had been expelled from Rome in connection with a tax revolt, and a new revolt was brewing under Nero. Paul's point is that the insurrectionist motives behind this are missing the gospel's methods of revolution. (See Klaus Wengst, *The Pax Romana and the Peace of Jesus Christ* [Philadelphia: Fortress, 1987], 82.)

of the Rings trilogy, the only thing that should be done with the ring of power is dissolve it in the fire, not put it in the hands of "a pious man."

If this ever becomes confusing, one need simply look at the example of Jesus' death at the hands of the powers to understand subordination. The way Jesus interacted with the temple courts and with Pilate displays a subordinate yet revolutionary heart. Jesus never obeyed their whims and wishes—indeed, his wild action in the temple precipitated his arrest—and yet he also nonviolently subordinated to arrest.[3] He understood the powers as fallen but lovingly navigated through their hands, speaking truth that their power had blinded them to. To overcome evil, he would not resist it but suffered and absorbed it.

(4) Many warrior Christians like to refer to the "just war tradition." And apparently Romans 13 is at the heart of this theory's constitution. As you read through the text, you'll notice there is no place where sanction is given to the Christian to take up arms or even try to become the one who "governs by the sword." Indeed, the Christian identity is upheld in this text, as it was a chapter before, as radically distinct from the powers. For Paul, the powers and the state are clearly a "they," because he pledges allegiance to another Lord. Much just-war reflection fails not only in its logic and application but also in its preconception: their "we" is not the church but the state. In response to the question, "What should we have done in World War II?" we must ask, "Who is we?" If you are a Christian and your citizenship is in Jesus' kingdom, reflection begins not with the powers but with the church. The church should not have religiously supported, fought for, and obeyed Hitler. The church should have been enacting the teachings of Jesus. The church should have been taking in

3 "The conscientious objector who refuses to do what a government demands, but still remains under the sovereignty of that government and accepts the penalties which it imposes, or the Christian who refuses to worship Caesar but still permits Caesar to put him or her to death, is being subordinate even though not obeying" (John Howard Yoder, The Politics of Jesus [Grand Rapids: Eerdmans, 1994], 209).

Jews and others who were hunted. In many instances the church *was* doing these things, but this is not the history we learn. Each of these instances, as in the case of Schindler or in our Celestin story or with the midwives in Egypt, are acts of holy subversion and disobedience. We are blessed to learn the lessons of history through the small faithful ones in the church, instead of through gigantic military history.

Not only does Romans 13 make no mention of Christians and the sword, it also doesn't talk about the state and war. When the text refers to the sword (v. 4, *machiara*: "short dagger"), the Greek word used refers not to war but to the symbol of local policing—the sword Roman officers would carry while accompanying tax collectors. There are many Greek words that refer to war, but *machiara* is not one of them.

But if we must talk about the state and war, "just war" is the most identifiable tradition in the church. If Christians actually held to this theory, they would never go off to war. Just-war theory isn't a "justify any war" theory. It defines a just war by stringent criteria and was intended to criticize governments, minimize violence, and define several reasons that wars were wrong. It should not be used to encourage Christians to abandon Jesus' teachings.

All major denominations, including just-war churches, declared the recent Iraq war unjust and illegitimate. (But why have many congregations in these denominations allowed their members to go off to war?) The only major denomination that we know of to officially sanction the war, the Southern Baptists, did so for reasons other than just-war criteria. (And we might ask whether this denomination would have sanctioned the war if the US president were an atheist and not a "born again Christian.")

(5) Only when the state resists evil and rewards good can the state be considered God's servant. The conditional word "attending" (also "give

their full," v. 6, *proskarterountes*) helps us read the verse to say, "They are servants of God *insofar as* they busy themselves with governing (resisting evil and rewarding good)." When this condition is met, it's not as if Christians would join in resisting evil—no, they are still called to *overcome* evil as agents of the gospel, not agents of wrath. And as we said before, if this condition is not met, it's not as if Christians are justified in overthrowing the government either![4]

In a similar way, the fact that the prophets speak of what a good king should do doesn't change the fact that kings were not part of God's original plan but a breaking of God's heart (1 Samuel 8). The condition is simply to define for the Christian a broad conception of what the state is doing, which is not what the Christian is doing.[5] The act of resisting evil is what Paul and Jesus explicitly prohibited for Christians (Romans 12; Matthew 5).

It may be argued that this reading of Romans 13 leaves the dirty work of violence to the state while Christians keep their hands clean. Paul, indeed, understands that the powers play a role. (Paul had been protected from riot violence by this pagan government. Doubtlessly he was grateful for this, but he also seemed to be indifferent to this protection when he declared, "To live is Christ and to die is gain.") The powers' role is simply part of the old order that is passing away and crumbling.

It's as if an old castle, deteriorating and full of holes in the walls from war, is being rebuilt. The powers, partly responsible for creating the cycles of

4 "The conception of a 'state properly so called,' in the name of which one would reject and seek to overthrow the state which exists empirically, is totally absent in the passage. In the social context of the Jewish Christians in Rome, the whole point of the passage was to take out of their minds any concept of rebellion against or even emotional rejection of this corrupt pagan government" (Yoder, *Politics of Jesus*, 200).

5 "Christians are told (12:19) to never exercise vengeance but to leave it to God and to wrath. Then the authorities are recognized (13:14) as executing the particular function which the Christian was to leave to God ... the function exercised by the government is not the function exercised by the Christians" (Ibid., 198).

war, protect the castle from further bombing and set up scaffolds and girders to keep the building from crumbling on everyone's heads. They mitigate the mess they haven't yet become convinced to stop making. Meanwhile, those committed (the church) to the renewed castle make peace between the warriors who destroyed the castle, redesign its architecture, rework the plumbing, and so on. But if the reworkers resort to constructing gun turrets on the walls, they simply assure the tightening of the cycle that destroyed everything. This analogy, like any, falls short. But the picture is that the old order plays a role, but it's a limited and largely negative role. Rather than trying to save a sinking ship, Christians are to be helping people get into lifeboats. To the extent that people play a part in the old order of violence and power, they prolong and maintain it. Put simply, "the most effective way to contribute to the preservation of society in the old aeon is to live in the new."[6]

Appendix 4

LITANY OF RESISTANCE

Compiled with the help of friends Jim Loney and Brian Walsh

One: Lamb of God, you take away the sins of the world.

All: Have mercy on us.

One: Lamb of God, you take away the sins of the world.

6 John Howard Yoder, *The Original Revolution* (Scottdale, PA: Herald Press, 2003), 83.

All: Free us from the bondage of sin and death.

One: Lamb of God, you take away the sins of the world.

All: Hear our prayer. Grant us peace.

· ·

One: For the victims of war.

All: Have mercy.

One: Women, men, and children.

All: Have mercy.

One: The maimed and the crippled.

All: Have mercy.

One: The abandoned and the homeless.

All: Have mercy.

One: The imprisoned and the tortured.

All: Have mercy.

One: The widowed and the orphaned.

All: Have mercy.

One: The bleeding and the dying.

All: Have mercy.

One: The weary and the desperate.

All: Have mercy.

One: The lost and the forsaken.

All: Have mercy.

One: O God, have mercy on us sinners.

All: Forgive us for we know not what we do.

One: For our scorched and blackened earth.

All: Forgive us.

One: For the scandal of billions wasted in war.

All: Forgive us.

One: For our arms makers and arms dealers.

All: Forgive us.

One: For our Caesars and Herods.

All: Forgive us.

One: For the violence that is rooted in our hearts.

All: Forgive us.

One: For the times we turn others into enemies.

All: Forgive us.

One: Deliver us, O God.

All: Guide our feet into the way of peace.

One: Hear our prayer.

All: Grant us peace.

One: From the arrogance of power.

All: Deliver us.

One: From the myth of redemptive violence.

All: Deliver us.

One: From the tyranny of greed.

All: Deliver us.

One: From the ugliness of racism.

All: Deliver us.

One: From the cancer of hatred.

All: Deliver us.

One: From the seduction of wealth.

All: Deliver us.

One: From the addiction of control.

All: Deliver us.

One: From the idolatry of nationalism.

All: Deliver us.

One: From the paralysis of cynicism.

All: Deliver us.

One: From the violence of apathy.

All: Deliver us.

One: From the ghettos of poverty.

All: Deliver us.

One: From the ghettos of wealth.

All: Deliver us.

One: From a lack of imagination.

All: Deliver us.

One: Deliver us, O God.

All: Guide our feet into the way of peace.

One: We will not conform to the patterns of this world.

All: Let us be transformed by the renewing of our minds.

One: With the help of God's grace.

All: Let us resist evil wherever we find it.

One: With the waging of war.

All: We will not comply.

One: With the legalization of murder.

All: We will not comply.

One: With the slaughter of innocents.

All: We will not comply.

One: With laws that betray human life.

All: We will not comply.

One: With the destruction of community.

All: We will not comply.

One: With the pointing finger and malicious talk.

All: We will not comply.

One: With the idea that happiness must be purchased.

All: We will not comply.

One: With the ravaging of the earth.

All: We will not comply.

One: With principalities and powers that oppress.

All: We will not comply.

One: With the destruction of peoples.

All: We will not comply.

One: With the raping of women.

All: We will not comply.

One: With governments that kill.

All: We will not comply.

One: With the theology of empire.

All: We will not comply.

One: With the business of militarism.

All: We will not comply.

One: With the hoarding of riches.

All: We will not comply.

One: With the dissemination of fear.

All: We will not comply.

* * * * * * * * * * * * * *   * * * *

One: Today we pledge our ultimate allegiance to the kingdom of God.

All: We pledge allegiance.

One: To a peace that is not like Rome's.

All: We pledge allegiance.

One: To the gospel of enemy-love.

All: We pledge allegiance.

One: To the kingdom of the poor and broken.

All: We pledge allegiance.

One: To a king who loves his enemies so much he died for them.

All: We pledge allegiance.

One: To the least of these, with whom Christ dwells.

All: We pledge allegiance.

One: To the transnational church that transcends the artificial borders of nations.

All: We pledge allegiance.

One: To the refugee of Nazareth.

All: We pledge allegiance.

One: To the homeless rabbi who had no place to lay his head.

All: We pledge allegiance.

One: To the cross rather than the sword.

All: We pledge allegiance.

One: To the banner of love above any flag.

All: We pledge allegiance.

One: To the one who rules with a towel rather than an iron fist.

All: We pledge allegiance.

One: To the one who rides a donkey rather than a war horse.

All: We pledge allegiance.

One: To the revolution that sets both oppressed and oppressors free.

All: We pledge allegiance.

One: To the way that leads to life.

All: We pledge allegiance.

One: To the slaughtered Lamb.

All: We pledge allegiance.

One: And together we proclaim his praises, from the margins of the empire to the centers of wealth and power.

All: Long live the slaughtered Lamb.

One: Long live the slaughtered Lamb.

All: Long live the slaughtered Lamb.

Contributor Credits

Thanks so much to all of you who donated their time, energy, photos, and talents to help this project along. Thanks also to those who sent us pics, drawings, paintings, and whatnot that were not used.

Cover art copyright © 2007 by Chico and Tatiana Fajardo-Heflin.

Photos of "Christina & Harvey" on pages 2 and 3 copyright © 1983 by Lavonne Dyck. Submitted by Christina Dyck.

Photo on page 6 copyright © 2007 by Cassie Haw.

Photo on page 7 copyright © 2007 by Andrea Ferich.

Photo on page 8 copyright © 2005 by Dan Chung / Guardian Newspapers Ltd.

Handsewn appliques on pages 15, 23, 63, 139, 225, and 368 copyright © 2007 by Daniel Dixon. www.myspace.com/danieldixon.

Ink and watercolor illustrations on pages 18, 19, 27, 34, 52, 53, 72, 73, 93, 95, 105, 113, 127–30, 134, 135, 150, 153, 156, 170, 176, 183, 184, 186, 229, 231, 246, 257, 262, 263, 265, 274, 300, and 315 copyright © 2007 by Paul Soupiset. More of Paul's illustrations may be viewed and purchased online at paulsoupiset.com.

Photo on page 46 copyright © by Paul Taggart / WpN. www.paultaggart.com.

Photo on page 49 copyright © 2007 by Collette Younan. Submitted by Rochelle Younan. www.idd.landolakes.com.

Photo on page 58 copyright © by Clive Shirley / Panos Pictures. www.panos.co.uk.

Photos on pages 74–75 copyright © 2007 by Optical Realities Photography. www.OpticalRealities.org.

Photos on pages 102, 118, 138, and 258 copyright © 2007 by Erik Stenbakken at Stenbakken Photography. www.stenbakken.com.

Photo on page 164 copyright © by Martin Roemers / Panos Pictures. www.panos.co.uk.

Photo on page 190 copyright © by Jacob Silberberg / Panos Pictures. www.panos.co.uk.

Photo on page 197 copyright © 2007 by Logan Laituri.
courageouscoward.blogspot.com.

Political cartoon on page 210 copyright © 2007 by Marvin Halleraker. www.marvin.no.

Photo on page 226 copyright © by Pep Bonet / Panos Pictures. www.panos.co.uk.

Photo on page 240 copyright © by Piotr Malecki / Panos Pictures. www.panos.co.uk.

Photo on page 253 copyright © 2007 by Mazzarello Media & Arts.
www.mazzarello.com.

Photo on page 254 and stitching on pages 140–224, 290–93, 313, and 329 copyright
© 2007 by Lora Burnett. viewfromthemiddleages.blogspot.com.

Photo on page 260 "Hurricane Relief Work in Arcadia Florida" copyright © 2003 by
Mary Reiff. Submitted by Christina Dyck.

Photo on page 271 copyright © by AP Photo / Jeff Widener.

Photo on page 272 copyright © by Charles Cherney / Chicago Tribune.

Photos on page 305 copyright © 2007 by Brian Lewis at Common Ground Community.
www.brianlewis.com.

Photo on page 309 copyright © by Lindsay Keating-Moore.

We used a few stock photos for images we couldn't find elsewhere. Some of these
photos have been altered, illustrated upon, etc. Thanks to istockphoto.com for making
stock photography accessible for a project like this.

Page 16 copyright © by www.istockphoto.com/sdgamez.

Page 24 copyright © by www.istockphoto.com/JoliJoellen.

Pages 28–29 copyright © by www.istockphoto.com/ntzolov.

Page 42 copyright © by www.istockphoto.com/Vasko.

Pages 64–65 copyright © by www.istockphoto.com/lucato.

Page 89 copyright © by www.istockphoto.com/mevans.

Page 91 copyright © by www.istockphoto.com/lucato.

Pages 99–101 copyright © by www.istockphoto.com/KateLeigh.

Page 114 copyright © by www.istockphoto.com/askhamdesign.

Pages 116–17 copyright © by www.istockphoto.com/LordRunar and www.istockphoto.com/billyfoto and www.istockphoto.com/ZE14361 and www.istockphoto.com/swilmor and www.istockphoto.com/ginosphotos.

Page 125 copyright © by www.istockphoto.com/MousePotato.

Pages 140–41 copyright © by www.istockphoto.com/AnitaPatterson.

Page 249 copyright © by www.istockphoto.com/JBryson and www.istockphoto.com/JPecha and www.istockphoto.com/RicciPhotos.

Page 252 copyright © by www.istockphoto.com/remem.

Page 268 copyright © by www.istockphoto.com/66North.

Page 272 *Chicago Tribune* photo by Charles Cherney. All rights reserved. Used with permission.

Pages 288–89 copyright © by www.istockphoto.com/MKucova.

Page 331 copyright © by www.istockphoto.com/mdesign_se.

Pages 360–61 copyright © by www.istockphoto.com/bibikoff.

Pages 362–63 copyright © by www.istockphoto.com/dem10.

Page 364 copyright © by www.istockphoto.com/AquaColor.

Page 367 photo of Holly and Ryan Sharp copyright © 2007 by Daley Hake.

All other photos, textures, illustrations, and whatnots are either copyright © 2008 by SharpSeven Design or copyright © 2008 by The Simple Way. Find out more at www.sharpseven.com or www.thesimpleway.org.

Bibliography

1

LET JUSTICE ROLL DOWN — Perkins

Dorothy Day: Selected Writings — Day

The Executed God — Taylor

MATTHEW AND EMPIRE — CARTER

THE PROPHETS — Heschel

GETTING IN THE WAY — Christian Peacemaker Teams

Agenda for Biblical People — Wallis

THE PROPHETIC IMAGINATION — BRUEGGEMAN

THE
VIOLENCE
OF LOVE

ROMERO

Jesus Christ Liberator

Sobrino

The Paradise of God

Wirzba

Cry of the Earth,
Cry of the Poor

Leonardo Boff

The Powers That Be

Wink

Peculiar People

Clapp

PAX ROMANA AND THE PEACE OF JESUS CHRIST

WENGST

The Rise of Christianity

Stark

Torture and Eucharist

Cavanaugh

Nolan

JESUS BEFORE CHRISTIANITY

GOD AND EMPIRE

Crossan

Powers, Weakness, and the Tabernacling of God

Marva Dawn

ANARC
AND
CHRISTI

Ellu

Jesus and Empire

rsley

BINDING THE STRONG MAN

Myers

Unveiling Empire

Howard-Brook and Gwyther

Does God Need the Church

Lohfink

Early Christians in Their Own Words

Arnold

POLITICS OF JESUS

Yoder

Resident Aliens

JESUS AND THE NONVIOLENT REVOLUTION

TROCME

McLaren

Everything Must Change

The Myth of a Christian Nation

Boyd

The
Kings
and
Their
Gods

Berrigan

Colossians
Remixed

Keesmaat
and Walsh

The Local Church, Agent of Transformation

Padilla

CHRISTIANITY FOR THE REST OF US

BASS

Sex, Economy,
Freedom &
Community

Wendell Berry

Wisdom Distilled From the Daily

Chittister

THE END

(but may we all continue to
study, imagine, and practice
the politics of Jesus)

About the Authors

Shane Claiborne is an author, activist, and recovering sinner—a Tennessee hillbilly with a love for bluegrass music. He is a founder of The Simple Way (www.thesimpleway.org) and a long-term partner in the Potter Street Community, an intentional community in Kensington, Philadelphia. Shane is a board member of the Christian Community Development Association and has helped birth and connect radical faith communities and intentional hospitality houses (newmonasticism.org). He's also a little rusty on his circus skills but has been known to do a little juggling and fire breathing on occasion.

Chris Haw is an aspiring potter, carpenter, painter, and theologian. He grew up Catholic, spent many years growing and serving at Willow Creek Community Church outside of Chicago, and spent a few months studying ecology and theology while living in Belize. A graduate of Eastern University with degrees in sociology and theology, he is currently working on his graduate degree in theology from Villanova University. Chris and his wife, Cassie, are members of Camden Houses, a multi-house community in Camden, New Jersey.

Holly and Ryan Sharp are both artists and musicians. When they're not designing (www.sharpseven.com) or playing with their son, Holly finds herself painting vignettes of the soul while Ryan writes and performs as The Cobalt Season (www.thecobaltseason.com). They live with their son, Paxton, and housemates in San Francisco's Mission District and are actively involved in a missional community called SEVEN.

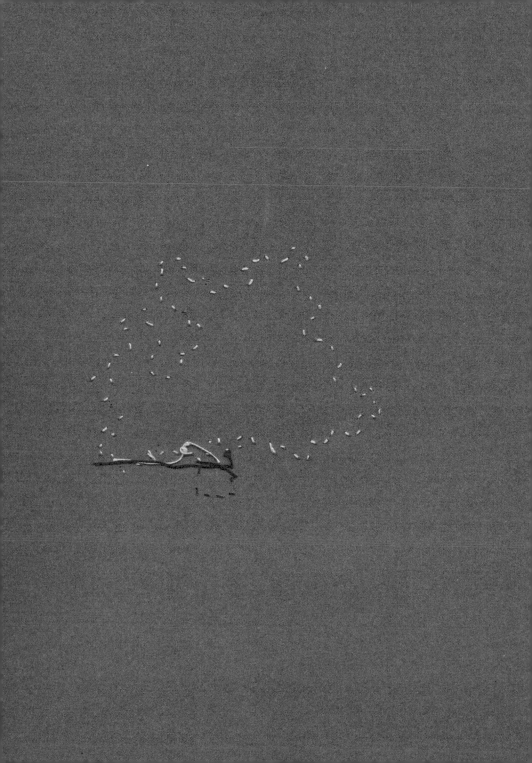